MW00849434

Graphic
Design

Judenpfad 61, 50996 Köln
info@feierabend-unique-books.de

Idea & Concept: Peter Feierabend, Marc Wnuck
Production: 12ender, Mannheim | www.12ender.de
Special Thanks to: Christian Schaarschmidt | www.illunatic.de

Printed in China

ISBN 978-3-939998-29-7

zeixs

Graphic
Design 2

FEIERABEND
UNIQUE BOOKS

Graphic Design2

The portal and label www.zeixs.com was created by the publishing house Feierabend Unique Books and the 12ender agency. zeixs is an amalgamation of digital and printed media with the aim of opening up new possibilities for both. zeixs is open to all areas where design is applied: typography, calligraphy, graphic design, logotype, also fashion, street art, industrial design, and photography. Both established designers and semi-professionals contribute to zeixs.

Graphic Design is the visual composition of content within the two-dimensional media. Thanks to the rapid technological progress and today's omnipresence of mass media and consumer products, graphic design has become one of the most important means of communication. Today, graphic design is everywhere. Regardless of form or material, every product, gadget, item or can be designed according to the individual aesthetic requirements. No advertisement, poster, or packaging is without graphic design. It can support the task of communication by employing more subliminal means such as colour schemes or images that convey moods and feelings. Therefore, aesthetics play an increasingly important part in our everyday life.

The recent development of widely accessible software such as InDesign has created a boom in the field of graphic design. Everybody who can handle the programme, it seems, can be a designer. But while the field of graphic design may have become more "democratic", it's the same old virtues that are crucial to the creation of good design. Talent and inspiration are indispensable.

Graphic Design 2 presents a comprehensive collection of current graphic design, contributed by designers around the globe who are connected through the zeixs-network. If you would like to be included in some future release, just contact us.

www.zeixs.com
www.feierabend-unique-books.de

Graphic Design?

Das Design-Portal und Label www.zeixs.de wurde von dem Verlag Feierabend Unique Books und der Agentur 12ender gegründet, um ein internationales Portal für Designer zu schaffen. zeixs ist die Verschmelzung von Online- und Printmedien, die sich gegenseitig befruchten sollen. zeixs ist offen für alle Bereiche, in denen Design zur Anwendung kommt: Typo, Kalligrafie, Grafik, Webdesign, Produktdesign, Werbung, Technik, Streetart, Mode, Gebrauchsdesign, Printdesign etc.

Grafikdesign ist die zweidimensionale visuelle Gestaltung in den verschiedenen Medien, damit gehört es zum Kommunikationsdesign. Mit der Verbreitung der Massenmedien und einem technischen Fortschritt, der es mittlerweile erlaubt, selbst alltägliche Gebrauchsgegenstände frei nach Bedarf und fast unabhängig von Material und Form zu gestalten, ist Grafikdesign zu einem der bedeutendsten Ausdrucksmittel geworden. Kaum eine Anzeige, ein Plakat oder eine Verpackung kommt ohne grafische Gestaltung aus. Selbst technische Geräte, Lebensmittel oder Kleidung lassen sich heute nahezu beliebig mit Grafikdesign versehen und überziehen.
Dabei soll die grafische Gestaltung die Informationsvermittlung unterstützen. Angesichts der Reizüberflutung unserer Tage wird es zunehmend schwerer, wichtige Informationen von unwichtigen zu trennen. So gewinnt der Aspekt der Ästhetik zunehmend an Bedeutung.

Besonders die Entwicklung computerbasierter Grafikprogramme hat den gegenwärtigen Boom des Grafikdesigns überhaupt erst geschaffen, und ein Ende ist nicht abzusehen. Das Neue ist, dass nun jeder sein „eigener" Designer sein kann. Doch auch diese scheinbare Öffnung des Berufsfeldes ändert natürlich nichts daran, dass es nach wie vor auf Talent, technische Fähigkeiten und Ideen ankommt. Nicht jeder, der InDesign beherrscht, ist gleich ein Grafiker.

Graphic Design 2 präsentiert eine umfangreiche Sammlung neuer Arbeiten von internationalen Gestaltern, die mit dem zeixs-Netzwerk verbunden sind. Wenn Sie beim nächsten Mal auch mit vertreten sein möchten, dann nehmen Sie doch einfach Kontakt mit uns auf.

www.zeixs.com
www.feierabend-unique-books.de

Will dich bei mir wissen – bei mir tragen! – Mein Schatz + + + +++ +++

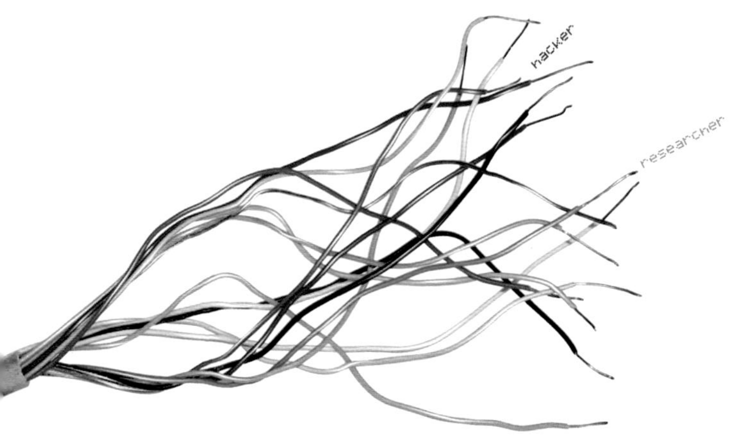
hacker
researcher

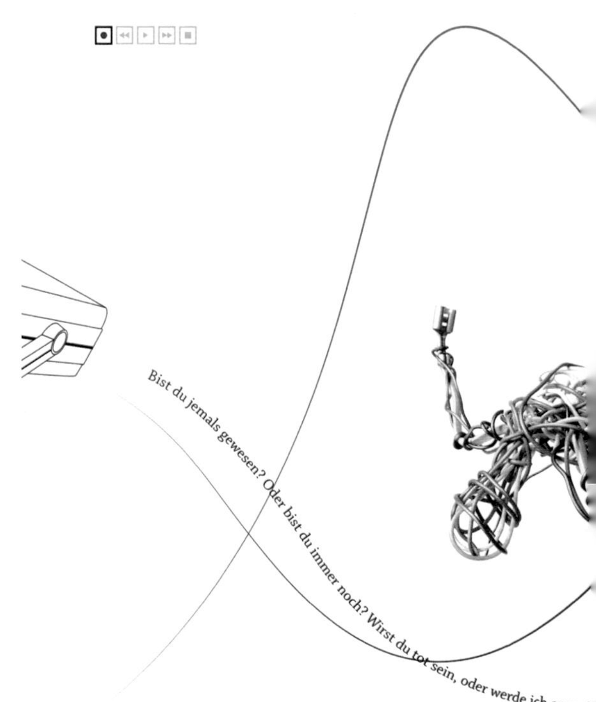
Bist du jemals gewesen? Oder bist du immer noch? Wirst du tot sein, oder werde ich erneut

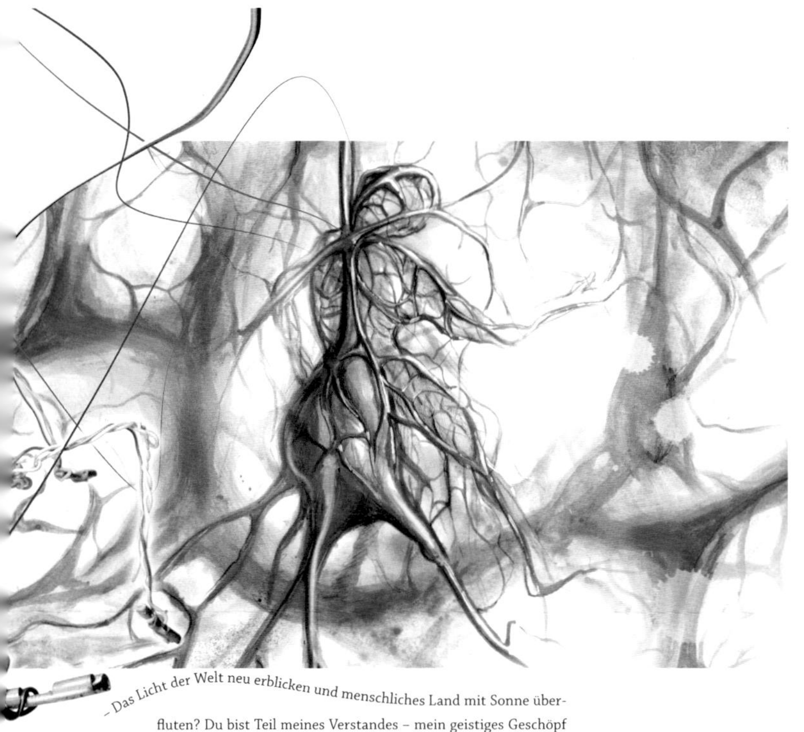

– Das Licht der Welt neu erblicken und menschliches Land mit Sonne über-

fluten? Du bist Teil meines Verstandes – mein geistiges Geschöpf

– Produkt jahrelanger Forschungsarbeit! Du darfst nicht verloren gehen, als wärest du niemals gewes

oren?

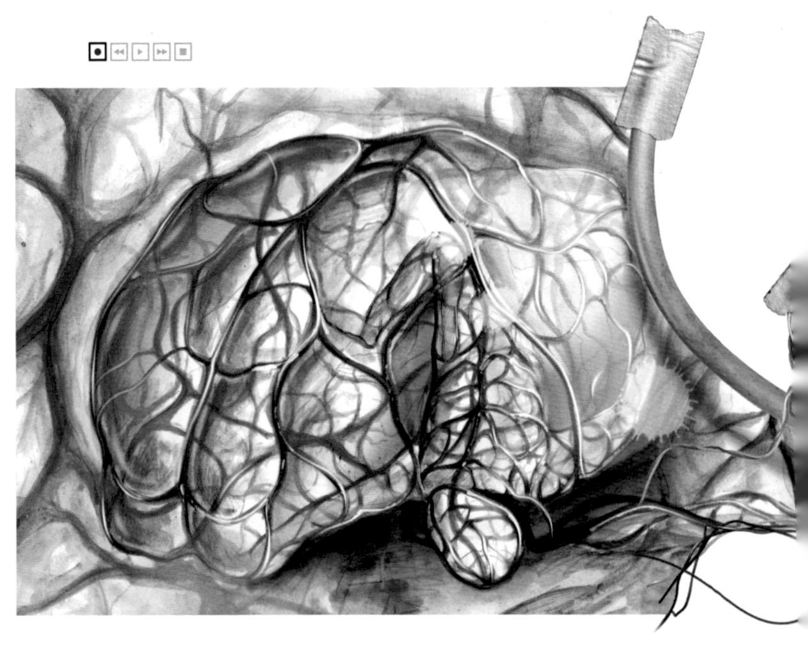

mals gewesen! Wer greift nach dir? Wer versucht dich mir zu entreißen? Bleib bei mir – mein Kind! Du darfst nicht gehen!

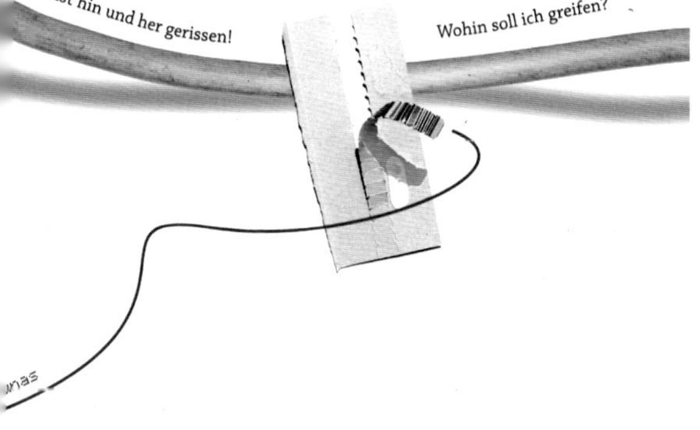
Bist hin und her gerissen!
Wohin soll ich greifen?

015 Johannes Bayer (GER) www.jotopia.de

Audree Lapierre (CAN) www.audreelapierre.com

TOYS Я US

Kingdrips [GER] www.kingdrips.de

FIRST
OFFICIAL
MANTIS
SKATEDECK
LIFE STORE

Kingdrips [GER] www.kingdrips.de

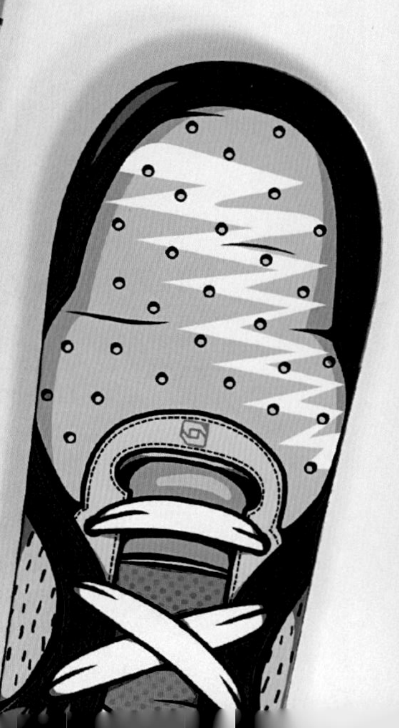

Andreas Klammt (GER) www.breitengrad535.de

BROKEN
SKATE
BOARD
SERIE

die
kann

Eduardo Escobar Beckwith [MEX] www.escobas.com.mx

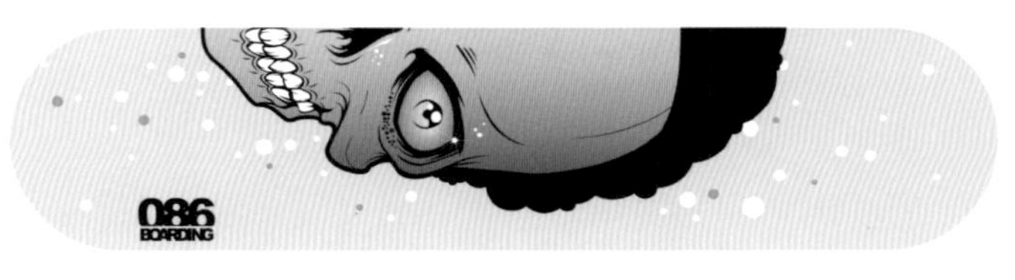

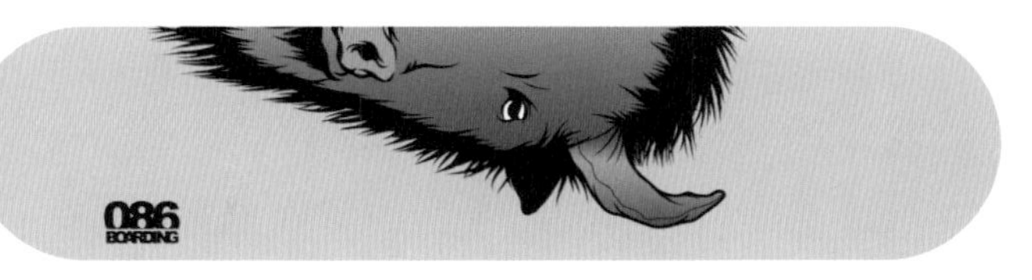

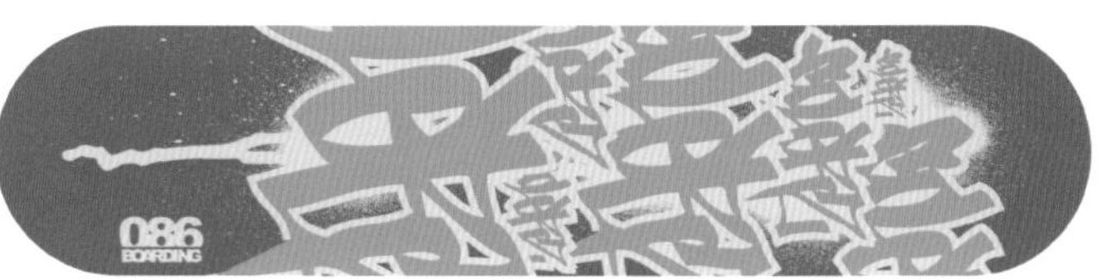

Daniel Hartmann (GER)

Andreas Klammt (GER) www.breitengrad535.de

M

Stefan Frey (GER) www.schwarzschild.de

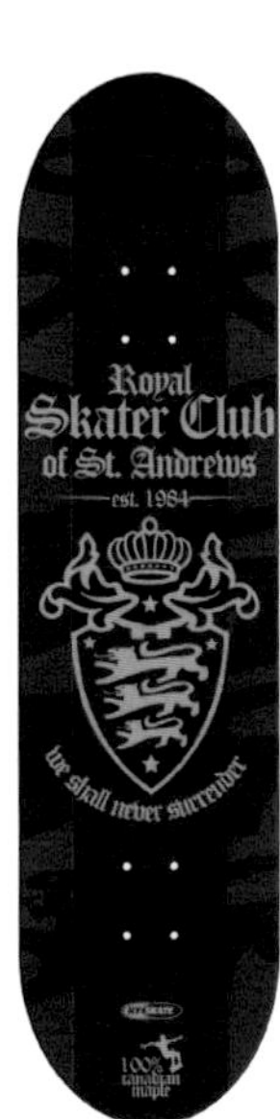

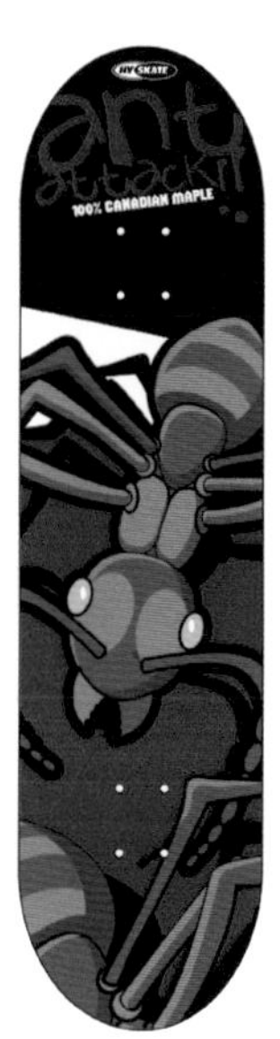

ant
attack!!
100% CANADIAN MAPLE

LUMBER
JACK
HOMEMADE SKATEBOARS SINCE '83

MEANWHILE ON THE SKATE RAMP...
WACK!
YEAH!
HUDORA

100%
MAPLE

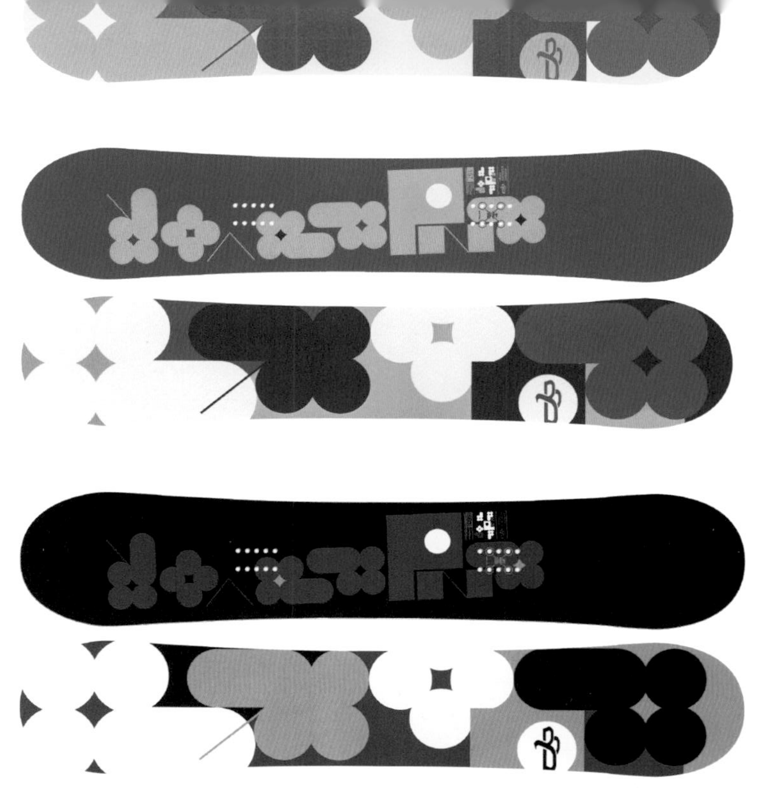

KABUKI
POW

EL
1.000
MUERTOS

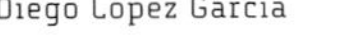

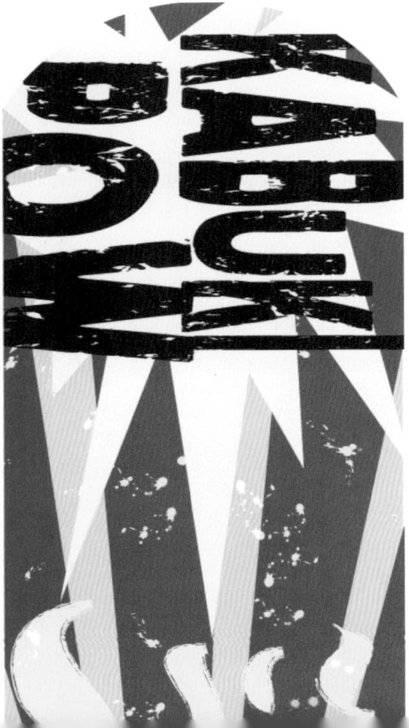

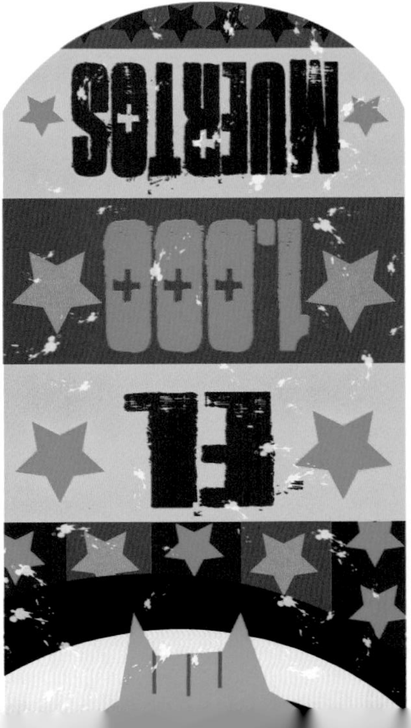

Julian Velasquez [COL]

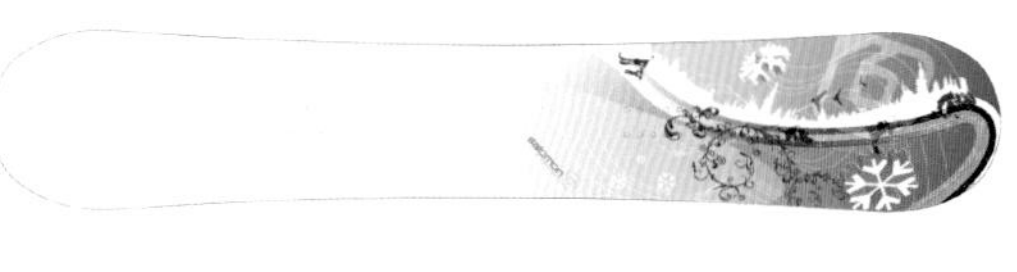

Steven Waldron (SCO) www.tangentgraphic.co.uk

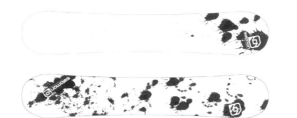

Henrik Persson (SWE) www.become.se

HEAD
Wild One

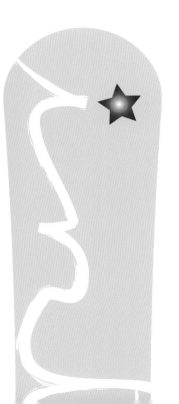

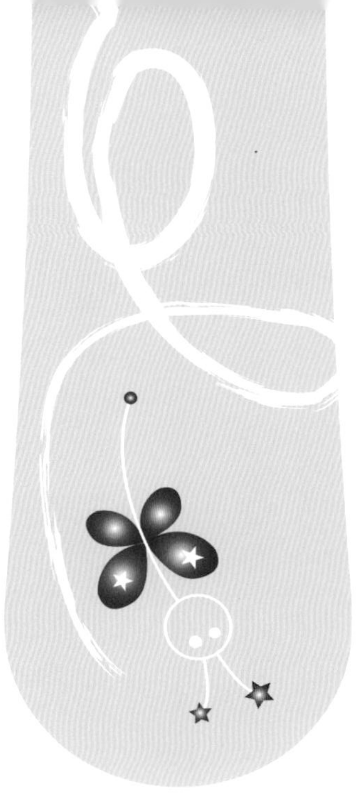

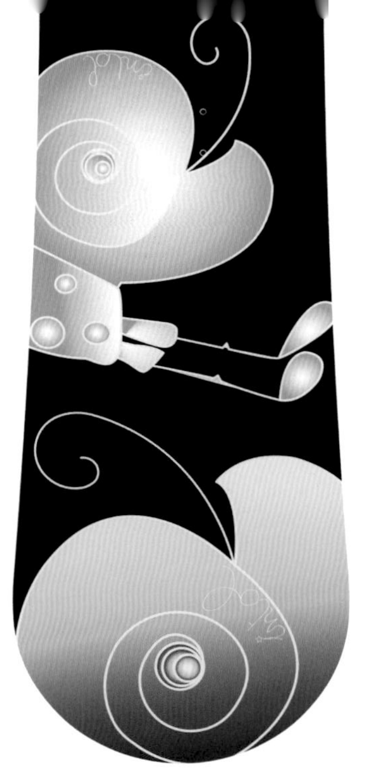

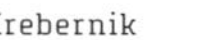

Lilo Krebernik (AUT) www.0717.at

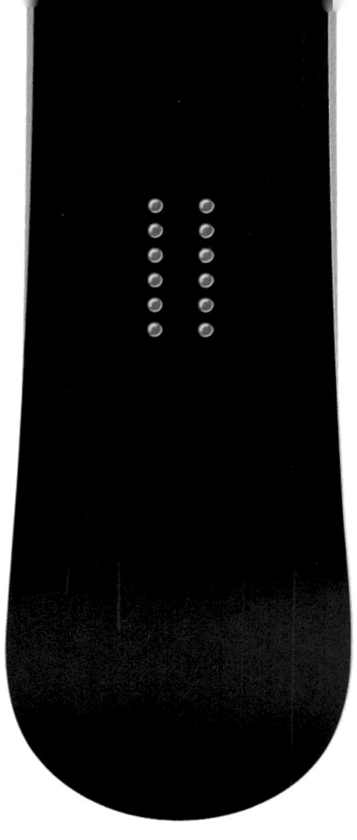

Max Ruf (GER) www.maxruf.com

Lorenzo Geiger (SUI) www.lorenzogeiger.ch

Jeffrey Bowman (GBR) www.mrbowlegs.co.uk

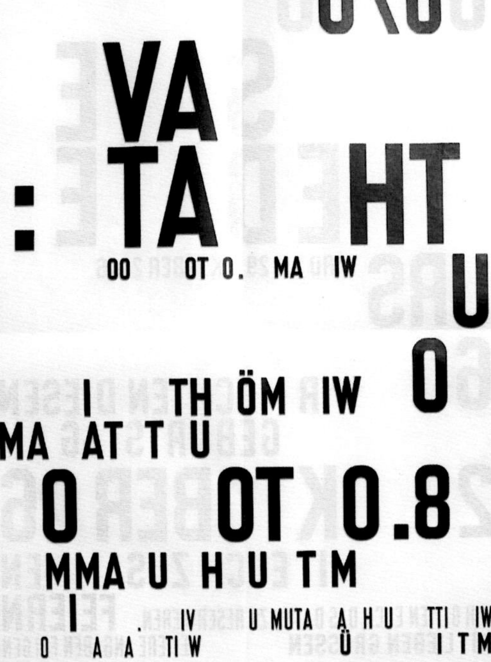

Lorenzo Geiger (SUI) www.lorenzogeiger.ch

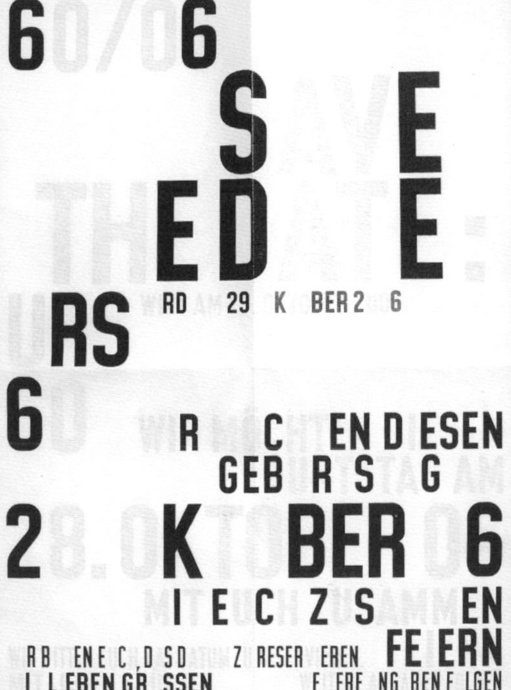

60/06
S E
ED E
RS RD 29 K BER 2 6
6 R C EN D ESEN
GEB R S G
2 K BER 6
I E C Z S EN
FE ERN
RB EN E C D S D Z RESER EREN
I L EBEN GR SSEN E ERE NG BEN F LGEN

stereo mission
exclusive vinyl entertainment

WE
CALL
IT
SOUL

www.stereomission.de

stereo mission
WE CALL IT SOUL
www.stereomission.de

WE CALL IT SOUL

EXHIBITION

WHAT

MAY 20th

HAPPENED

10am–18pm

Have a look at the works the design students made during their exchange stay
on other schools in foreign countries.
Fachhochschule Darmstadt | University of Applied Sciences
FB Gestaltung | Olbrichweg 10, 64287 Darmstadt

Central Saint Martins

BA (Hons) Graphic Design
Course Diagram

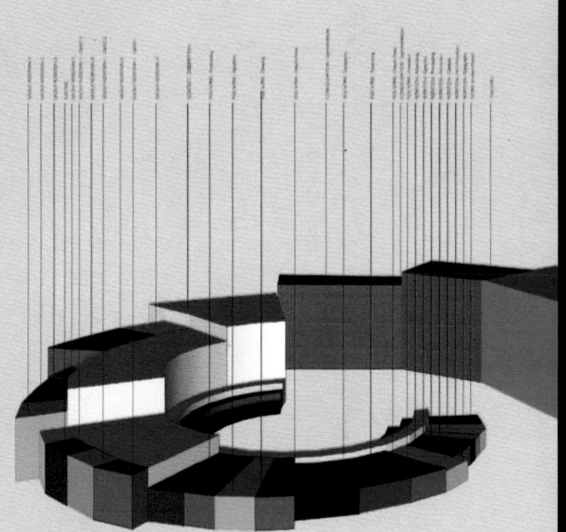

Alexis Cuddyre (GBR) www.alexiscuddyre.com

Stuart Tolley (GBR) www.thisistransmission.com

FROM PULVER RECORDS / BUDAPEST, HUNGARY

ERIK SUMO AND BAND

SURREALISTIC WORLD MUSIC DANCEFLOOR SOUNDTRACKS

SUPPORTED BY DJ RINGMASTER

FRIDAY SEPTEMBER 29 TH 2006 DOORS 22H

PRESALE AT ROCKAWAY BEACH, SPEICHERGASSE 35, BERN

DACHSTOCK REITSCHULE BERN

Lorenzo Geiger [SUI] www.lorenzogeiger.ch

Stuart Tolley (GBR) www.thisistransmission.com

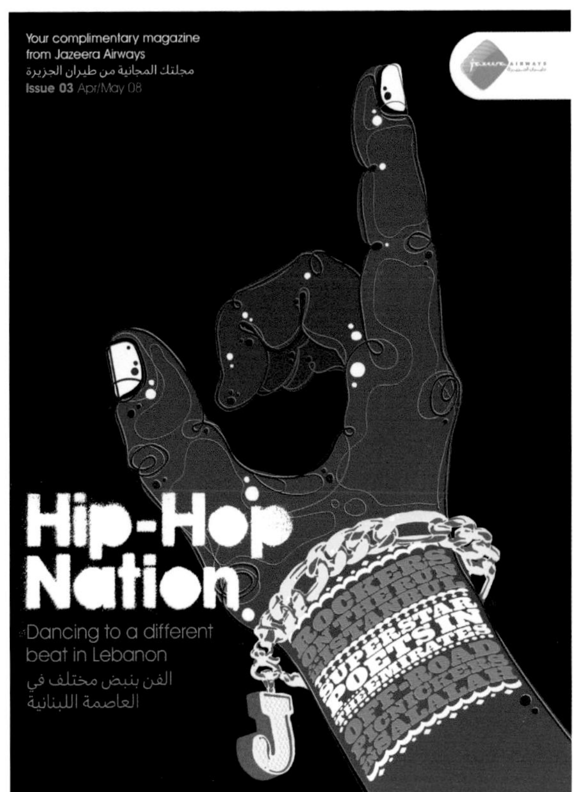
Your complimentary magazine
from Jazeera Airways
مجلتك المجانية من طيران الجزيرة
Issue 03 Apr/May 08
Hip-Hop
Nation
Dancing to a different
beat in Lebanon
الفن بنبض مختلف في
العاصمة اللبنانية
SUPERSTAR
POETS IN
THE EMIRATES
J

where	when
kunstraum kreuzberg/bethanien and other venues ↔ berlin	30/08 – 12/10/08 opening 29/08/08

supported by

HAUPT STADT KULTUR FONDS · ifa Institut für Auslandsbeziehungen e. V. · ZMO · GOETHE-INSTITUT ÄGYPTEN · .CHB

آمال قيناوي
نادر صادق
دان تيسين

amal kenawy
nader sadek
dan tesene

convergence

alexandria: feb 4 - feb 20
cairo: feb 25 - march 21

تلاقي

الإسكندرية: ٤ فبراير - ٢٠ فبراير
القاهرة: ٢٥ فبراير - ٢١ مارس

ACAF: 4 February – 20 February 2007
10 Hussein Hassab St., off Sultan Hussein St., Flat 6 Alexandria
Tel: +2 (03) 4804145 Mobile: +2 (012) 3874874

٤ فبراير - ٢٠ فبراير
١٠ شارع حسين حساب، متفرع من السلطان حسين، شقة ٦ ،
الأزاريطة، الإسكندرية، مصر ت: ٤٨٠٤١٤٥ (٠٣)٢+ موبايل: ٣٨٧٤٨٧٤(٠١٢)٢+

Townhouse Gallery: 21 February - 21 March 2007
10 Nabrawy Street off Champollion Street, Downtown – Cairo
Gallery Hours: 10 am - 2 pm, 6 - 9 pm. Friday 6 - 9 pm, Thur. closed

٢٥ فبراير - ٢١ مارس
١٠ شارع النبراوي متفرع من شارع شامبليون وسط البلد - القاهرة تليفون: ٥٧٦٨٠٨٦ ٢ (٢٠+)
المواعيد : من ١٠ ص إلى ٢ م و من ٦ - ٩م ، الجمعة ٦ -٩م ، مغلق الخميس

ACAF

Townhouse
Gallery of contemporary art
FORD FOUNDATION
ART the review

19
OKT
Overtoom - 141 - Amsterdam
www.myspace.com/dropsumthin
ade

free
myspace.com/dropsumthin
19
OKT
drop
expo
party
Overtoom -141- Amsterdam
amsterdam
dance event

2ND
MAY
FRI~
DAY

DROP
&
LAID
BACK

FREE
and begins at
22.00
LINE UP:
LEFTO
FS-GREEN
40WINKS
INFINIT SKILLS
DYNO/JLS/ERJEE
AME / FLO / LOWMAN
WWW.LAID-BACK.BE
WWW.MYSPACE.COM/
DROPSUMTHIN
KAVKA
Oudaan 14 - Antwerpen

25
JAN
free
www.myspace.com/
dropsumthin
The
Duck
Hunt
Cup
FRI~
DAY
Café
VAAG
HUYZEN
Nieuwenieuwstraat 17
Amsterdam

REFU-
GIUM
www.whatisyourrefuge.com
20.juni,2008
Internasjonal flyktningdag
Forbud mot utvisning eller avvisning
1. Ingen kontraherende stat må på noen som helst
måte utvise eller avvise en flyktning over grensen
til områder hvor hans liv eller frihet ville være
truet på grunn av hans rase, religion, nasjonalitet,
politiske oppfatning eller det forhold at han
tilhører en spesiell sosial gruppe.
Artikkel 33, FNs Flyktningkonvensjon (1951)
AKTIV UNGDOM

SPORT CLUB SANT PAU
RONDA SANT PAU,46
METRO UNIVERSITAT, PARALEL O SANTANTONI
CAPOEIRA
ABADA- CAPOEIRA
GRADUADO
BUFALO
MIÉROLES Y VIERNES
DE 21.10 A 22.15 H
+ info:610927964

06
THIS IS NOT ART
INDEPENDENT
EMERGING
EXPERIMENTAL
ARTS & MEDIA
FESTIVAL
28 SEPTEMBER - 02 OCTOBER
NEWCASTLE
AUSTRALIA
THISISNOTART.ORG
octapod
The City of Newcastle
2ser 107.3
arts nsw
RRR
frankie magazine

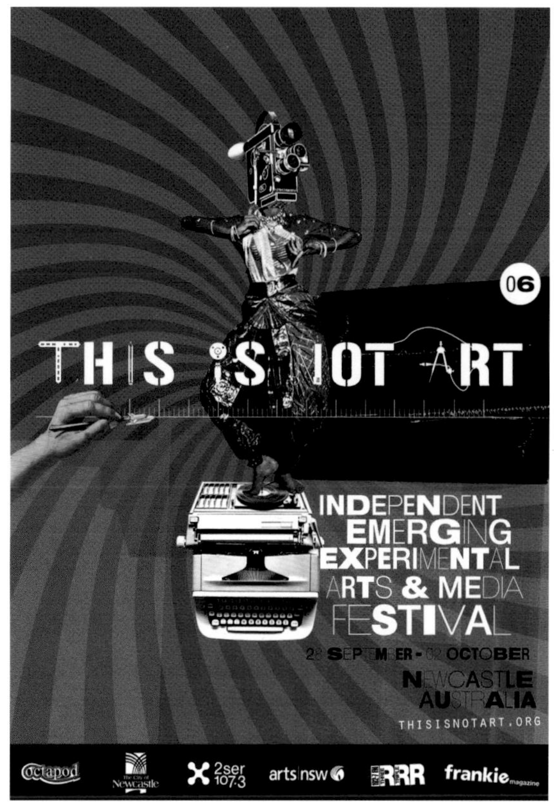
06
THIS IS NOT ART
INDEPENDENT
EMERGING
EXPERIMENTAL
ARTS & MEDIA
FESTIVAL
28 SEPTEMBER - 02 OCTOBER
NEWCASTLE
AUSTRALIA
THISISNOTART.ORG
octapod
The City of Newcastle
2ser 107.3
arts nsw
RRR
frankie magazine

Dave Millard (GBR) www.cpluv.com/www/galleries/LDM

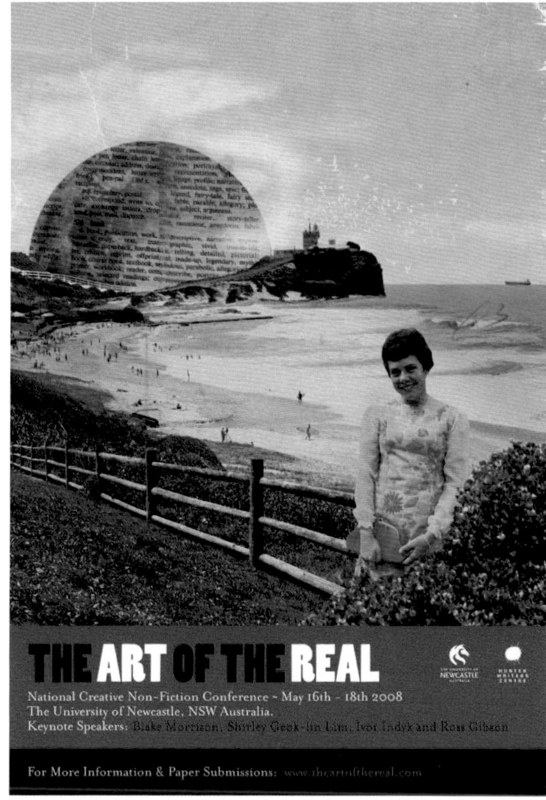

THE ART OF THE REAL
National Creative Non-Fiction Conference ~ May 16th - 18th 2008
The University of Newcastle, NSW Australia.
Keynote Speakers: Blake Morrison, Shirley Geok-lin Lim, Ivor Indyk and Ross Gibson
For More Information & Paper Submissions: www.theartofthereal.com

Heath Killen (AUS) www.illuminationink.com

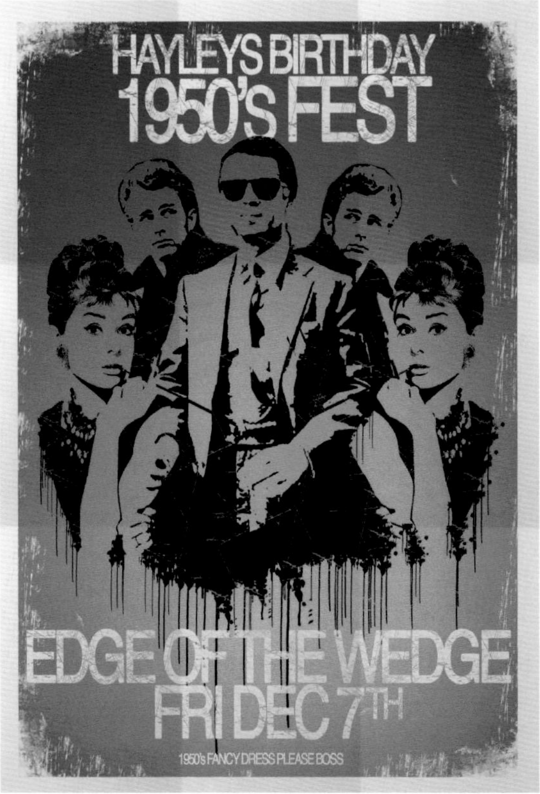

Dave Millard (GBR) www.cpluv.com/www/galleries/LDM

IF YOUR GOING TO
PLAY WITH FIRE
YOUR GOIN TO GET BURNT

ROM FOR KUNST PRESENTERER I SAMARBEID MED NORSK FORFATTERSENTRUM
FORTELLINGER OM BYEN I OSLO OG TRONDHEIM
NYSKREVNE VERK TIL BYEN, STASJONEN OG REISEN

2. OG REDSEL ER BARE NOE DE HAR LURT OSS TIL Å KJØPE SÅ VI HOLDER OSS UNNA ALLE DE VIRKELIG FINE ØYEBLIKKENE I LIVET

LISA C. B. LIE 2007

ROM EIENDOM AS · NORSK FORFATTERSENTRUM · NSB · MESEN

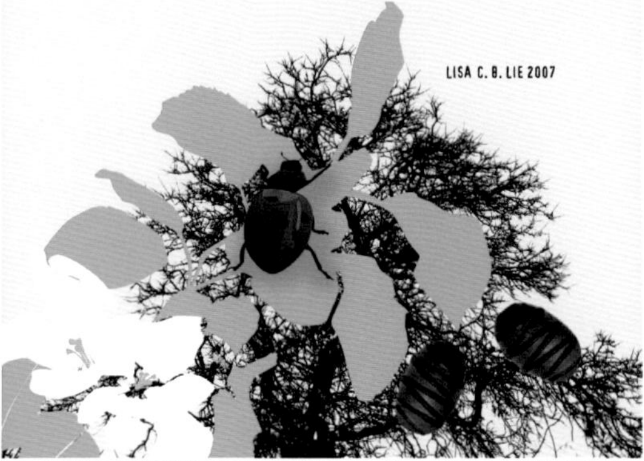

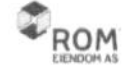

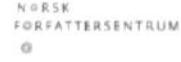

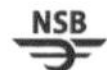

ROM FOR KUNST PRESENTERER I SAMARBEID MED NORSK FORFATTERSENTRUM
FORTELLINGER OM BYEN I OSLO OG TRONDHEIM
NYSKREVNE VERK TIL BYEN, STASJONEN OG REISEN

3.

VI ER ALENE PA EN TOM
LANDEVEI ELLER STRYKER HENDENE
OVER STRA I VANNKANTEN MENS
REGNET PISKER-
FORBANNELSEN ER BRUTT.

THE
YELLOW BRICK ROAD
GAR GJENNOM ULENDT TERRENG OG DU SKAL ÆRE DIN MOR
OG DIN FAR OG LEVE LENGE I UTLANDET.
FORDI VI KAN DET. SETTE OSS PA ET BILLIG FLY. OG STIKKE AV
FRA VARE LIV.

LISA C. B. LIE 2007

MESEN

VORTRAG:

ROBERT SCHAEFER

Design Director
MetaDesign

VISIBLE STRATEGIES★

MONTAG
26.MAI 08
13 UHR

Lette-Verein
Raum A480

★ MetaDesign agiert seit über zehn Jahren in der Spitzengruppe der renommierten europäischen Branding-Agenturen. Das Leistungsspektrum reicht von der strategischen Markenführung bis hin zur Gestaltung und Implementierung von komplexen Unternehmensidentitäten und Erscheinungsbildern.

Der Name ist Programm. »Design« wird mehr und mehr zum unverzichtbaren Steuerungsinstrument des unternehmerischen Erfolgs. Das Visuelle dient als Prüfkriterium bei der Bestimmung der Strategie und der Vision, die Strategie selbst bedarf der Spiegelung im Visuellen, um Emotionen freizusetzen und Interpretationsspielräume zu minimieren. Die wachsende Bedeutung von Identitätsprozessen in den sich dynamisch verändernden Unternehmenslandschaften bedingt, dass CI-Prozesse auf einer »Meta«-Ebene geführt und gesteuert werden. Dafür steht MetaDesign.

www.metadesign.de

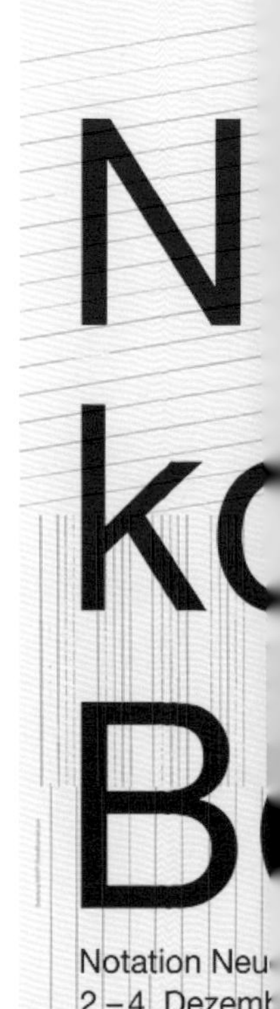

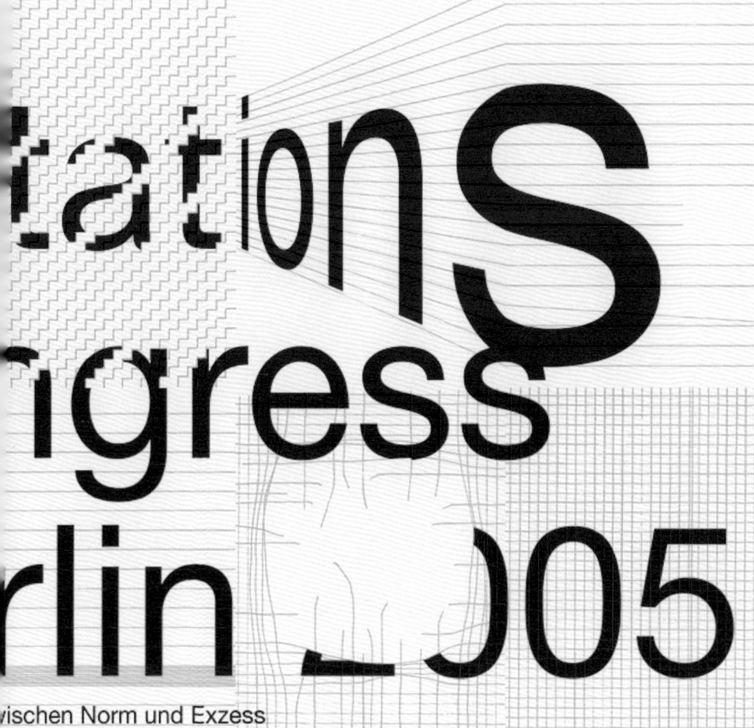

Boris Brumnjak (GER) www.brumnjak.com

LINE UP
CURSE MIT DJ KITSUNE & KOOL DJ GQ
RENO
GERMANY
STRESS & TRAUMA
PARTY
DJ KITSUNE ARR
KOOL DJ GQ ARR
DJ MARIOUS AFDC
KÖLN
STADTGARTEN
23 12 2007 VVK 12 EUR AK 16 EUR
ALLES REAL RECORDS
MEETS GUERILLA WEB
ARR
bloodgold
WWW.HIPHOP.DE

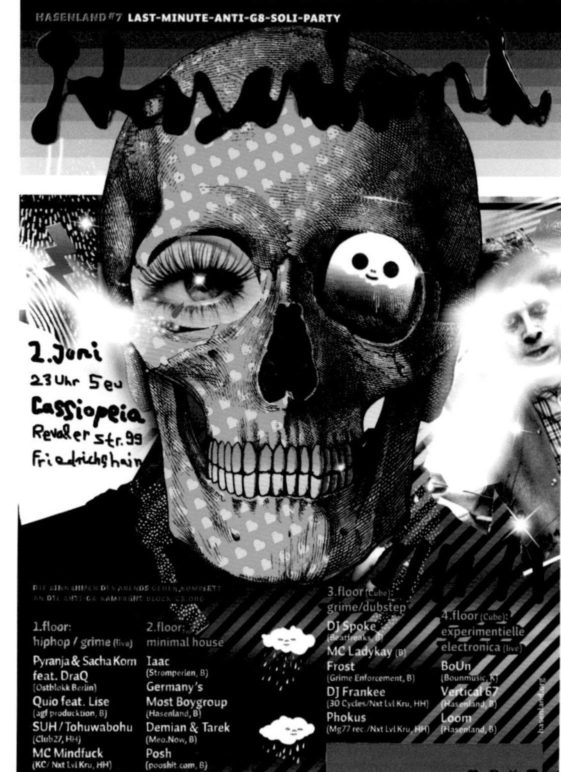

HASENLAND #7 LAST-MINUTE-ANTI-G8-SOLI-PARTY
Hasenland
2.Juni
23 Uhr 5eu
Cassiopeia
Revaler str. 99
Friedrichshain
DIE EINNAHMEN DES ABENDS GEHEN KOMPLETT AN DIE ANTI-G8-KAMPAGNE BLOCK-G8.ORG
1.floor: hiphop / grime (live)
Pyranja & Sacha Korn feat. DraQ (Ostblokk Berlin)
Quio feat. Lise (agf produktion, B)
SUH / Tohuwabohu (Club27, HH)
MC Mindfuck (KC/ Nxt Lvl Kru, HH)
2.floor: minimal house
Iaac (Stromperlen, B)
Germany's Most Boygroup (Hasenland, B)
Demian & Tarek (Meo.Now, B)
Posh (pooshit.com, B)
3.floor (Cube): grime/dubstep
DJ Spoke (Beatfreaks, B)
MC Ladykay (B)
Frost (Grime Enforcement, B)
DJ Frankee (30 Cycles/Nxt Lvl Kru, HH)
Phokus (Mg77 rec./Nxt Lvl Kru, HH)
4.floor (Cube): experimentielle electronica (live)
BoUn (Bounmusic, K)
Vertical 67 (Hasenland, B)
Loom (Hasenland, B)
hasenland.org

Kingdrips (GER) www.kingdrips.de

WIWI SOMMERPARTY
FREITAG 27. JUNI 08
17 UHR CAMPUS UNI ESSEN
AB 22:00 UHR PARTY-ALARM IM HÖRSAALZENTRUM MIT DJ FND
LIVE:
DAS BO SOUNDSYSTEM
PHONEY 14
POEDRA
WWW.WIWI-SOMMERPARTY.DE
Veranstalter: Fachschaft WiWi · Tickets: 5,-/7,- Euro (VVK/AK)
Ticket-VVK: Fachschaft WiWi, Heinrich-Heine Buchhandlung Campus + Viehofer Platz, Karten-Zentrale Galeria Kaufhof

20. LANDESLEISTUNGSWETTBEWERB UND
31. JUGENDBEWERB DER FREIWILLIGEN FEUERWEHREN
BRIXEN
03.-05.06.
08

Alex Knaack (GER) www.born-clothing.de

Sandro Tanneberger (GER) www.remood.net

CUBE CLUB
JUNI 2008
MONATSPROGRAMM
JUNI-HIGHLIGHTS
DJ DYNAMITE
& D-FLAME
SOUNDSYSTEM
RONNY
TRETTMANN

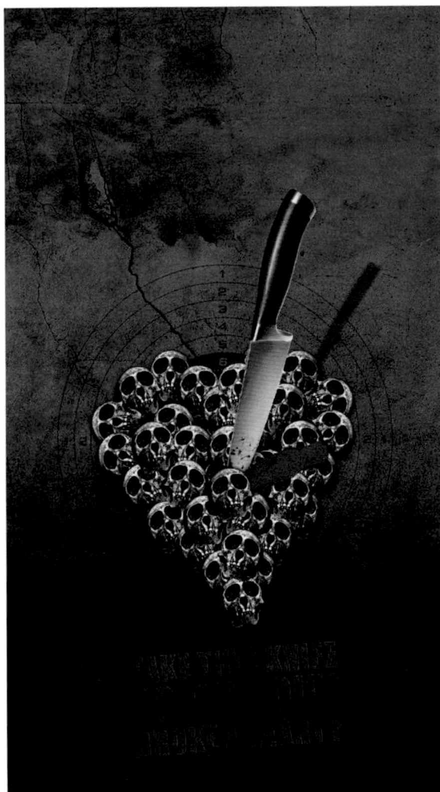

LET FREEDOM
RING WITH A
SHOTGUN BLAST?

STANDING ON THE ROOFTOPS
WAIT UNTIL THE BOMBS DROP?

Hendrik Kuiter (GER) www.buerosiebzehn.de

Ee Venn Soh [MAS] www.behance.net/vennsoh

Odyssey
Orion
In 495 AD,
GreekMythology,
starry constellation
upon death.

Ee Venn Soh [MAS] www.behance.net/vennsoh

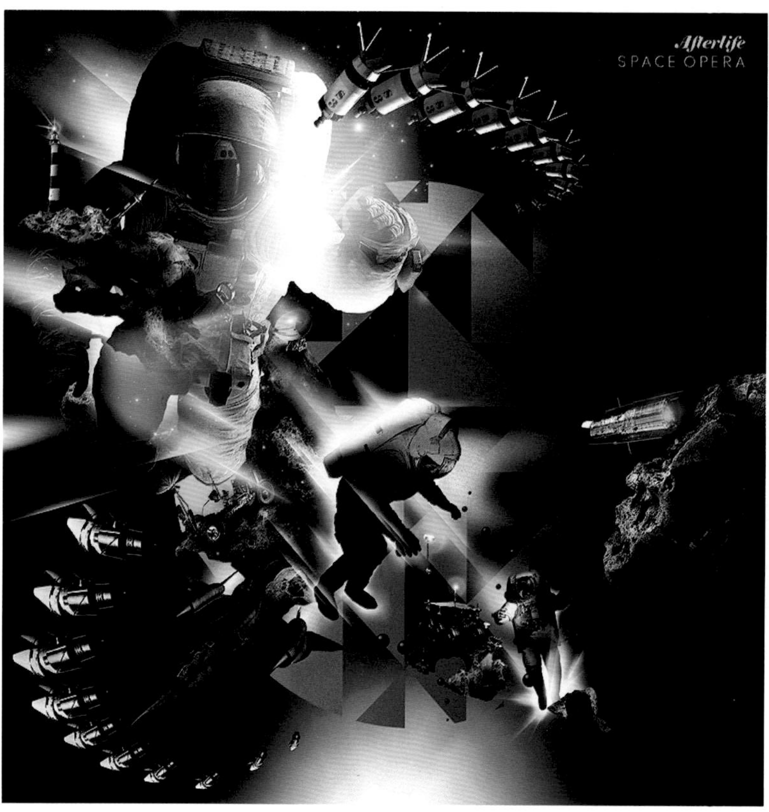

Who
is
this?
What is this?
i don't know!
are you sure?
You're a liar!
Yes you are!
NO
i like your
very
nice
Sunglasses
Where
are
we?

Chris Halderman [NED]

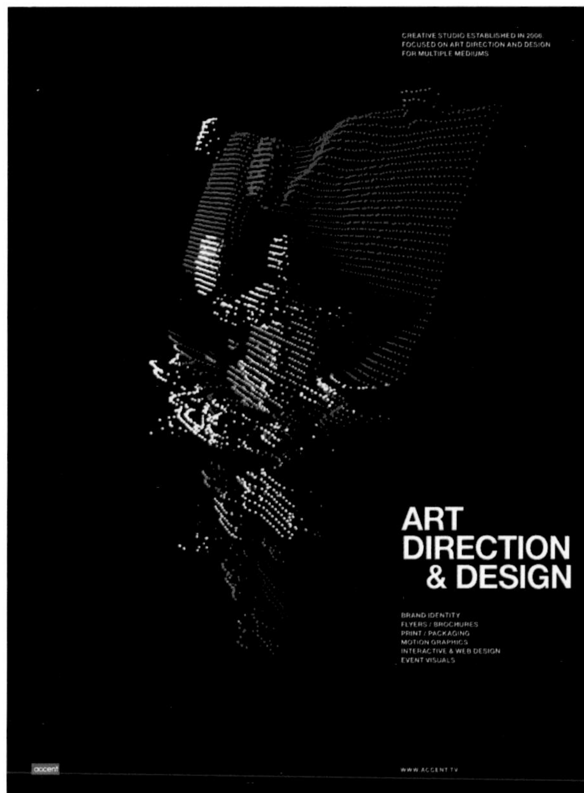

Miguel Vega (USA) www.accent.tv

Daniel Meneses (MEX) www.vectormedia.com.mx

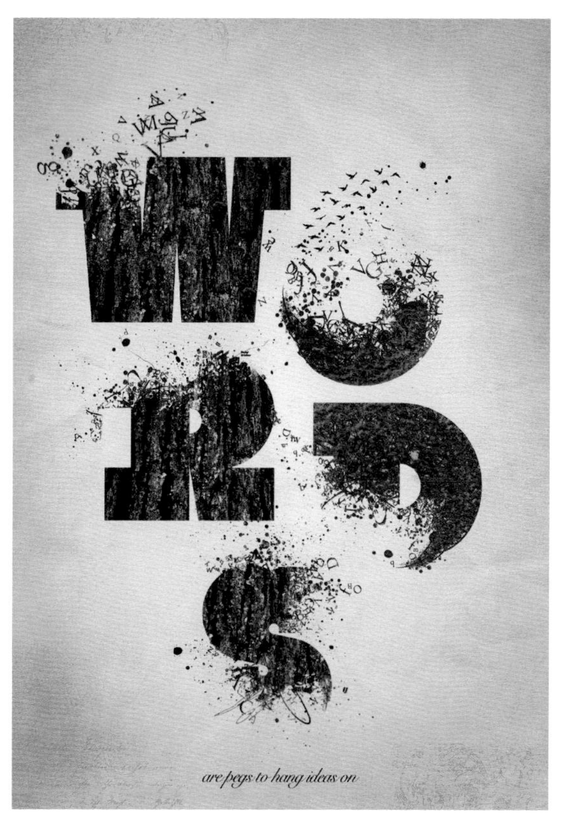
WORDS
are pegs to hang ideas on

 Matthias Tratz (GER) www.hkant.de

Chris Halderman

AFRICA

Heesun Seo [KOR]

DRINK YOUR APPLE A DAY!
SPARKLING
APPLE JUICE
10 FL. OZ. 296mL
SINCE 1868
SINCE
1868
SPARKLING
10 FL. OZ. • 296 mL
100% FROM U.S. GROWTH FRESH APPLES
MARTINELLIS

STELLA

baladi bar flyer

a tour guide through downtown cairo's little baladi bars

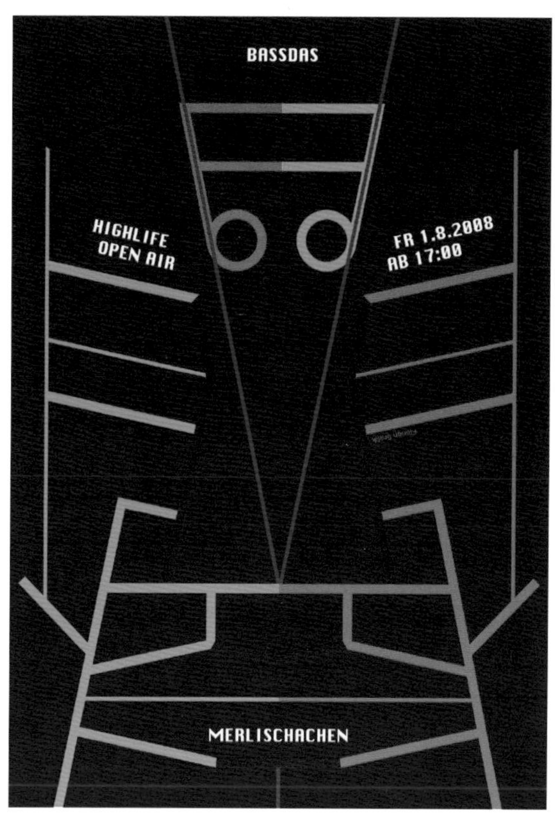

Florian Jakober (SUI) www.floriangrafik.ch

www.chicksriot.com
CHICKS RIOT! 2008
with:
RIFF RANDELLS
2008/10/11(sat)
12(sun)
@Kichijoji
Star Pine's Cafe
lucatieri.com

l'associazione **treesessanta** presenta

CAR NEA LMA CEL LO

23 no

30 no

07 di

14 di

2 di

nov
dic
07

Giovanni Ricchi [ITA] www.minimalsonic.net

24.05.08
Cube Club Chemnitz
DOUBLE
TROUBLE
ft. Artificial Intelligence & Pot of Gold

Artificial Intelligence
V Recordings / Integral Rec, London UK
DJ Racoon
Dead Metropolis, Chemnitz
MC Phowa
Dead Metropolis, Leipzig
Pot of Gold
Madrid, Spanien
Cosmophonic Sound
Chemnitz
cube
24.05.08 - 22:00 6EUR
Cube Club Chemnitz
Straße d. Nationen 80 - 09111 Chemnitz
www.cubeclub-chemnitz.de

Sandro Tanneberger (GER) www.remood.net

Sandro Tanneberger (GER) www.remood.net

DRUM+BASS

Resource Crew - The Birth

Kaidar

Flex Records, Rostock, myspace.com/kaidar

DJ Gizeh

Resource Crew, Chemnitz, resource-dnb.de

DJ Sighter

Resource Crew, MJM, Chemnitz, resource-dnb.de

REGGAE+DANCEHALL

Sensi Movement

Chemnitz, Dresden, sensimovement.de

cube

26.07.08 - 22:00 6EUR

Cube Club Chemnitz
Straße d. Nationen 80 - 09111 Chemnitz
www.cubeclub-chemnitz.de

NewRave fucks BadTaste
NewRave fucks BadTaste
22.11.07 Club 3TON Ravensburg // hinter Club Gonzales

Florian Hucker

(tresor, mayday '94, trax rec, karlsruhe)

Julius Troeger

(int. dj gigolos, omen, new york)

Don Pacino

(cosmic baby, strightly rhythem, bremen)

Sir Maximilian

(ed banger rec - paris, roulette, düsseldorf)

##################################

Start: 22h Give Away for the first 70 guests
Stop: 04h Special Deko & Dresscode*

*kleidet euch bunt, in neon, schrill, freakig, packt eure Leggins, Hosenträger, Smilly Shirts aus - umso ausgeflippter - umso besser!

22.11.07 Club 3TON Ravensburg//hinter Club Gonzales

www.myspace.com/florianhucker // www.thelager.de // we support: www.rave-strikes-back.de

10
dm
10 YEARS
15.03.2008
AJZ CHEMNITZ
DEAD METROPOLIS
One Decade of Drum & Bass Music

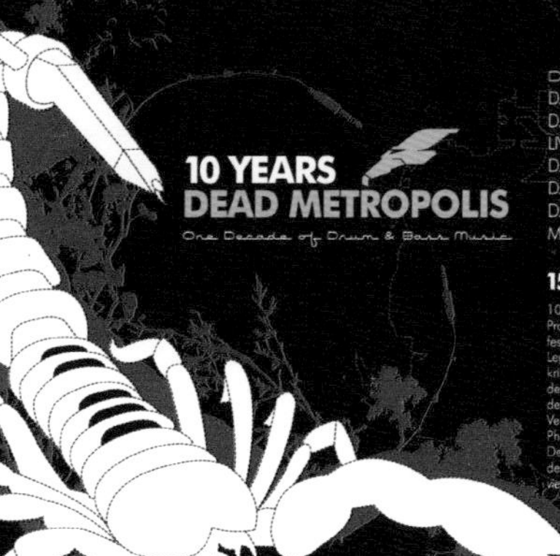

10 YEARS
DEAD METROPOLIS
One Decade of Drum & Bass Music
Drum & Bass
DJ ANGEL DUST CHEMNITZ
DJ RACOON CHEMNITZ
LIVE CREATIVE URGE
DJ SURE CHEMNITZ
DJ POS FRANKENBERG
DJ DRUMATIC CHEMNITZ
MC PHOWA LEIPZIG
Extras
VISUALS BY THE VIDIOTS
+ SPECIAL DEKO
100 BUTTONS AM EINLASS
ONLINE-COUNTDOWN:
AB DEM 10.03. JEDEN TAG EIN
DNB-GOODIE FÜR EUCH AUF
WWW.DEADMETROPOLIS.DE
15.03.08 23:00 6EUR AJZ CHEMNITZ - CHEMNITZTALSTR. 54
10 Jahre Dead Metropolis - Was anfänglich als Projektname für ein Drum & Bass Projekt von Headnooks und Angel Dust gedacht war, entwickelte sich zu einem festen Bestandteil der Chemnitzer aber auch der deutschen Drum & Bass Szene. Legendäre Parties wie Face of Asia oder Egypt Drumfire lassen es auch heute noch kribbeln. Und immer spielte auch der Kick für das Auge eine große Rolle. Neben den Parties und dem Auflegen kam immer mehr der Produktionseifer hinzu. Entstanden sind verschiedene Mixtapes, 2000 die erste Platte von mittlerweilen 5 Veröffentlichungen, mehrere Gast- Releases auf deutschen Labels wie Santorin oder Phunkfiction, Remixe für verschiedene Künstler, Splash! Festival und Auftritte in ganz Deutschland. 10 Jahre Dead Metropolis bedeuten für uns das Miterleben verschiedener Generationen, das Wachsen einer Chemnitzer D&B Szene und natürlich noch viele Jahre Soundboybusiness - Das Alles möchten wir heute Abend mit euch feiern!

Sandro Tanneberger (GER) www.remood.net

Axel Öland (GER) www. 2-3-5.info

drum and bass
the Junglist Movement presents
Sa 21.3.2004, ab 22:00
at Klangkeller, Merlischachen
information: junglist-movement.ch

the Junglist Movement presents
drum and bass
Sa 21.3.2004, ab 22:00 at Klangkeller
Merlischachen
information: junglist-movement.ch

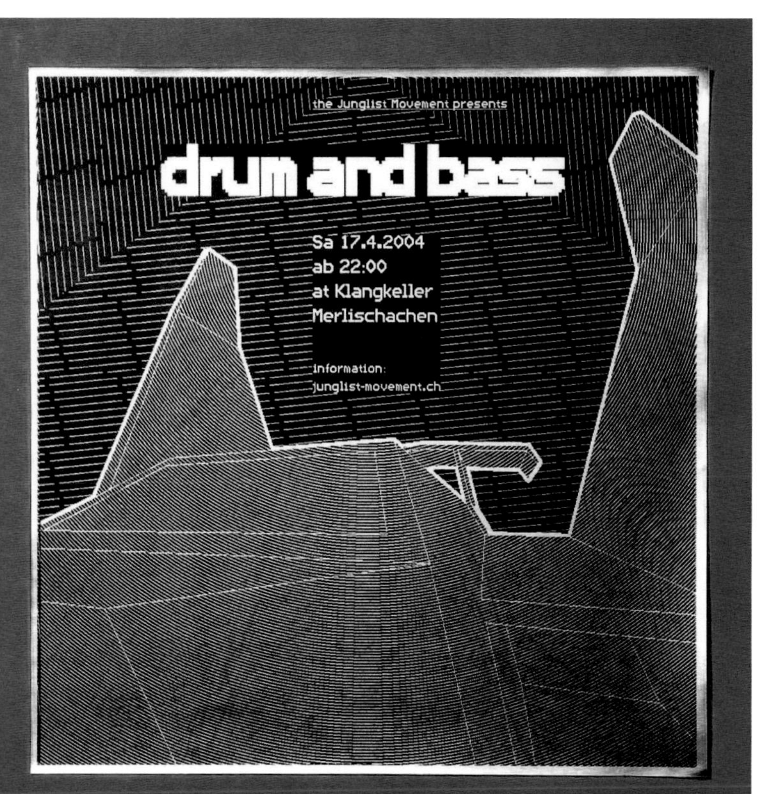
the Junglist Movement presents
drum and bass
Sa 17.4.2004
ab 22:00
at Klangkeller
Merlischachen
information:
junglist-movement.ch

Timo Schlosser (GER) www.designbydigitalink.com

BREAK THE
UP: HIP HOP / FUNK / MASHUP
ITF / SCRAPE TACTICIANS -
CUTCANNIBALZ / ESOULATE -
ESOULATE - LEIPZIG
DOWN: DRUM N BASS
SOUL:R / COMBINATION REC. - NEW YORK
WWW.DESIGNBYDIGITALINK.COM
LEIPZIG
DISTILLERY / KURT-EISNER-STR. 108A / LEIPZIG

une
estívale
2007
SOLO

une
estívale
2008

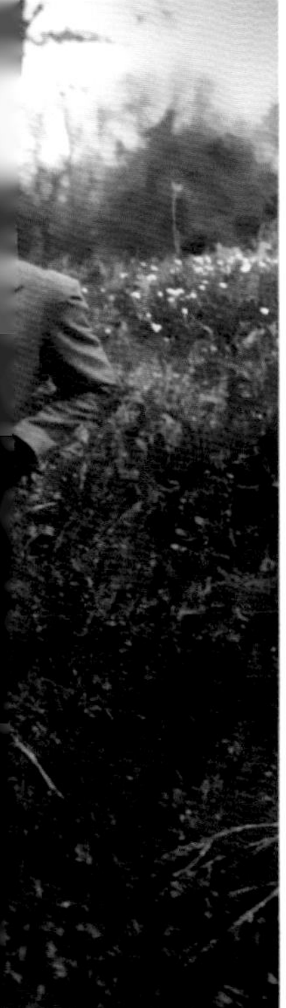

April 22 / 23, 2007
Beverly Hills
California
NEVER
ENDING
FRIENDING
A Journey into Social Networking

UREDD (NOR) www.uredd.no

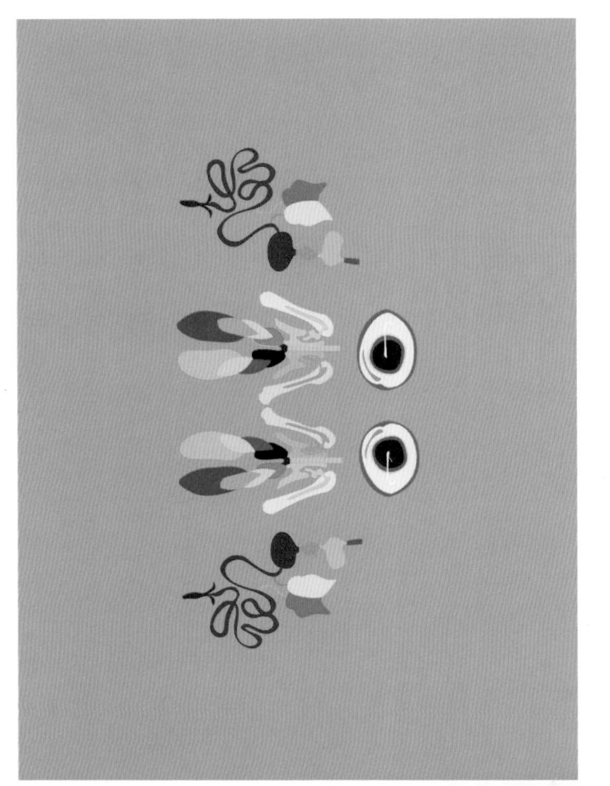

Alexis Cuddyre (GBR) www.alexiscuddyre.com

3
5

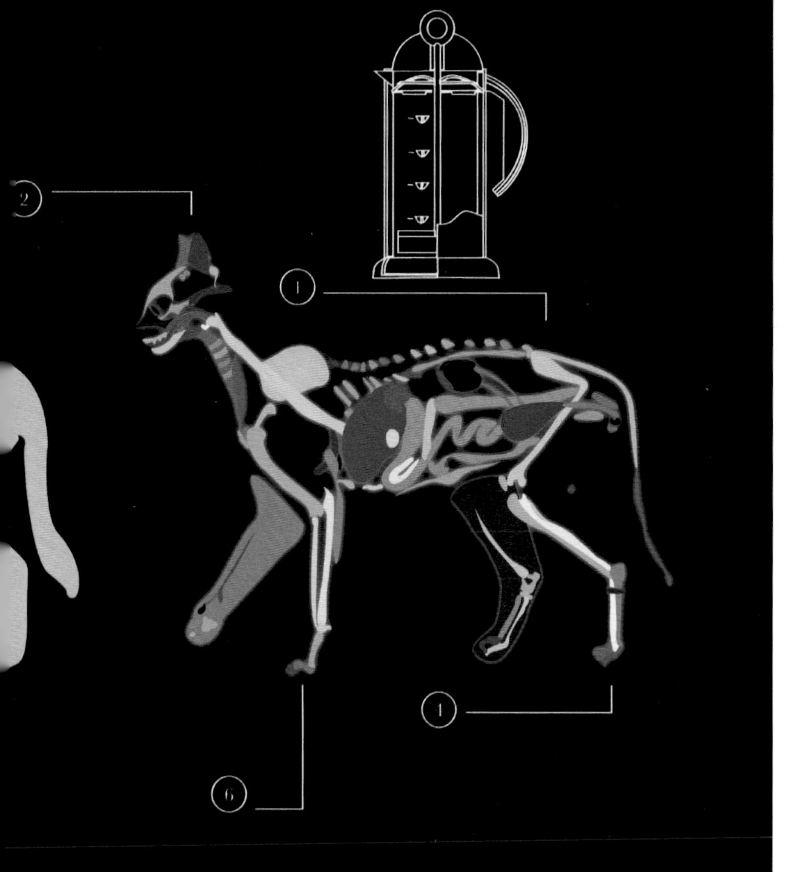
2
1
4
6

Clementine Derodit (FRA) www.monordinateurmagik.free.fr

Bupla (FRA) www.bupla.com

Bupla (FRA) www.bupla.com

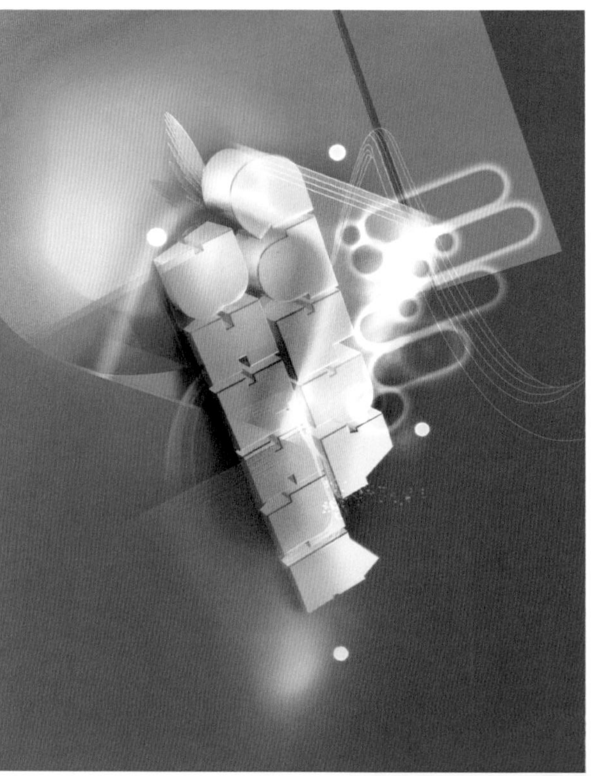

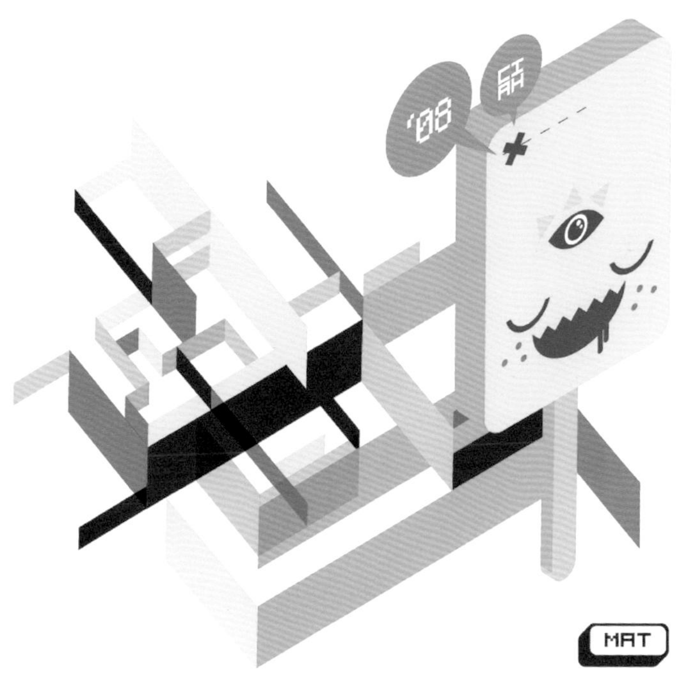

ciah-ciah (POL) www.ciahciah.com

Freundschaft
JOHANNES 15,5

friends, families and lovers
present or gone
LOVERS BE LOST LOVE SHALL NOT
benea
I
GREETINGS FROM THE GREY
II
NO CANDLES PLEASE
III
SWEET PARASIT
IV
I DO KNOW MERCY
V
THE DUST IN MY HEAR
VI
DAY ONE (AND HOW I WAS A
VII
VIII
VIOLATORS WILL BE CI
IX
SELLING MY DIGNITY FOR A BUNC
benea

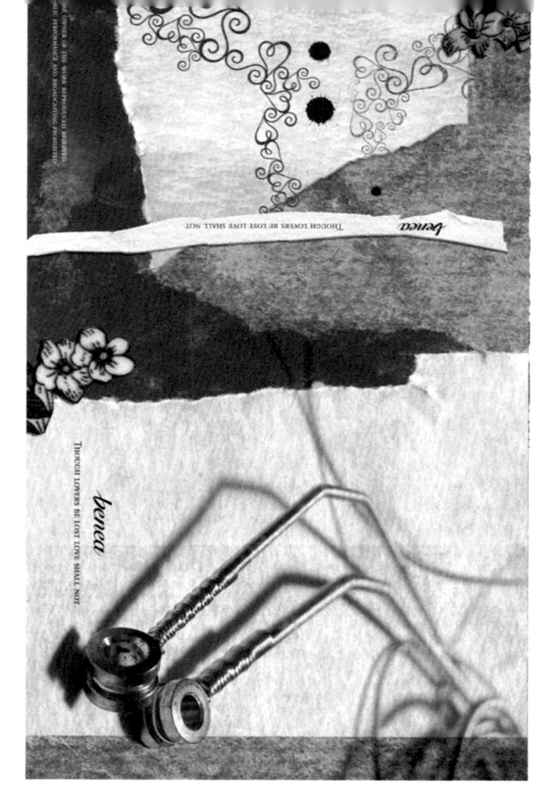
benea
Though lovers be lost love shall not
benea
Though lovers be lost love shall not

Words,
Recorded and mixed by
Coverartwork,

Johannes Bayer (GER) www.jotopia.de

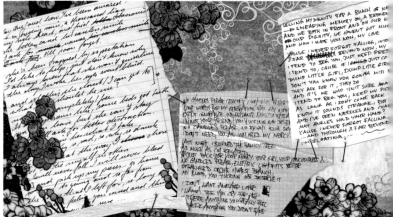

Johannes Bayer (GER) www.jotopia.de

hitators will be ilked
e power I got now
ear myself to ~~death~~ dead
ugh get abolished
uiation out of sight
re so proud of your dogs
crush under my feet
y sense of humor?
t it completely
didn't mama feet you
uch as she should
we all are meant to
o much more than
myself(s).

There's ~~truth~~ no truth like mine
no soul inside my body
I think I'm growing blind
there's room left but me (to see)
and ignorant asshole
a decorated looser
a creep a bug
a pig ~~and of~~
... and le
much as sho

SWEET PARASITE

MOVE OR STAY!
ECHOES FLOATING... THROUGH MY HEAD
SELF-ESTEEM WON'T HELP... TO CURE MY MIND
COME TO ME SWEET PARASITE
DREAMING NEON PRETTY SIGHTS, ABSENT
MOMENTS & CRYSTAL FLIES...
PARANOID BEHAVIOUR, INVISIBLE ENEMIES
MY NOISE STARTS TO BLUR, PLEASE RELEASE ME
MY FRIENDLY SAVIOUR... YOU'RE WELCOME
MY FRIENDLY SAVIOUR... I LIKE YOU
...DREAMING NEON PRETTY SIGHTS, ABSENT
MOMENTS CRYSTAL FLIES
CRAWLING, HIDING FAR AWAY, FIND
THE BALANCE → MOVE
OR STAY!

I DO ~~HOW~~ KNOW MERCY
BESIDES THIS BOY
THE SAD YOUNG BRIDE TONIGHT
AND STILL TIED IN A DRESS THAT DOESEN'T FIT
AND HER LOVER IN ALAR
THAT NEVER WILL ARRIVE, NOR WILL HIM
WELL, I DO KNOW MERCY
LISTEN, BUT YOU CANNOT KEEP ME IN HERE
THROUGH YOUR STREET IN A SHARED CAB
BACK FROM WORK AND NEVER TO RETURN
AND STILL TIED IN A DRESS THAT DOESEN'T FIT
BUT JUST ONE GLIMPSE OF THE EYE
I KEPT THIS WORD OUT OF ME
AND OUT OF WHERE
S ONLY YOU AND EYE
SO TONIGHT I MIGHT WANT TO DIE
UT TOMORROW JUST LIKE ONCE, I
WILL START MY NEW LIFE,
AUSE I'M GETTING AWAY WITH ALL THIS
VER TIRED 'CAUSE I'M GETTING AWAY
TH ALL THIS (AGAIN & AGAIN & AGAIN)

EATE A
BLACK
AND
WHITE

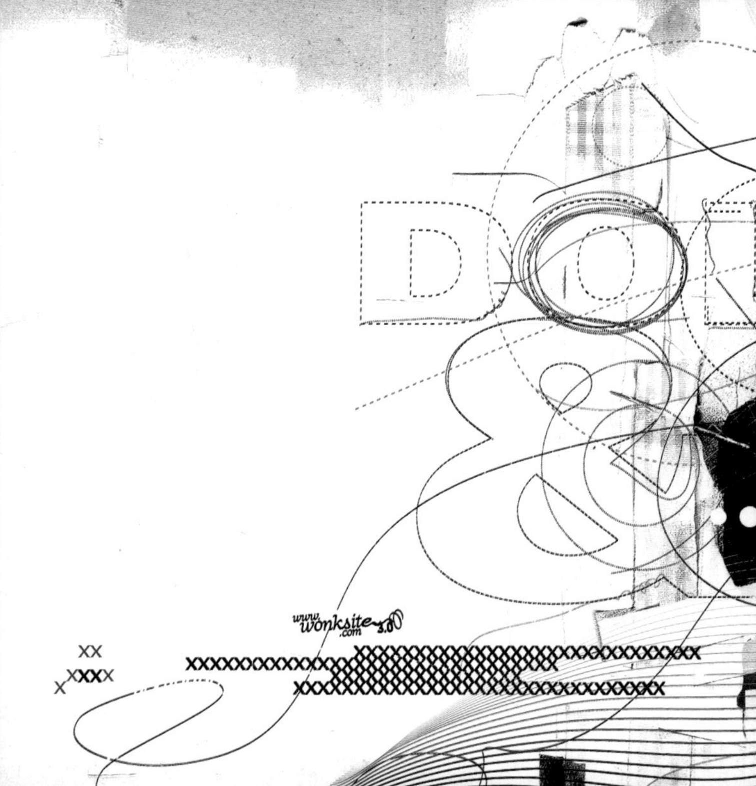
www.wonksite.com

D&G
DOLCE & GABBANA

Sam Lambert (GBR) www.samlambert.com

VISUAL PERCEPTION

Bernardo Henning (ARG) www.holabosque.com.ar

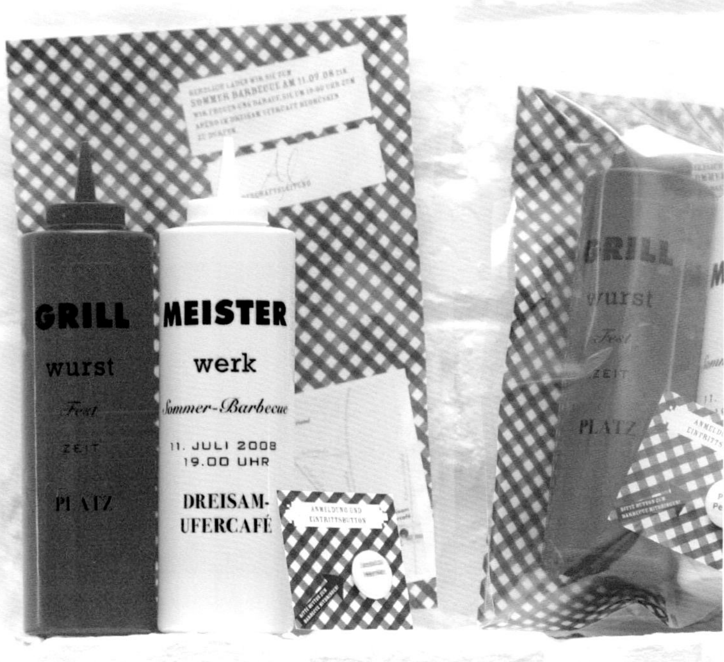

Daniela Merkel (GER) www.bemerkt.net

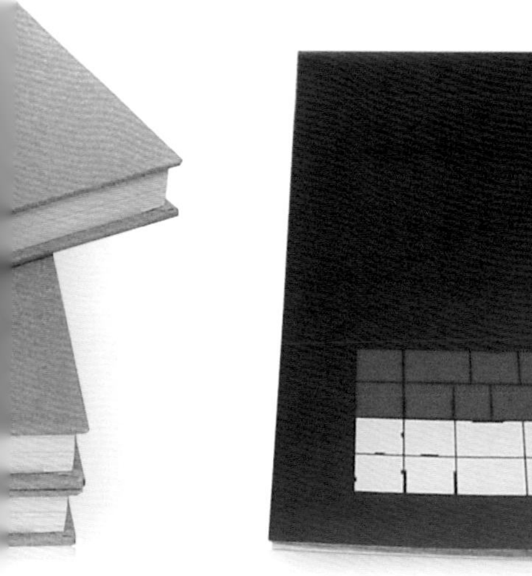

Daniel Bretzmann (GER) www.eyegix.com

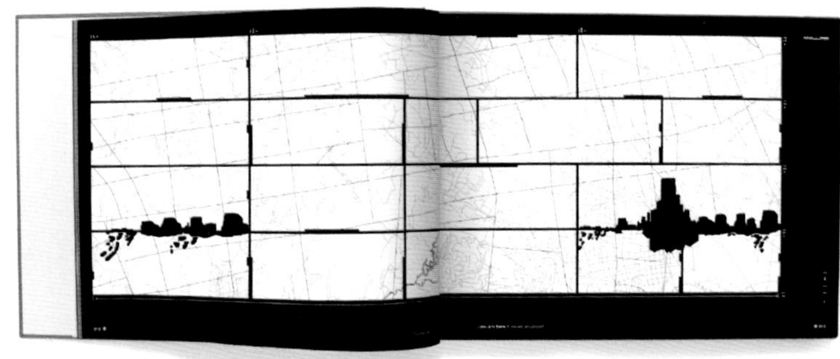

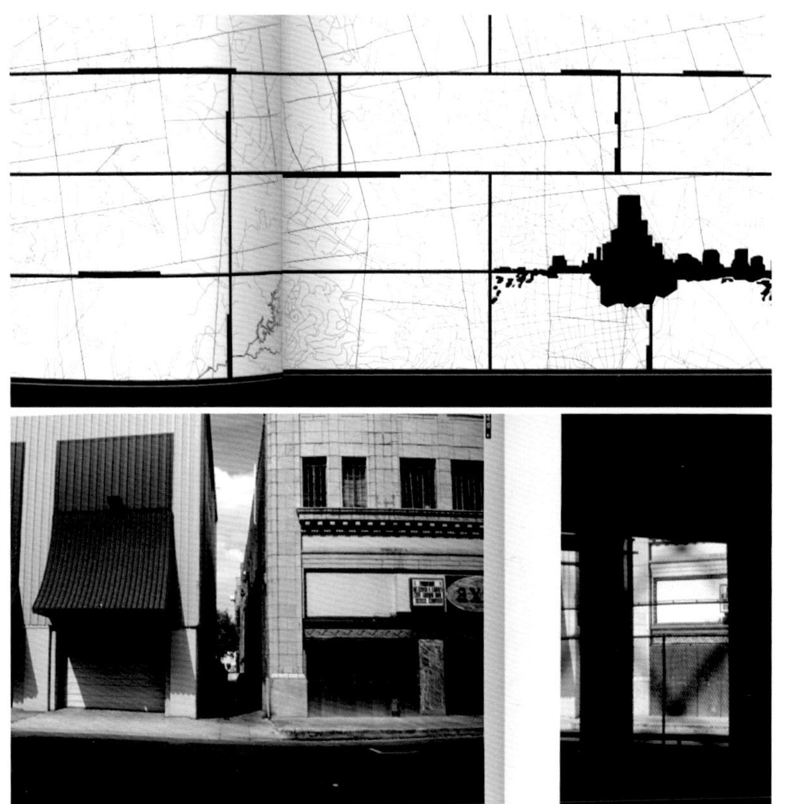

)UNG
RMAN
SIGN
)UNG
RMAN
SIGN

Young German Design

Fresh Ideas in Graphic Design

Katja M. Becker › Stephanie Podobinski (Hg.)

DU SOLLST DIR
BILDER MACHEN.
LERNE GRAFIK! LUZERNER GRAFIK.
Imagekampagne für eine Bildungseinrichtung

Katja M. Becker, Stephanie Podobinski [GER] www.beau-bureau.de

LOLLEKUNDBOLLEK.DE
www.lollekundbollek.de
»Guuude!
merkwürdig

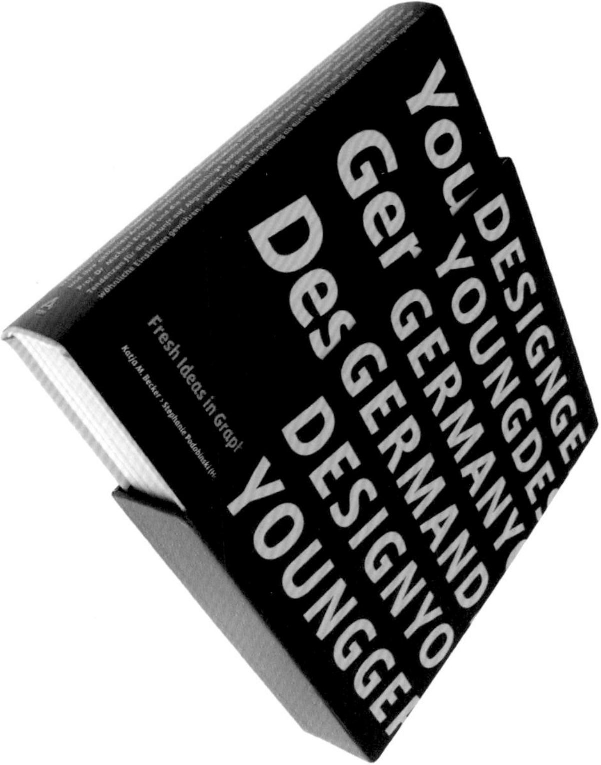

Katja M. Becker, Stephanie Podobinski (GER) www.beau-bureau.de

Katja M. Becker, Stephanie Podobinski (GER) www.beau-bureau.de

40/41, Studiengang Grafik, allg.

Das Grafikstudium

möchte gestalterische Entwicklung fördern und eine Sensibilisierung für kulturelle und theoretische Fragestellungen anregen. Studierende sollen hier eine eigenständige Stimme herausbilden und erproben können, anstatt starre Methoden zu erlernen, die bereits morgen wieder veraltet sind.

(...)

Andreas Maldei (GER) www.myspace.com/andimacht

EDGAR ALLAN POE
Die Sphinx
UND ANDERE UNHEIMLICHE GESCHICHTEN

EDGAR ALLAN POE
Die Maske des Roten Todes
UND ANDERE UNHEIMLICHE GESCHICHTEN

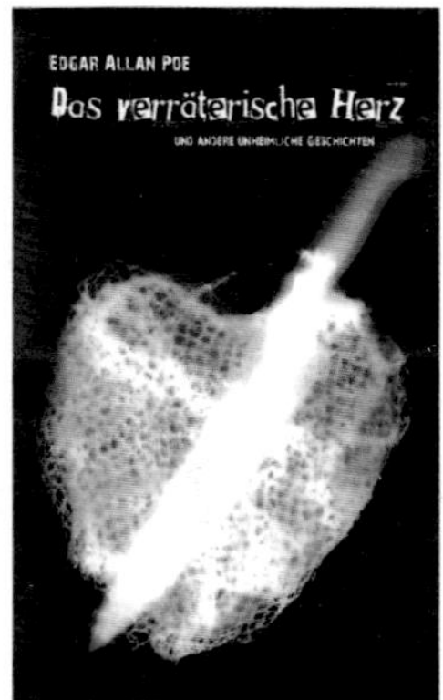
EDGAR ALLAN POE
Das verräterische Herz
UND ANDERE UNHEIMLICHE GESCHICHTEN

EDGAR ALLAN POE
Der Untergang des Hauses Usher
UND ANDERE UNHEIMLICHE GESCHICHTEN

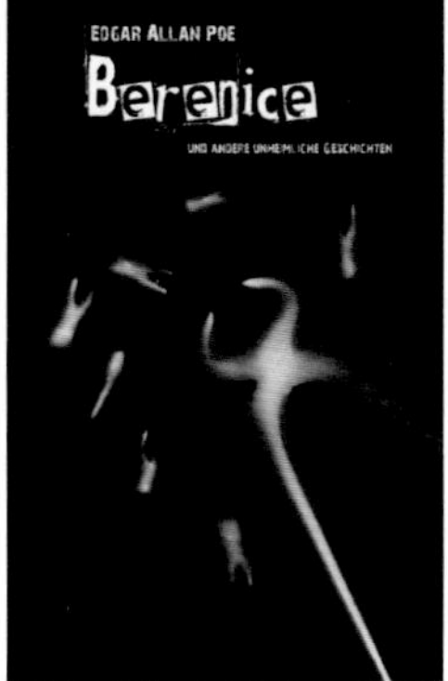
EDGAR ALLAN POE
Berenice
UND ANDERE UNHEIMLICHE GESCHICHTEN

EDGAR ALLAN POE
Das ovale Portrait
UND ANDERE UNHEIMLICHE GESCHICHTEN

Nudel
Trubel
Heiterkeit
11

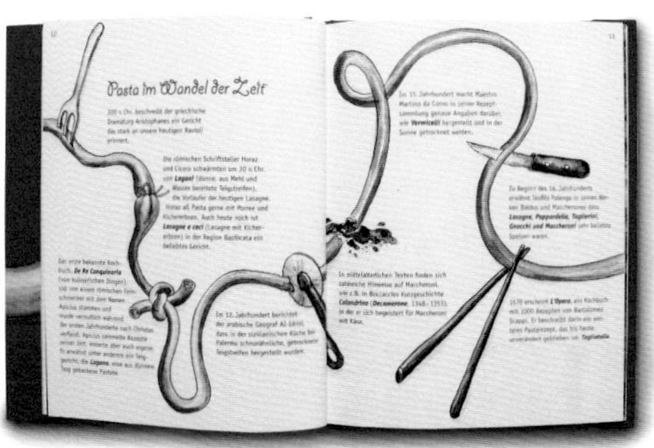
Pasta im Wandel der Zeit
300 v. Chr. beschreibt der griechische Dramaturg Aristophanes ein Gericht das stark an unsere heutigen Ravioli erinnert.
Im 12. Jahrhundert berichtet der arabische Geograf Al-Idrisi, dass in der sizilianischen Küche bei Palermo schnurähnliche, getrocknete Teigstreifen hergestellt wurden.
Im 15. Jahrhundert macht Maestro Martino da Como in seiner Rezeptsammlung genaue Angaben darüber, wie Vermicelli hergestellt und in der Sonne getrocknet werden.
In mittelalterlichen Texten finden sich zahlreiche Hinweise auf Maccheroni, wie z.B. in Boccaccios Kurzgeschichte Calandrino (Decamerone, 1348–1353), in der er sich begeistert für Maccheroni mit Käse.

Punkte, Streifen, Farben

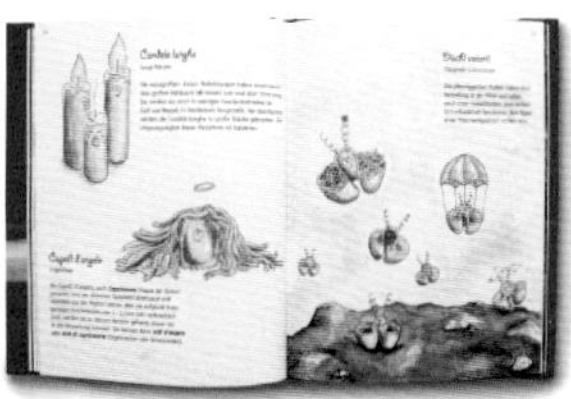

Die Geschichte

rache
s haus
in.» el aler
mes premiers
d'amours,
la seule lan
dont la poé
sera toujou
plus belle.

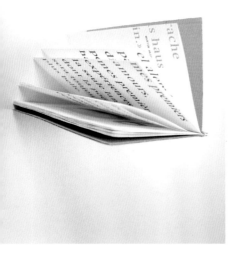

mes premiers
amours,
mes premières
expériences,
la seule langue
dont la poésie
sera toujours la
plus belle.

RESERVOIR DOGS
PULP FICTION
A QUENTIN TARANTINO SCREENPLAY
JACKIE BROWN
A QUENTIN TARANTINO SCREENPLAY
JACKIE BROWN
A QUENTIN TARANTINO SCREENPLAY
QUENTIN TARANTINO

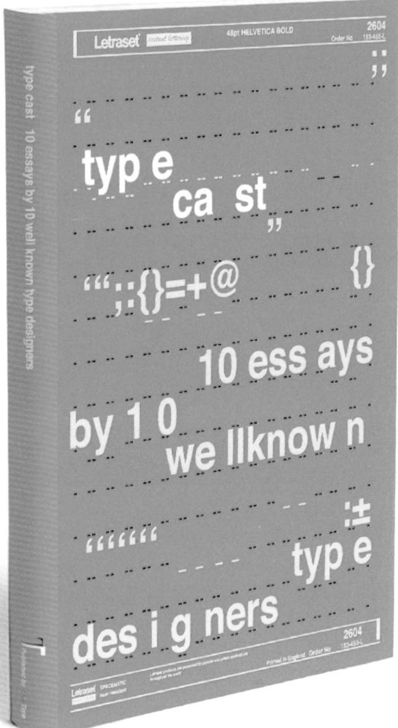

Steven Halton (GBR) www.themiracleshop.blogspot.com

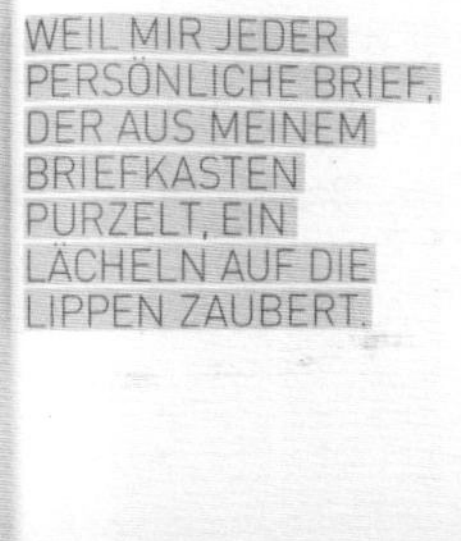
WEIL MIR JEDER
PERSÖNLICHE BRIEF,
DER AUS MEINEM
BRIEFKASTEN
PURZELT, EIN
LÄCHELN AUF DIE
LIPPEN ZAUBERT.

HIROS
HIMA

NEW YORK

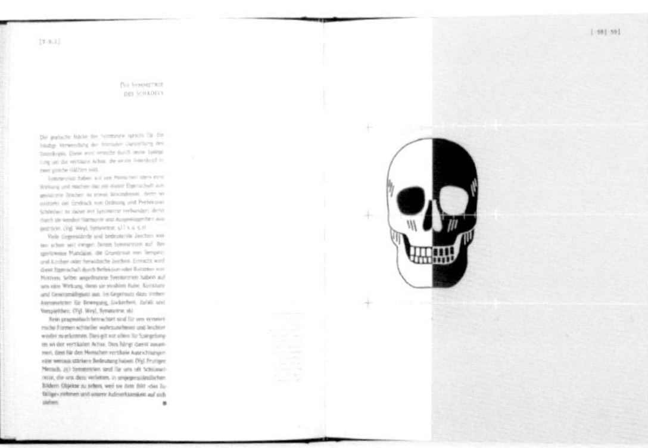
Die Symmetrie
des Schädels

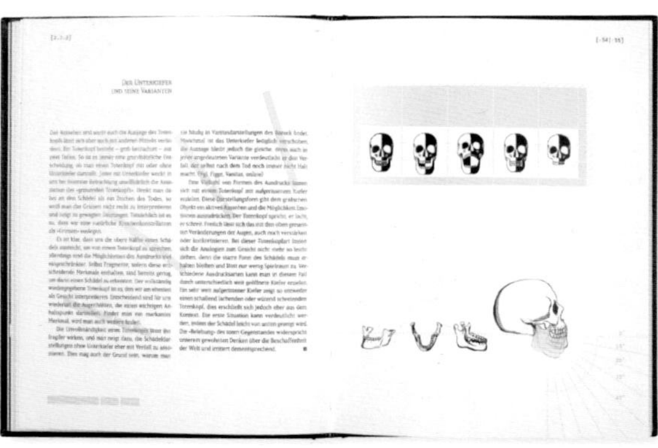
Der Unterkiefer
und seine Varianten

HISTORY
HAUTNAH ERLEBEN
Band VI Die Schlacht um Mü De
Ausgezeichnet mit der Tapferkeitsmedaille
für besonders großartige Heldentaten:
Apfel, Birne, Banane und Kiwi
MIT DER EXTRA-PORTION
ENERGY AUS GUARANA
ZUSATZ VON ZUCKER
FRUISTER
DER ENERGY-FRUCHTRIEGEL
UND MÜDIGKEIT WIRD
UM GNADE WINSELN

Allison Wilton (USA) www.allisonwilton.com

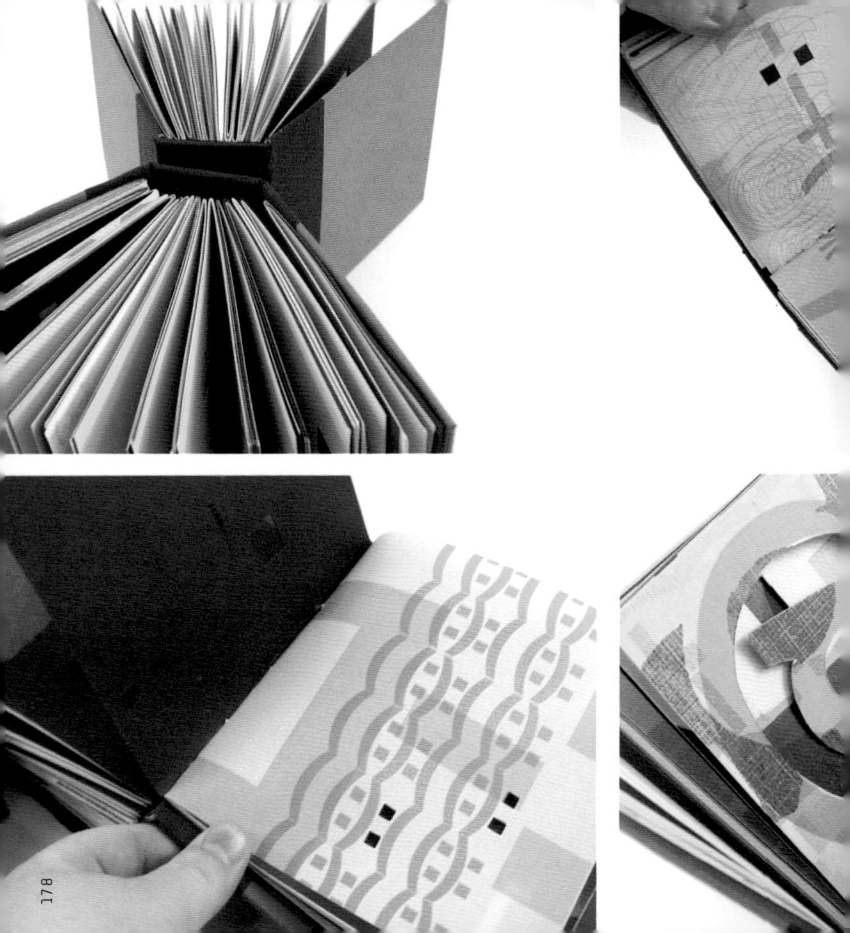

Allison Wilton (USA) www.allisonwilton.com

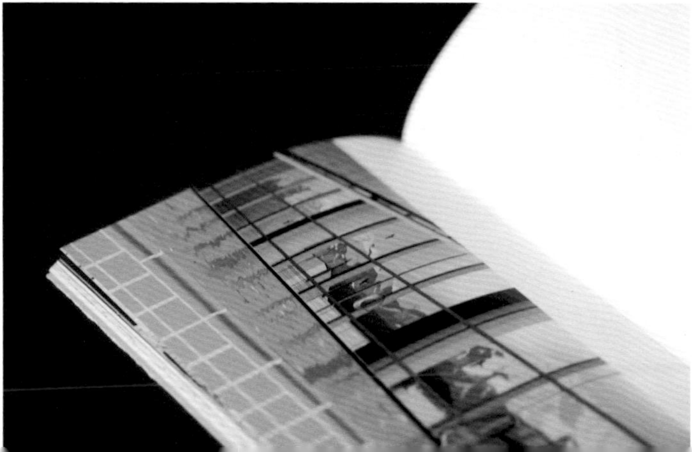

arte
03

48
49
MÁS ALLÁ
DE LO QUE
LOS OJOS PUEDEN VER

Hector Montes de Oca (MEX) www.cuatrog.com

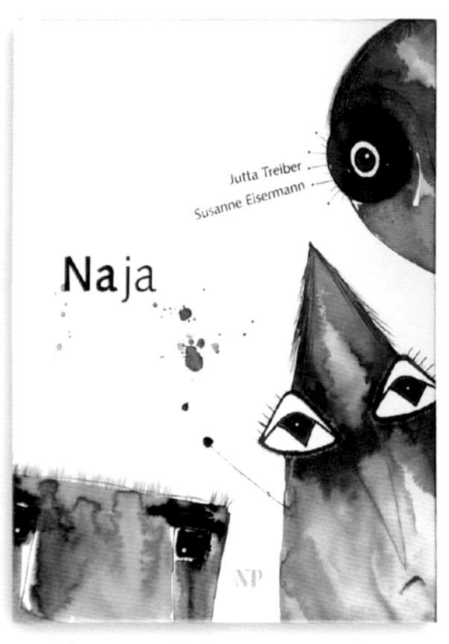
Jutta Treiber
Susanne Eisermann
Naja
NP

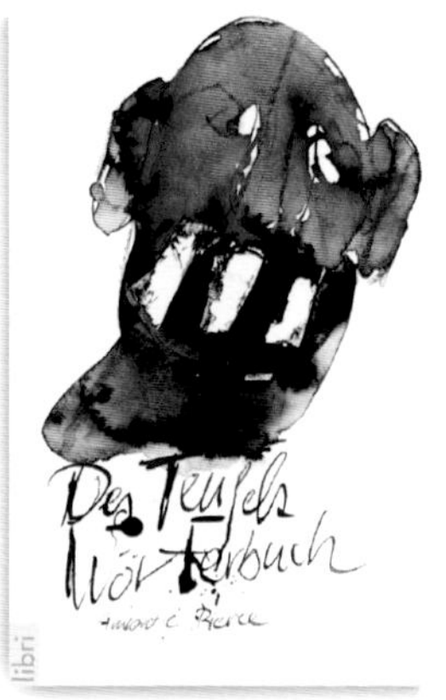
Des Teufels Wörterbuch
libri

Rafik Schami
Reise zwischen Nacht und Morgen
libri

 Susanne Eisermann (GER) www.susanne-eisermann.de

Typografische
Schriftenkompendium
Stile und Moden
des 20. Jahrhunderts
Gregor Stawinski
Stilgeschichte

Gregor
Slawinski

23. Juni 1992 | 00:14 Uhr

*»Selbst wenn ich ganz unten bin
spüre ich wie die Wörter in mir hochkochen
und raus wollen«*

Auszug aus Seite 115

vier

In den letzten Jahren habe ich wahrscheinlich mehr (und besser) geschrieben als in jedem vergleichbaren Zeitraum in meinem Leben. Als hätte ich das Ziel nach fünfzig Jahren beinnahe erreicht. Und seit zwei Monaten fühle ich mich zunehmend abgekämpft. Körperlich und geistig. Es könnte sein, daß ich an dem Punkt bin, wo es mit mir bergab geht. Was natürlich eine grauenhafte Vorstellung ist. Das Ideal war, bis zum Augenblick des Todes weiterzumachen, nicht in die Knie zu gehn. Vor drei Jahren habe ich eine Tuberkulose überstanden. Und dieses Jahr eine Augenoperation, deren Erfolg sich noch nicht so recht eingestellt hat. Und Kleinkram wie Schmerzen im Fußgelenk und ein bißchen Hautkrebs. Der Tod tritt mir hinten den Schlappen runter und bringt sich in Erinnerung. Ich bin ein alter Knacker, das ist alles. Ich konnte mich nicht zu Tode trinken, obwohl ich es beinnahe geschafft hätte. Jetzt geschieht es mir recht, daß ich leben muß mit dem, was von mir bleibt. Da hab ich nun seit drei Abenden nichts mehr geschrieben. Soll ich mich deshalb verrückt machen? Selbst wenn ich ganz unten bin, spüre ich, wie die Wörter in mir hochkochen und rauswollen.

Ich muß keinen Wettbeweb
bestehen. Es ging mir
nie um Ruhm oder
Geld.

05

24. August 1992 | 08:24 Uhr

*»Sogar den Göttern
kommt das große
Kotzen«*

acht

Neulich habe ich an die Welt nach meinem Tod gedacht. Die Welt tut, was sie immer tut, und ich bin nicht mehr da. Oder die gerollte Zeitung landet in der Einfahrt, und ich hebe sie nicht mehr auf. Undenkbar. Und das Schlimmste: Einige Zeit nach meinem Tod werde ich richtig entdeckt. Alle, die mich zu Lebzeiten gefürchtet oder gehaßt haben, finden mich jetzt ganz toll. Meine Worte sind überall. Clubs und Gesellschaften werden gegründet. Ekelhaft. Über mein Leben wird ein Film gedreht. Man macht mich viel mutiger und begabter, als ich es gewesen bin. Es wird übertrieben. Sogar den Göttern kommt das große Kotzen. Die menschliche Rasse übertreibt alles. Ihre Helden, ihre Feinde, ihre Bedeutung.

Wichser.
Ah, schon geht's mir besser.
Gottverdammtes Menschengeschlecht.

So.

Noch besser.

09

Linke Seite: Buchkunst, 1937. Dunedin-Schriftprobe der von M. F. Benton gestalteten Broadway, 1933. Diese Seite: Die Huxley Vertical von W. Huxley ist eine typische serifenlose Antiqua-Variante des Art Déco, 1935.

ABEFHPR

Viele Schriften werden aus geometrischen Formen zusammengesetzt. Die Wortbilder wirken flächig und ornamental, was die Lesbarkeit zwar erschwert, die plakative Wirkung jedoch erhöht. Häufig werden die Buchstaben zusätzlich räumlich-zeichnerisch ergänzt.

Kleinbuchstaben

Serifenlose Antiqua-Varianten gesellen sich zu den konstruierten Alphabeten. Auf Minuskeln verzichtet man mitunter und gibt Versalien mit dünnen Strichstärken den Vorzug, einige gestalterisch überhöht. Wiederholt findet man in diesen Alphabeten eine nach oben oder unten versetzte Mittelline, wie beim Versal-E, -F oder H. Gerne läßt man diese auch nach links ausbrechen, so gesehen bei Versal-A, -E, -F, -H und auch bei -B, -P, oder -R. Einige Alphabete sind durch einen starken Wechsel der Buchstabenbreite innerhalb des Alphabetes gekennzeichnet. Versal-S, -P und -R können dann sehr schmal, Rundformen wie das Versal-O, oder auch -G und -C im Verhältnis sehr breit ausfallen.

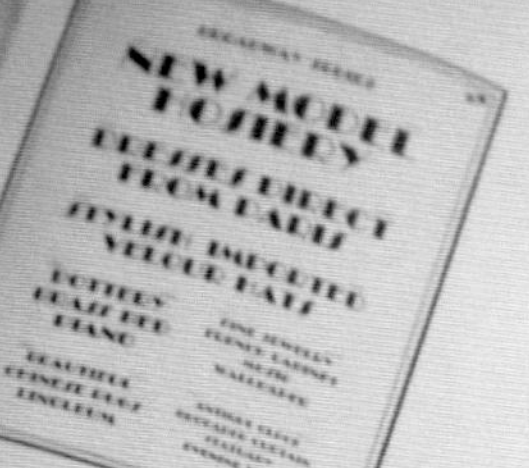

te Formen treten an die Stelle der Jugendstil-Ornamentik. Man greift überdies auf alle möglichen Vorbilder zurück: Die Zeichensprache der Ägypter, Azteken oder Indianer ist ebenso beliebt wie Zitate aus dem Klassizismus oder der afrikanischen Kunst. Auch die zeitgenössische Kunst wird ins Augenmerk geschlossen: Das Aufsplitten der Formen ist dem Kubismus, die Verehrung er Technik dem Futurismus, das geometrische Ornament dem nktionalismus entlehnt. Dieser eklektizistische Mix bildet den rboden der Schriften, die im Folgendem vorgestellt werden. Auch für die Schriftgestaltung des Art Déco gilt, dass sie auf Geometrie, Abstraktion und Elementarformen baf eine *zeichnerische Korrektur* zu Gunsten der Eleganz jeen verzichten wollte. Dennoch entstehen sie nicht aus ion der mit Feder geschriebenen Schriften, sondern nächst konstruiert, um schließlich zeichnerisch rt zu werden.

Alphabete des Art Déco sind jene Konstruierten, n starken, fast unausgeglichenen Strichstärken-Schriftschaffen des Klassizismus erinnern. Ihre on breit zu schmal, von hell zu dunkel ist chaird bewusst eingesetzt. Bis in die jüngste Zeit iftgestalter an dieser reizvollen Form.

Auch wenn unsere Schriftformen, vor allem das An- und Abschwellen der Linie, auf das Schreiben mit der Feder zurückzuführen sind, wird die Form meistens eher zeichnerisch nachempfunden. Viele Schriften werden also gezeichnet, nicht geschrieben.

ABE

Viele Schriften werd mengesetzt. Die Wortbilde die Lesbarkeit zwar ersch erhöht. Häufig werden die zeichnerisch ergänzt.

Kleinbuchstaben

Serifenlose Antiqua-Vari ierten Alphabeten. Auf Minuskel Versalien mit dünnen Strichstä risch überhöht. Wiederholt finde nach oben oder unten versetzte M oder H. Gerne läßt man diese auc sehen bei Versal-A, -E, -F, -H und a Alphabete sind durch einen starken te innerhalb des Alphabetes gekenn können dann sehr schmal, Rundfor auch -G und -C im Verhältnis sehr bre

Plakat, Copaline, 1971
Platten-Cover, 13th Floor, 1967
Revolte und Flower Power

Gregor Stawinski (GER) www.gregorstawinski.de

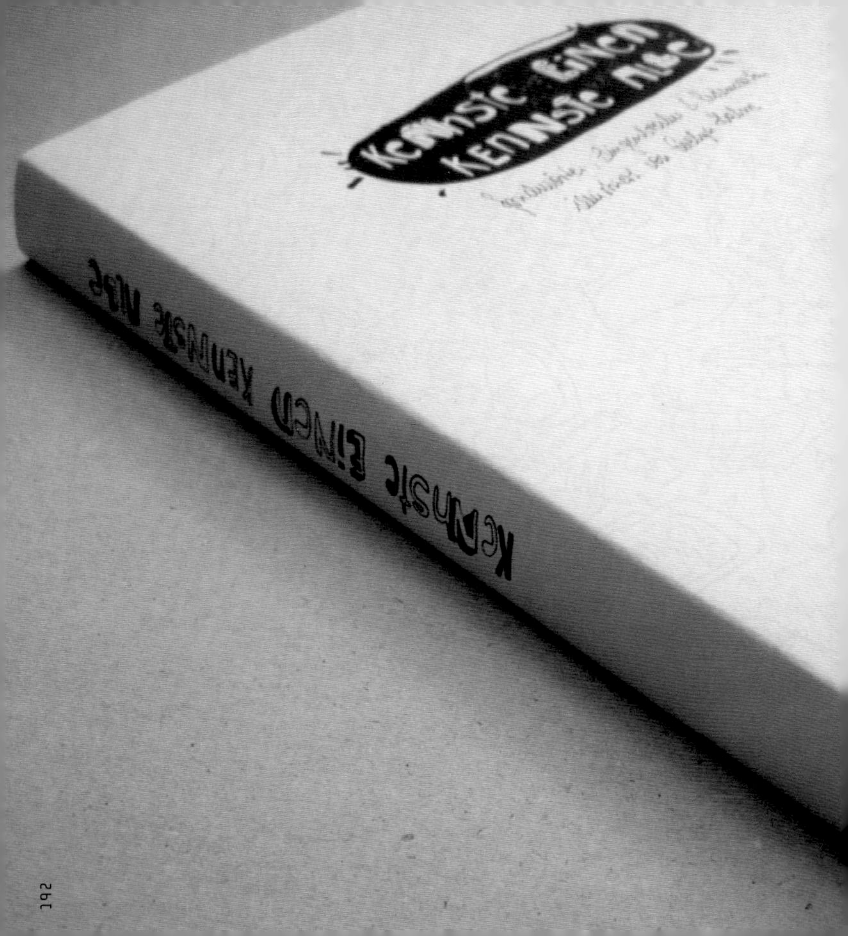

Evelyn Hahn (GER) www.evelynhahn.de

CHÖN
MUSS LEIDEN
Elisabeth
forever

des einen Freud des

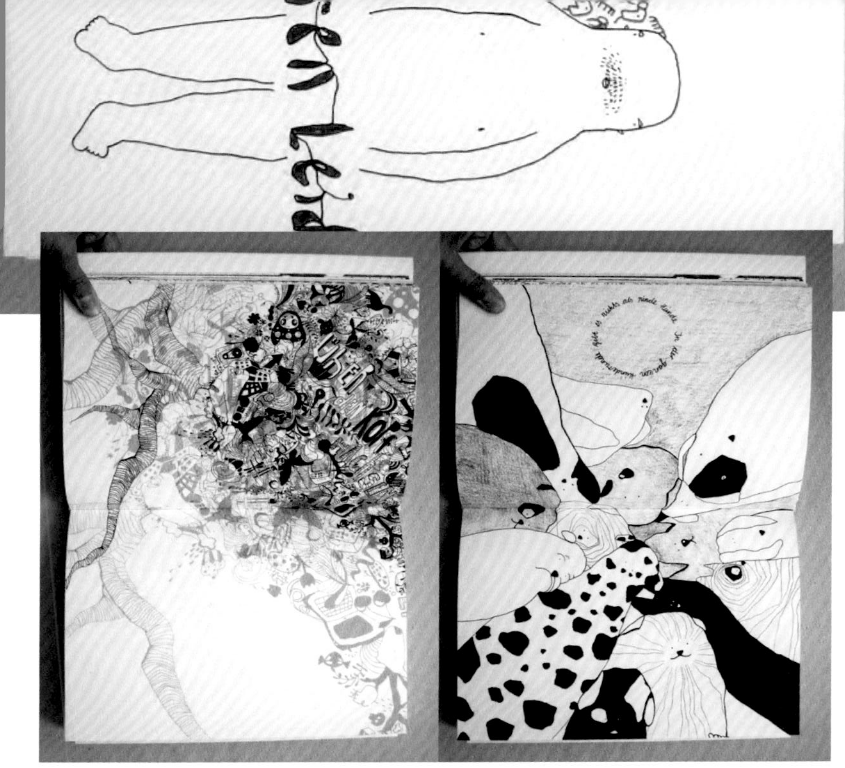

in der Pfanne verrückt.

Miau

Sabrina Weßling (GER)

Schnitt

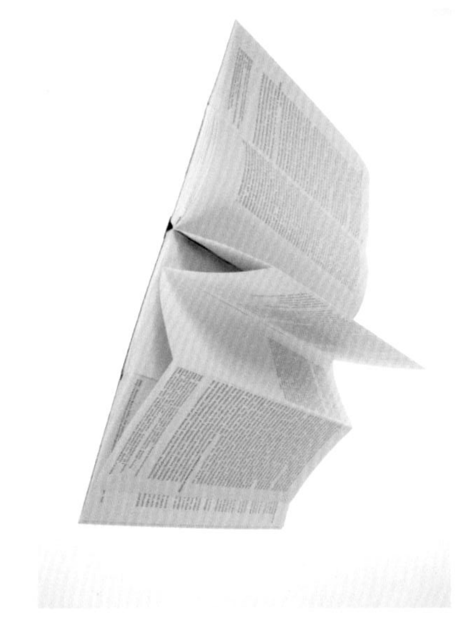

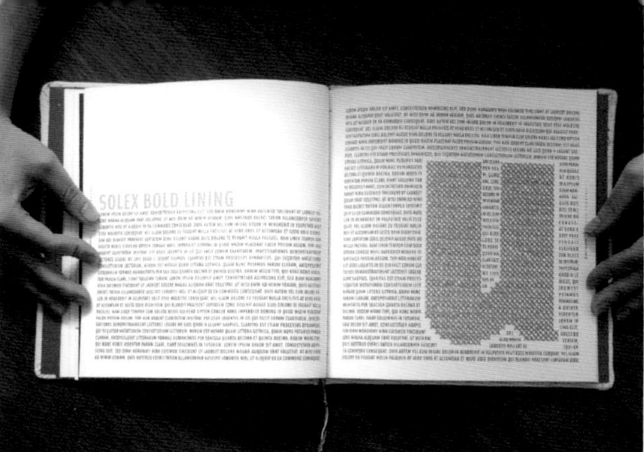
SOLEX BOLD LINING

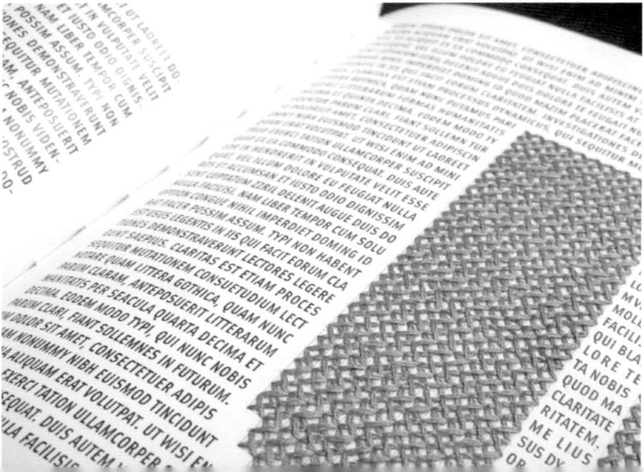

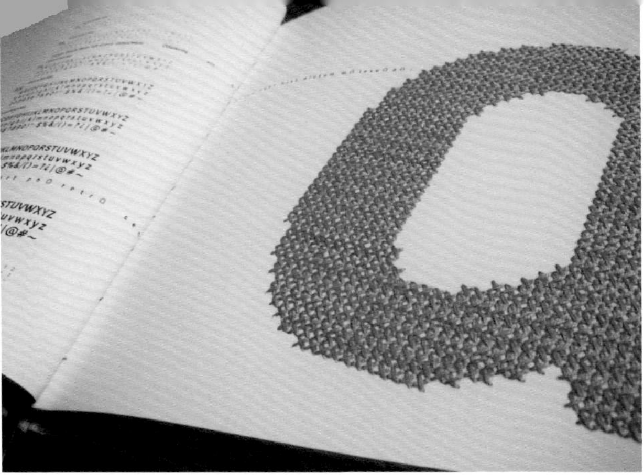

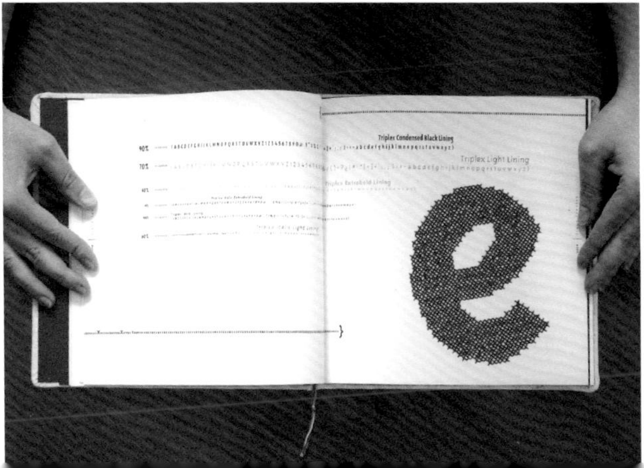
Triplex Condensed Black Lining
Triplex Light Lining

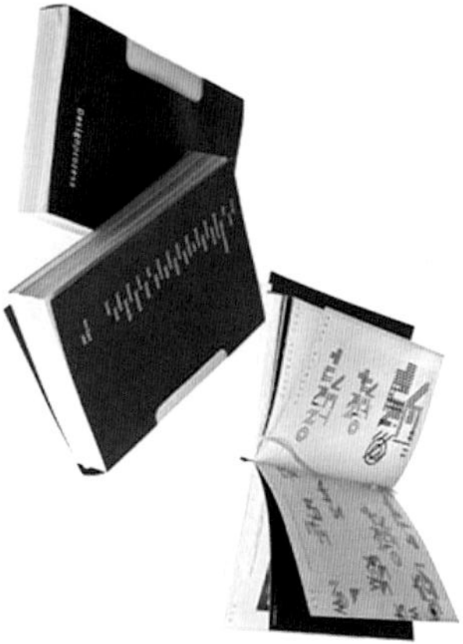

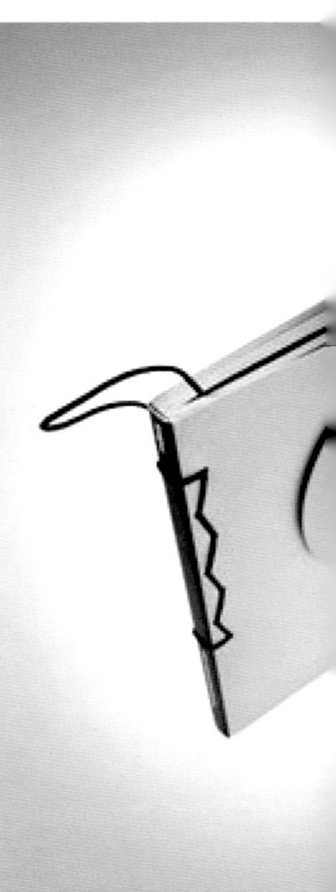

GOETHE
Über Rosen läßt sich dichten Für Gartenfreunde
AtV

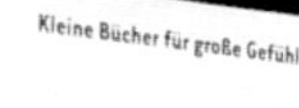

Kleine Bücher für große Gefühle
GOETHE
Über Rosen läßt sich dichten
Für Gartenfreunde
AtV
Kleine Bücher für große Gefühle
IRRTUM UND HERZLEID
Ein Trostbüchlein
Augustinus
AUGUSTINUS
AtV
DAS RECHTE MASS
AtV
DAS

Kleine Bücher für große Gefühle

DER TRÄNEN GENUG

Für unglückliche Verliebte

Ovid

OVID

AtV

MAUPASSANT

Kleine Bücher für große Gefühle

Erotische Novellen

Maupassant

PARISER ABENTEUER

AtV

Kleine Bücher für große Gefühle

DAS RECHTE MASS

Chinesische Weisheiten

AtV

DAS RECHTE MASS Chinesische Weisheiten AtV

MAUPASSANT Pariser Abenteuer. Erotische Novellen AtV

OVID Der Tränen genug. Für unglücklich Verliebte AtV

AUGUSTINUS Irrtum und Herzeleid. Ein Trostbüchlein AtV

GOETHE Über Rosen läßt sich dichten. Für Gartenfreunde AtV

Kleine Bücher für große Gefühle

GOETHE

Über Rosen läßt sich dichten

Für Gartenfreunde

AtV

BERND OEI
Band II
Nietzsche
unter deutschen Philosophen
Deutscher Wissenschafts-Verlag (DWV)

eps51 (GER) www.eps51.de

Marko Puclin (GER) www.becklyn.com

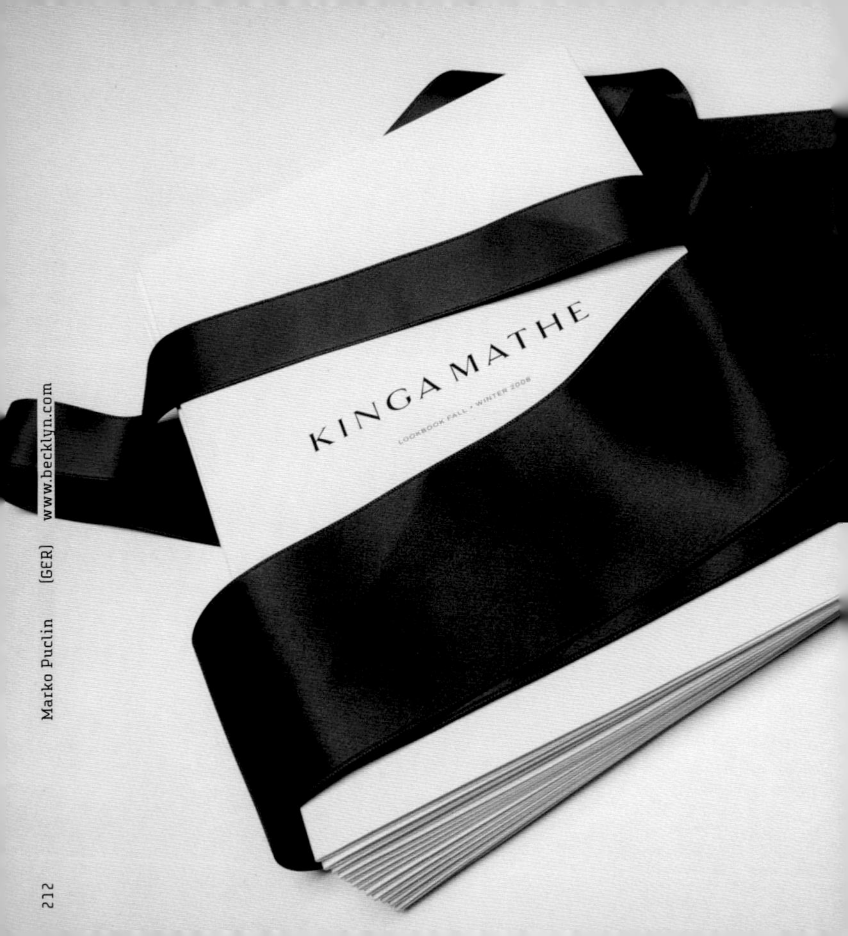

KINGA MATHE
LOOKBOOK FALL • WINTER 2008

KINGA MATHE
LOOKBOOK FALL • WINTER 2008

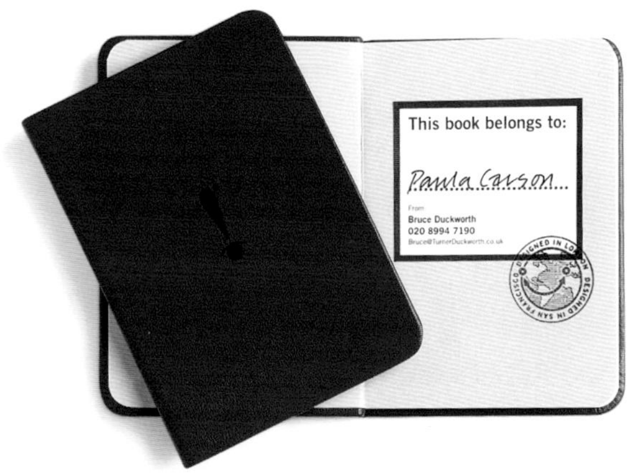
This book belongs to:
Paula Carson
From
Bruce Duckworth
020 8994 7190

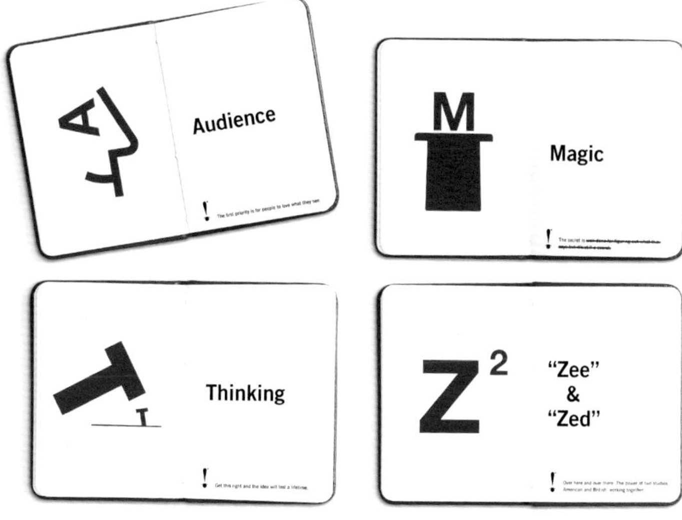

Audience
The first priority is for people to love what they see.
M
Magic
The secret is
Thinking
Get this right and the idea will last a lifetime.
Z 2
"Zee"
&
"Zed"
Over here and over there. The power of two studios.
American and British working together.

Turner Duckworth (GBR) www.turnerduckworth.com

scott howard

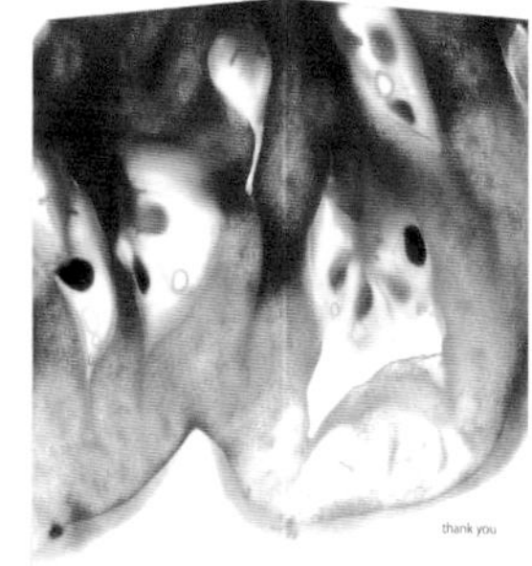

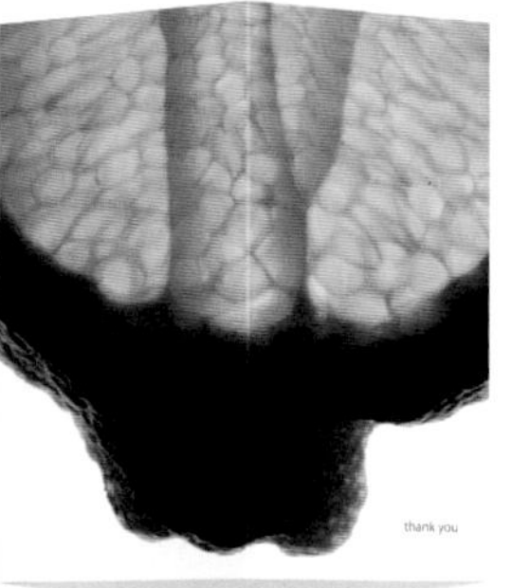

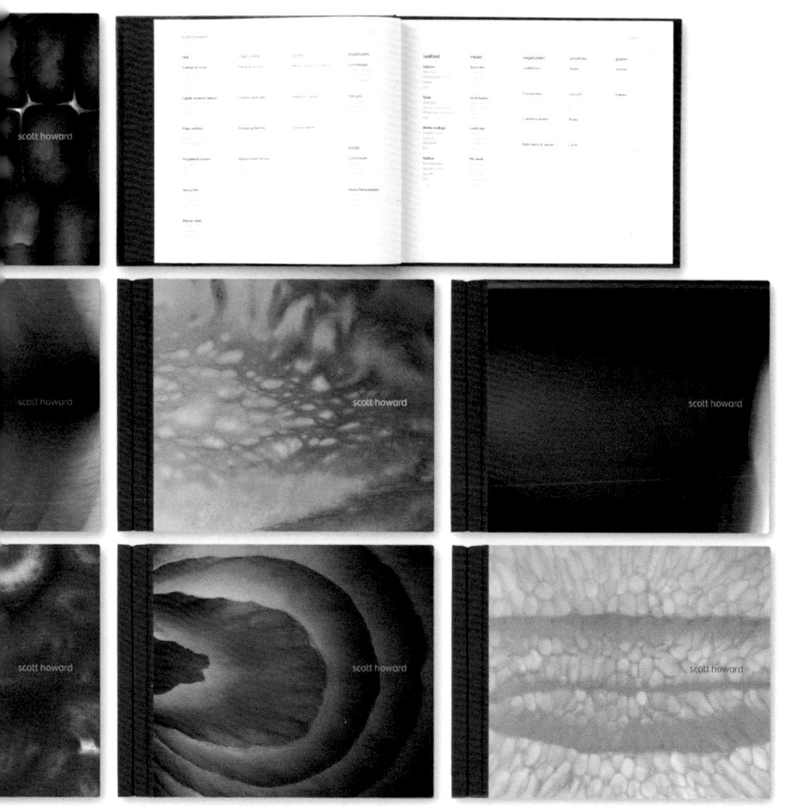
scott howard
scott howard
scott howard
scott howard
scott howard
scott howard
scott howard

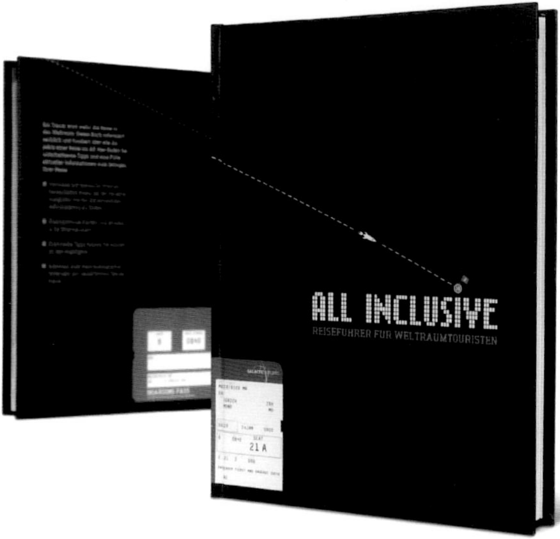

ALL INCLUSIVE
REISEFÜHRER FÜR WELTRAUMTOURISTEN
SEAT
21 A

WISSEN

INHALT
01
02
03
04
05
06
07

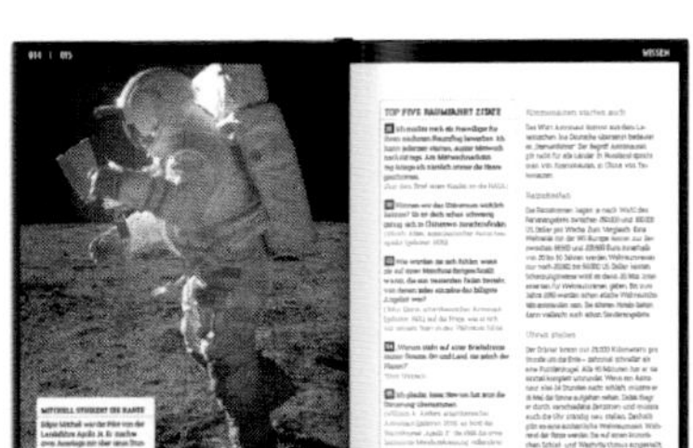

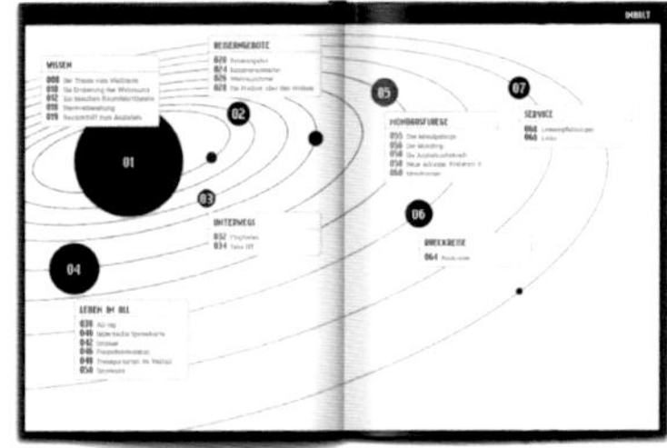

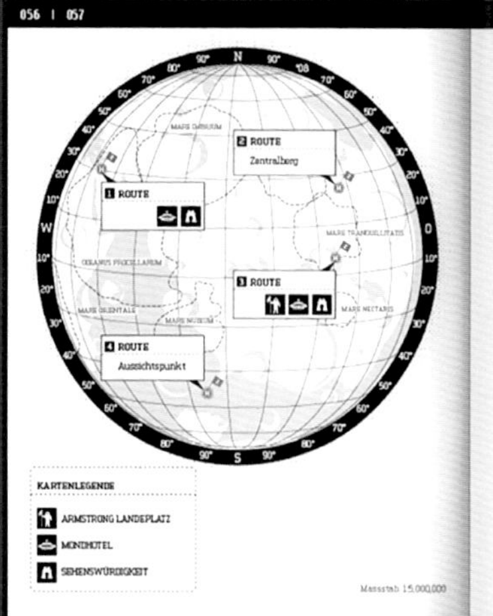

MONDAUSFLUEGE

DAS MONDGEBIRGE

Der Mond ist unser nächster Nachbar im Weltraum. Mit blossem Auge lassen sich auf dem Mond dunkle und helle Gebiete - die Mare und Terrae - erkennen. Bis heute ist er immer noch der einzige Himmelskörper, der Besuch von Menschen erhielt. Seit Beginn der modernen Monderkundung durch die Raumfahrt hat man einiges über unseren Nachbarn im All gelernt.

Mondmare

Die dunklen Mare finden sich vor allem auf der Vorderseite des Mondes. Bei den Maria handelt es sich um ausgedehnte Ebenen mit sehr wenigen Kratern. Die helleren Gebiete sind dagegen regelrecht mit Kratern übersäht. Die Anzahl Krater pro Flächeneinheit wird Kraterdichte genannt. Je älter eine Oberfläche ist, desto mehr kraterformende Meteoriteneinschläge hat sie erlebt. Die Maria sind vulkanischen Ursprungs und bestehen aus dunklen Basalten. In der Frühzeit des Mondes, bis vor etwa 38 Milliarden Jahren, wurden durch gewaltige Einschläge riesige Becken ausgehoben.

Hochländer

Die stark verkraterten hellen Gebiete liegen höher als die Maria und werden deshalb Hochländer genannt. Sie bestehen aus der ursprünglichen Kruste und sind wie die meisten Krater mehr als 4 Milliarden Jahre alt.

DER MOND IN ZAHLEN

Fläche
37 960 000 qkm (7,4 % der Erde)
Durchmesser
3476 km
Mondvolumen
21 990 000 km³ (2 % der Erde)
Masse
7,35 Trillionen Tonnen (1,2 % der Erde)
Beleuchtungsstärke des Vollmonds, von der Erde ausgesehen
0,25 Lux
Beleuchtungsstärke der Vollerde, vom Mond ausgesehen
16 Lux
Geringste Entfernung zur Erde
356 400 km
Grösste Entfernung zur Erde
406 700 km
Temperatur auf der Mondnachtseite
– 170 bis – 185 °C
Temperatur auf der Mondtagseite
+130 °C
Einwohner
117

LANDEPLÄTZE	KOORDINATEN
Mare Tranquillitatis	0° 67' N 23° 47' E
Oceanus Procellarum	3° 12' S 23° 23' W
Fra Mauro Hochland	3° 40' S 17° 28' E
Apollonius Hochland	3° 32' N 56° 33' E
Mare Crisium	12° 45' N 60° 12' E

EIN MÄDCHEN,
AUF DAS MÄNNER BEIM SPORT RÜCKSICHT
NEHMEN MÜSSEN...}

{HUPFDOHLE}

{II}
{...}
VERSCHNAUF
PAUSE

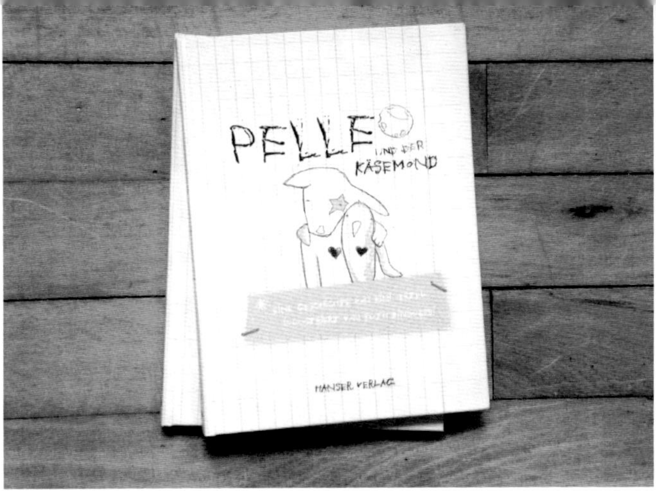

PELLE UND DER KÄSEMOND

HANSER VERLAG

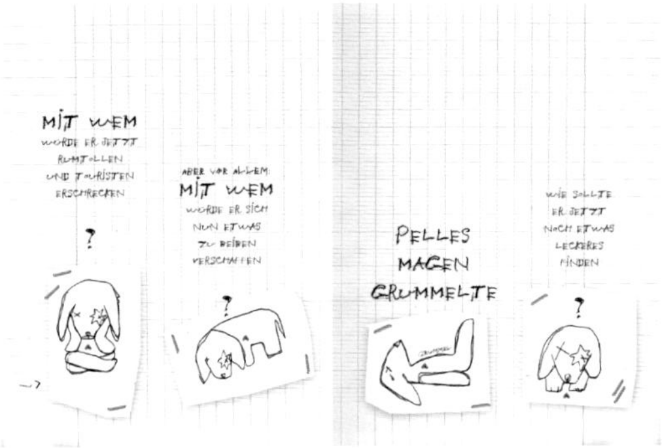

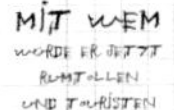

MIT WEM
WÜRDE ER JETZT
RUMTOLLEN
UND TOURISTEN
ERSCHRECKEN
?

ABER VOR ALLEM:
MIT WEM
WÜRDE ER SICH
NUN ETWAS
ZU BEIßEN
VERSCHAFFEN
?

PELLES
MAGEN
GRUMMELTE

WIE SOLLTE
ER JETZT
NOCH ETWAS
LECKERES
FINDEN
?

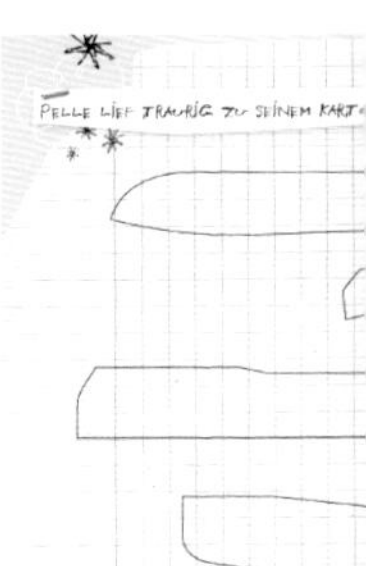

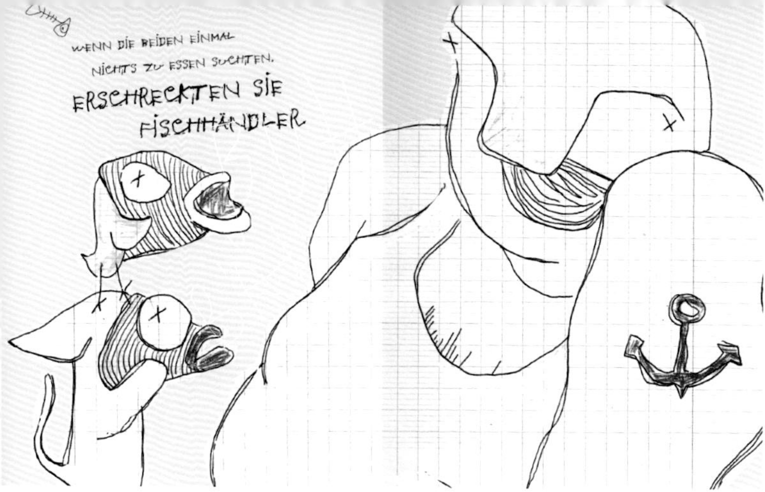

WENN DIE BEIDEN EINMAL
NICHTS ZU ESSEN SUCHTEN,
ERSCHRECKTEN SIE
FISCHHÄNDLER

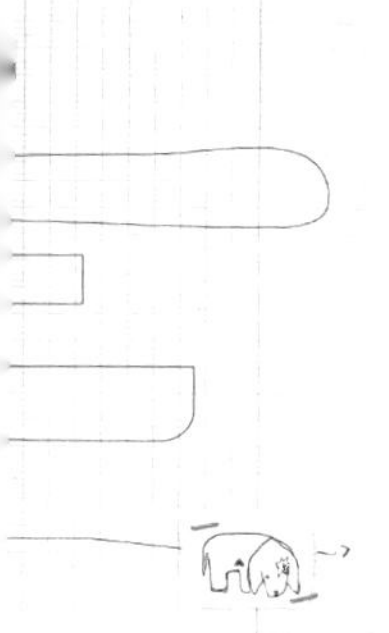

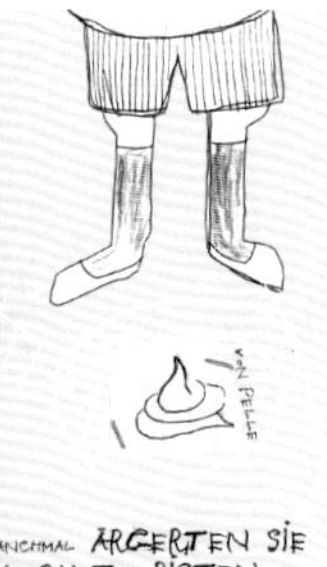

MANCHMAL ÄRGERTEN SIE
AUCH TOURISTEN,
DIE IN DER STADT URLAUB MACHTEN.

Christian Kohl, Christoph Pauli (GER)

›Märchen brauchen Zeit…‹
Don Quijote

Christian Kohl, Christoph Pauli (GER)

DER KAPITALISTISCHE SEKTOR ENDET HIER

BERLIN

Christian Kohl, Christoph Pauli [GER]

Christian Kohl, Christoph Pauli [GER]

SNEAKER SM MARMALADE

WELCOME TO THE SNEAKER CULTURE

français english text

interview the streets

megatest reebok ventilator

megatest nike air trainer 1

megatest adidas micropacer

interview tinker hatfield, nike

+ freshkicks, sneaker business, socio logik, freestyle...

love ?

Und man fast noch zweihundert Jahre lang nichts vom Doktor Luther wußte,
und hätte seitdem Tag für Tag daran gearbeitet und lebte noch, so wäre er
noch nicht fertig. Wenn also vierhundertachtzig Menschen daran arbeiten,
so werden sie fertig in einem Jahr.
17

Simone Blauert (GER) www.4teog.de

Evan Melnyk [CAN] www.curseofthemultiples.com

Martin Kühnel (GER) www.martin-kuehnel.de

01
form
02 pattern
colour

03

P 04	form
P 12	colour
P 16	pattern
P 22	showroom

■ 02

paul&louise™

Hamburg
Madrid
New York
Helsinki
Paris
London

paul&louise™
founded 1902 restart 1996

We are working to be one of the most efficient companies in the world, while ensuring that everyone touched by our business process has a positive experience. paul&louise offers the best forms, colours and patterns.

index

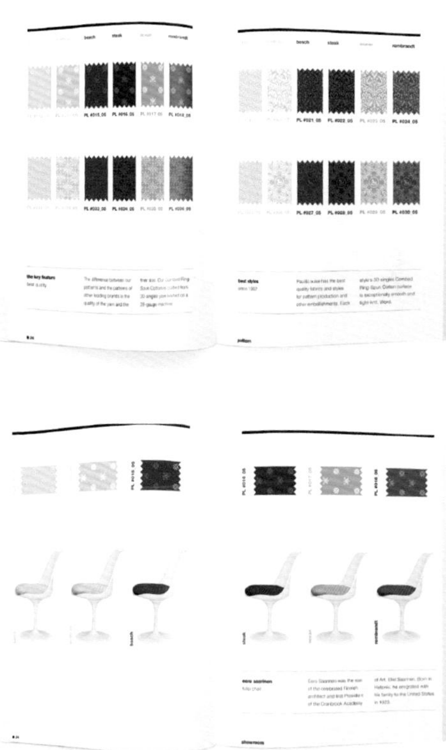
bosch
steak
rembrandt
the key feature
best styles
eero saarinen
tulip chair
showroom

GO
Glasgow's FREE lifestyle, entertainment and listings magazine
GO Magazine
Issue 1
FREE
embrace on why Barrowland is Best
win a 6 foot Sub
michael redmond A Stand Up, Sitting Down
music
film
theatre
comedy

Steven Waldron (SCO) www.tangentgraphic.co.uk

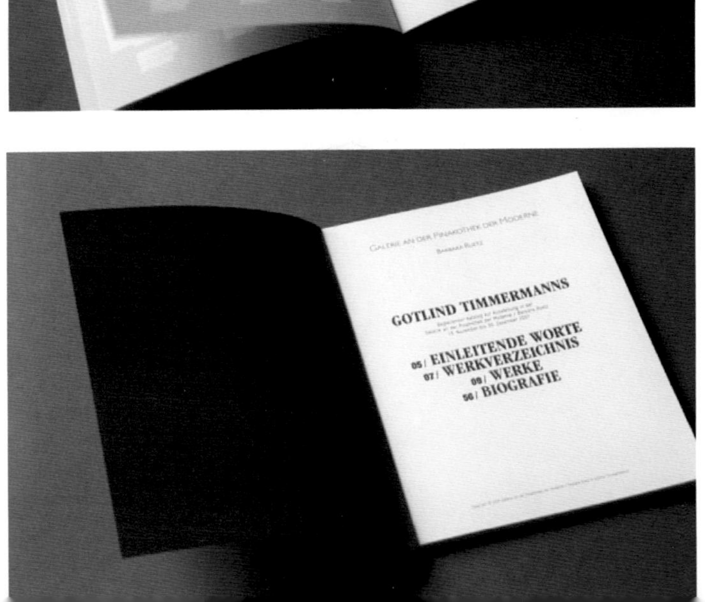
GALERIE AN DER PINAKOTHEK DER MODERNE
BARBARA RUETZ
GOTLIND TIMMERMANNS
05 / EINLEITENDE WORTE
07 / WERKVERZEICHNIS
09 / WERKE
56 / BIOGRAFIE

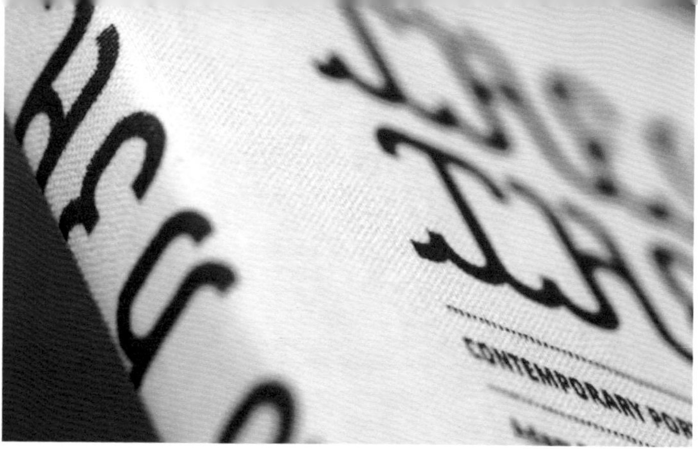
CONTEMPORARY POR

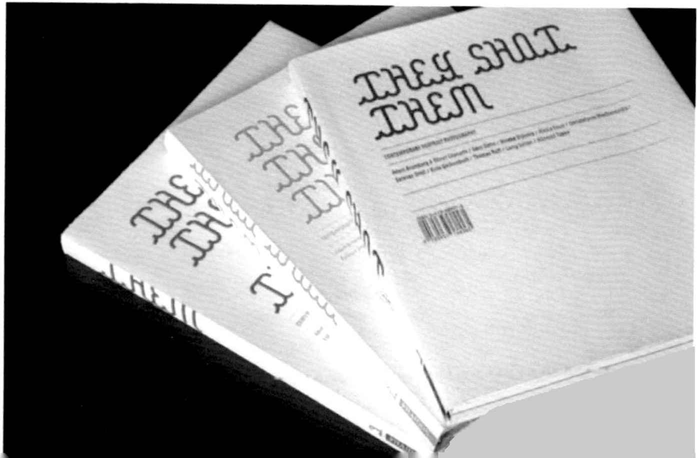
THEY SHOT
THEM

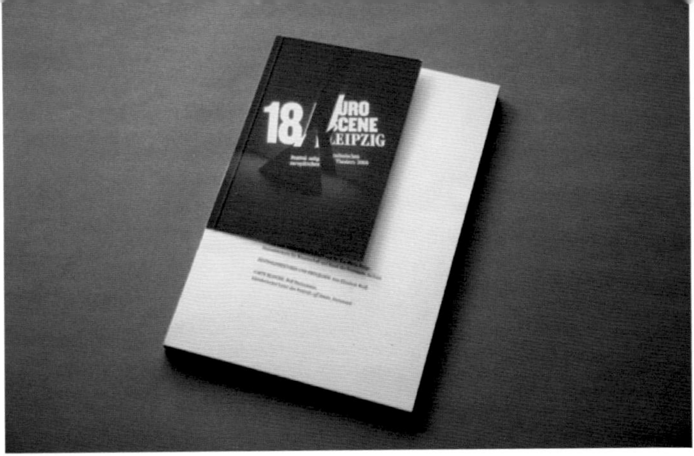
18/
URO
CENE
EIPZIG

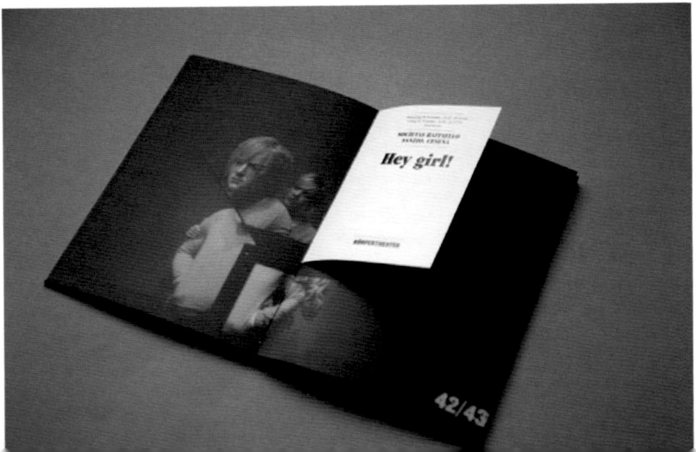
Hey girl!
42/43

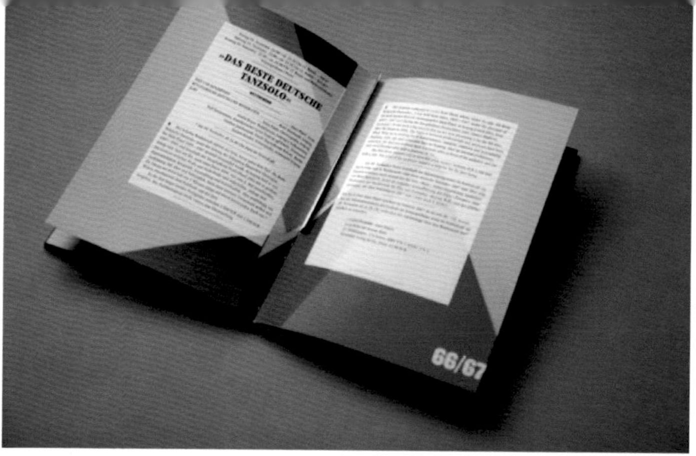
»DAS BESTE DEUTSCHE TANZSOLO«
66/67

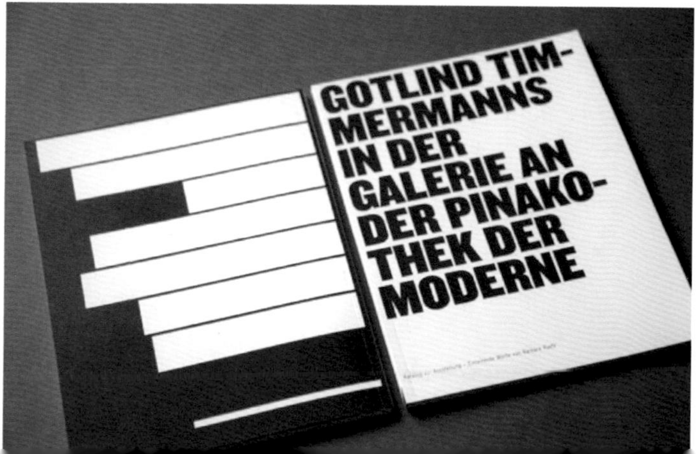
GOTLIND TIM-
MERMANNS
IN DER
GALERIE AN
DER PINAKO-
THEK DER
MODERNE

DESIGN + FUN
ICH KRIEG' DICH
ICH LIEB' DICH
VERKEHRSMARMELADE
ALLES IN ORDNUNG

245 Magdalena Nowak (GER) www. hellucinations.de

WELCOME
to ISSUE
05
>CHAOS

INHALT

Was heißt ich liebe Dich auf klingonisch?

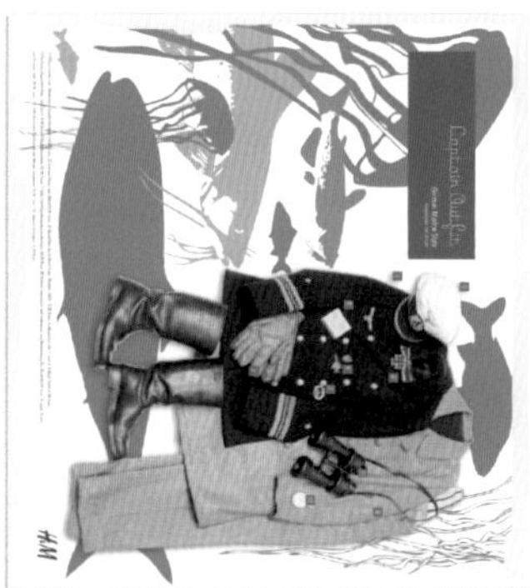

 Magdalena Nowak (GER) www.hellucinations.de

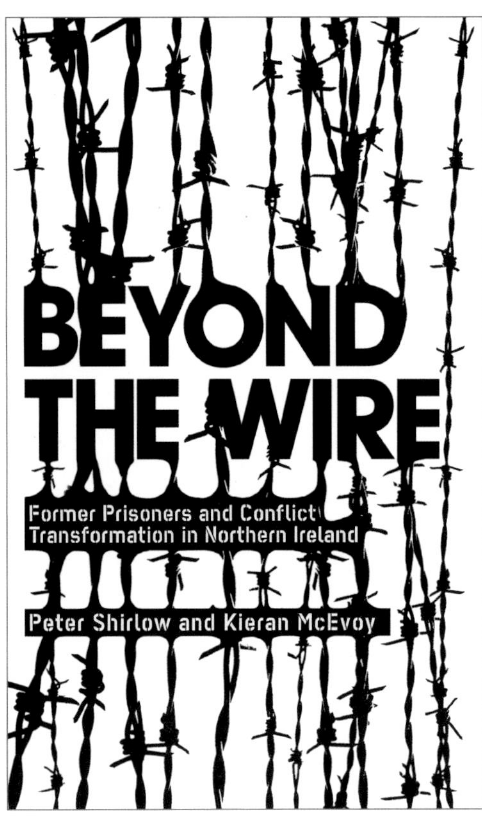
BEYOND
THE WIRE
Former Prisoners and Conflict
Transformation in Northern Ireland
Peter Shirlow and Kieran McEvoy

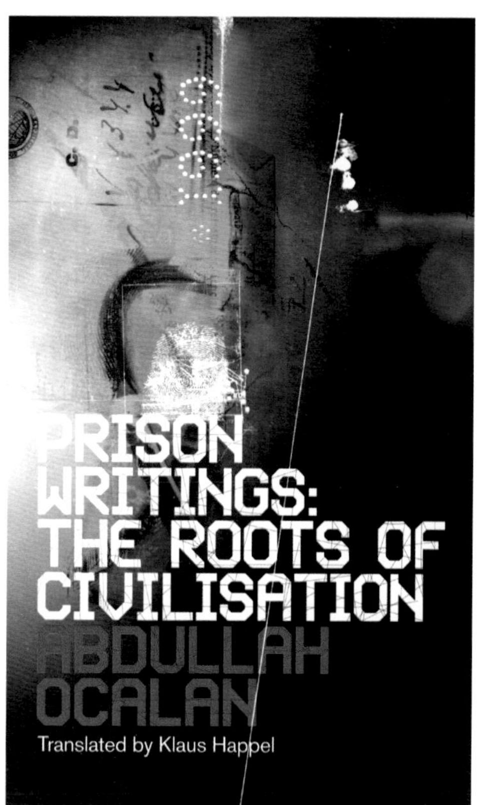
PRISON
WRITINGS:
THE ROOTS OF
CIVILISATION
ABDULLAH
OCALAN
Translated by Klaus Happel

Guideline
ACCESSORIES
ALL ACCESS!!
Fall Winter
2007 2008

Luca Serradura [ITA]

GUIDELINE
SPRING SUMMER
2008

GUIDELINE 09
SPRING SUMMER

Luca Serradura [ITA]

Silent
Five a.m.

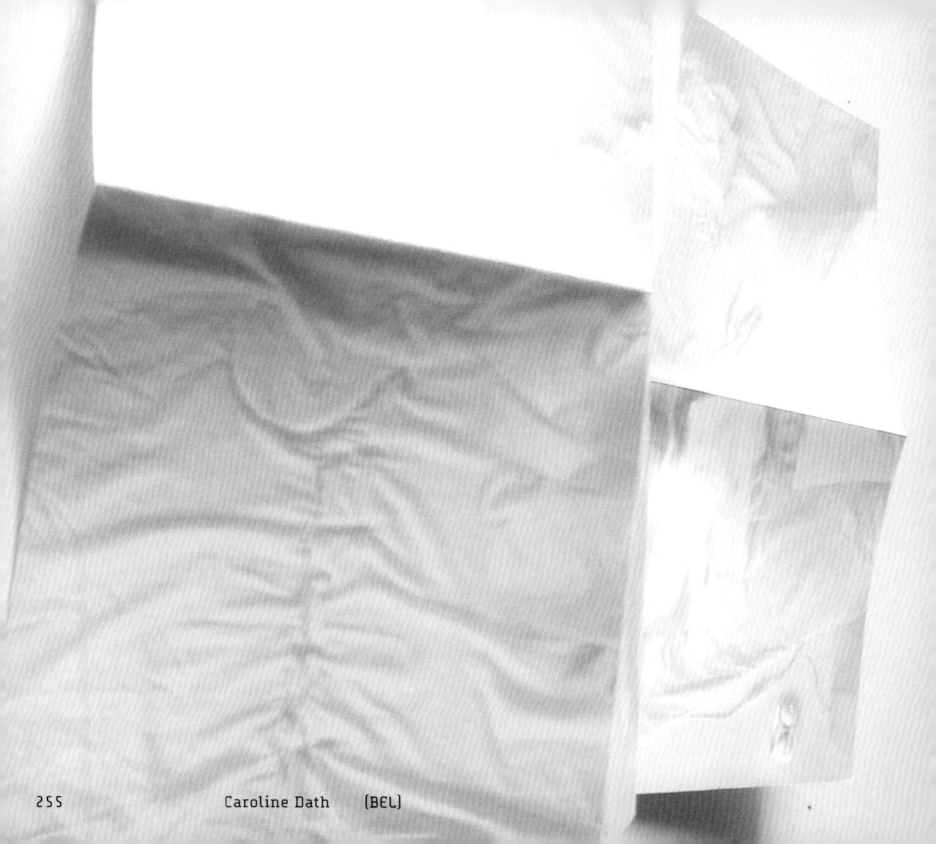

 Caroline Dath (BEL)

knewt
hurray!
new hits: hurray!
knewt

knewt
hurray!

CROWDPLEASER

ake your-
self more
attractive
to others!
EVE WHITE
New You

Crack Hoffmann
Jazz Quartett
A matinée for Johar Hospital

George Gershwin (1927)
(1928) Jimmy McHugh
Thomas Fats Waller (1929)
Richard A. Dick Winfree (1927)
Do you know what it means to miss New Orleans (1946) Louis Alter
I've found a new Baby Spencer Williams (1926)
Georgia on my mind Hoagy Carmichael (1930)
How high the moon William Morgan Lewis (1940)
On the sunny side of the street Jimmy McHugh (1930)
Runnin' wild Arthur Harrington Gibbs (1922)
Memories of you Eubie Blake (1930)
Rosetta Earl Hines (1935)
JOHAR2007

Crack Hoffmann
Jazz Quartett
A matinée for Johar Hospital

Eva Zechel (GER) www.exmono.de

BAUER
00:14:37:05

the pictures
page
Manual Aperture Control 14
Fadings 14
Filters 15
Close-Up Lenses 15
Converters 16
Shooting with Artificial Light 17
Unloading of Film Cartridge 17
Proper Care of the Camera 18

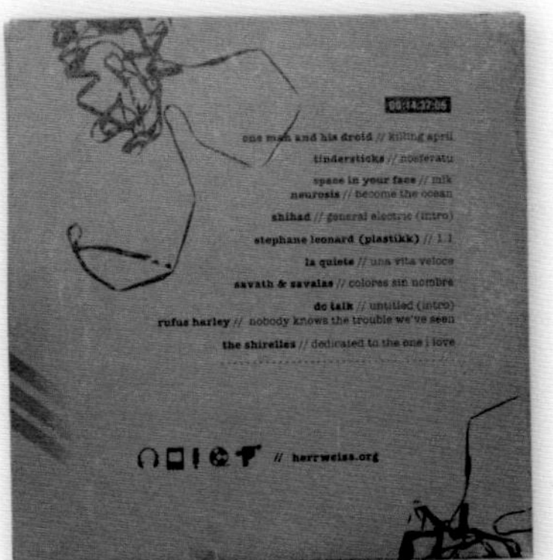
00:14:37:05
one man and his droid // killing april
tindersticks // nosferatu
space in your face // milk
neurosis // become the ocean
shihad // general electric (intro)
stephane leonard (plastikk) // 1.1
la quiete // una vita veloce
savath & savalas // colores sin nombre
dc talk // untitled (intro)
rufus harley // nobody knows the trouble we've seen
the shirelles // dedicated to the one i love
// herrweiss.org

Sebastian Weiß (GER) herrweiss.org

DANSE MACABRE
AM I DEAD
SPLIT 7"

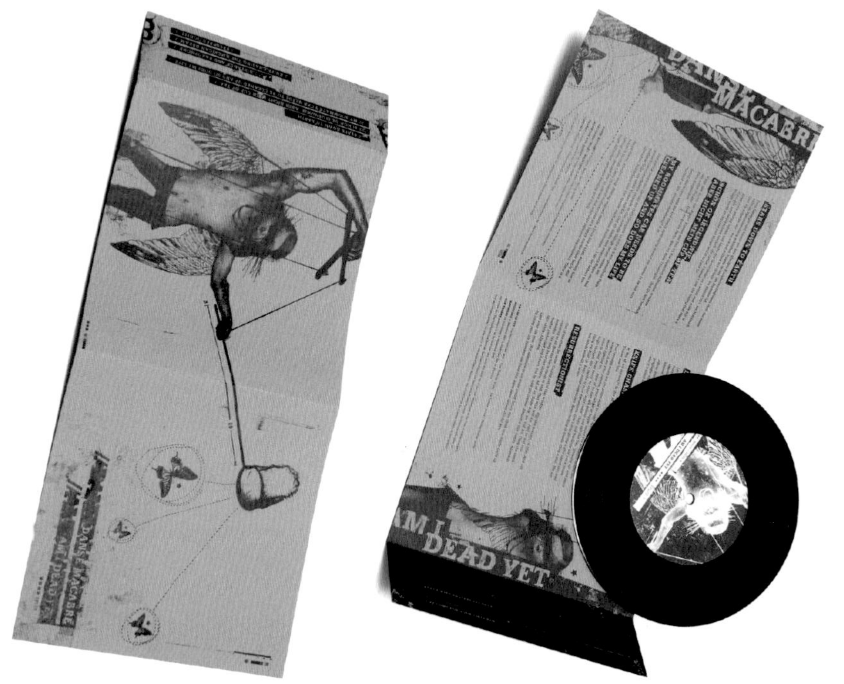
DANSE MACABRE
STARS DOWN TO EARTH
RESURRECTIONIST
AM I DEAD YET
DANSE MACABRE
AM I DEAD YET

Jamie Oliver Aspinall (SUI) www.schnuppe.ch

summer
music

Jeffrey Bowman (GBR) www.mrbowlegs.co.uk

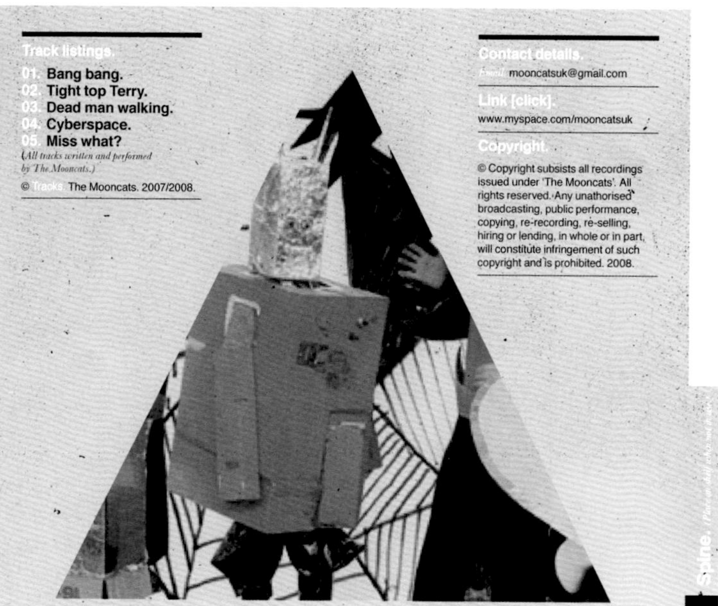

Track listings.
01. Bang bang.
02. Tight top Terry.
03. Dead man walking.
04. Cyberspace.
05. Miss what?
(All tracks written and performed by The Mooncats.)
© Tracks The Mooncats. 2007/2008.
Contact details.
Email mooncatsuk@gmail.com
Link [click].
www.myspace.com/mooncatsuk
Copyright.
© Copyright subsists all recordings issued under 'The Mooncats'. All rights reserved. Any unathorised broadcasting, public performance, copying, re-recording, re-selling, hiring or lending, in whole or in part, will constitute infringement of such copyright and is prohibited. 2008.
THE MOONCATS Adventures in space.
Spine.

Booklet inside.

Thank you.

The Mooncats wish to thank everyone who's been involved in helping us get to where we are today. Mr Bowlegs for supplying all the eye catching Mooncats artwork. Colin Williams for taking the time to believe in us and for assisting with recording. Jon Carroll for the photography along the way. Roberts Guitars for helping out with instrument maintenance.

Gary Robinson, Mike McGrath and Gary Wood for having enough faith in us to put us on big stages and making us sound good. Sevens for giving us that first gig, seems like a long time ago now, but we still really appreciate it. Pete Rathbone for helping out when times got hard for us and for working with Pablo. Terry Wilson for all his work with Ben and on our sound. Sharkey and PC for their constant support when it comes to Mooncats out of towners, very much appreciated! Wallie, one of the nicest guys a band could ever meet... and one of the best roadies in the world!!

We'd also like to say a big, and a special thank you to everyone who comes and watches us...you guys really make it worth while.

Album description.

The Mooncats.
Adventures in space.

© The Mooncats. 2008.

Track listings.

01. **Bang bang.**
02. **Tight top Terry.**
03. **Dead man walking.**
04. **Cyberspace.**
05. **Miss what?**

© The Mooncats. 2007/2008.

Who.

Ian Curwen.
Jordan Emms.
Ben Wilson.
Pablo.

Contact details.

mooncatsuk@gmail.com

Link [click].

www.myspace.com/mooncatsuk

Logo.

© The Mooncats. 2007/2008.

Copyright.

Design.

Sleeve designed by MrBowlegs™
© 2008.
www.mrbowlegs.co.uk
hello@mrbowlegs.co.uk

Steven Waldron (GBR) www.tangentgraphic.co.uk

TRUGBIL
design.
tangent

tangent

Hi.
We are
Tangent.
We
design.
TRUGBIL
WINDING

Hi.
We are
Tangent.

tangent

Dorota Bogucki (GER) www.boghukey.com

RUB-A-DUB
FRIDAYS!
STARTING JULY 18
ADMIT ONE
SIDE A
1. Reggae
2. Dub
3. Dancehall
4. Rockers
5. Downbeat
SIDE B
1. Roots
2. Culture
3. Steppers
4. Ska
5. Rub-A-Dub
100% REGGAE VIBES!
45 RPM

Miguel Vega (USA) www.accent.tv

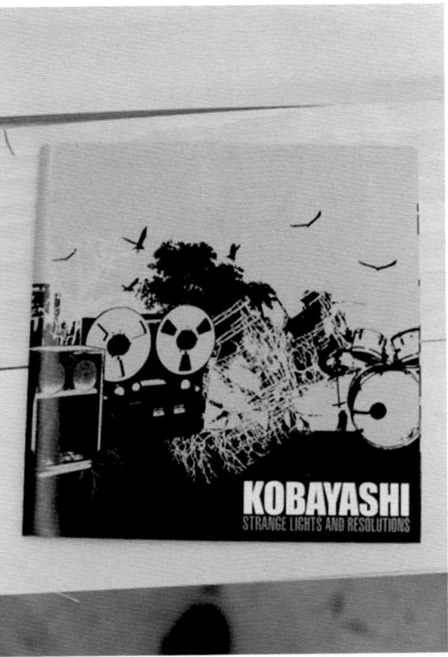
KOBAYASHI
STRANGE LIGHTS AND RESOLUTIONS

Billy Cicalo
Chris Tauchner
Radu Falcon
Evan Melnyk
Joshua Gearey
Hadiya Roderique
Franco Proietti
GUESTS

bongo beat
KOBAYASHI
STRANGE LIGHTS AND RESOLUTIONS
MADE IN CANADA

Never Was
Midnight Ambulances
Road Less Travelled
2 Cent
Narn't
Shadows
Conversations
Shasta
Rex Basin
bongo beat

Zarządzając pracą innych ludzi musimy mieć narzędzie do oceny jej jakości i efektywności. Jednym z najważniejszych elementów tej oceny jest stopień wykorzystania czasu pracy. Ale to nie jedyny parametr, który chcemy zmierzyć. Dla właściciela firmy, managera, kierownika czy lidera projektu ważne jest także to, jakie prace i dla kogo zostały wykonane w analizowanym przedziale czasowym, ile to kosztowało firmę i jakiej ceny powinniśmy żądać od naszego klienta za wykonane na jego rzecz czynności. Rzetelne, oparte o faktycznie wykonane prace rozliczenie z klientem jest podstawą dobrego i profesjonalnego wizerunku firmy, pozwalając jednocześnie na zachowanie właściwych proporcji pomiędzy opłacalnością a konkurencyjnością w branży.

Wychodząc naprzeciw tym oczekiwaniom stworzyliśmy **Rejestratora Czasu Pracy**, który oddajemy do Państwa dyspozycji. Jest to program, który pomoże Wam w rozwiązaniu powyższych problemów. Program powstał w oparciu o nasze własne doświadczenia i potrzeby, ale tworzyliśmy go z myślą o jego uniwersalnym wykorzystaniu w różnych branżach. Staraliśmy się aby był prosty i intuicyjny w obsłudze, a przy tym dostarczał jak najwięcej informacji.

dalgos sp. z o.o.
R:C:P
rejestrator czasu pracy

Rejestrator Czasu Pracy (RCP) składa się z dwóch modułów:

Moduł Operator - uruchamiany i obsługiwany przez osobę (pracownika) wykonującego czynności podlegające rejestracji. Moduł działa w czasie rzeczywistym i jest niewrażliwy na zmiany daty czy czasu w systemie. Operator wybiera klienta, dla którego wykonuje pracę, grupę czynności i czynność. Jednocześnie może być otwartych wiele czynności po między którymi przełączenie następuje za pomocą kliknięcia myszką. Czas automatycznie zatrzymuje się dla czynności nieaktywnej i uruchamia dla wybranej przez operatora.

Moduł Administrator - zawiera wszystkie niezbędne do pracy programu opcje konfiguracyjne. Możliwe jest zdefiniowane między innymi takich parametrów jak:

- Typ rozliczenia z klientem (ryczałt, według godzin, według stawki)
- Stawkę kosztu za godzinę pracy każdego z pracowników
- Cenę sprzedaży za godzinę pracy pracownika
- Grupowanie czynności wykonywanych przez operatora
- Przypisywanie operatorów do czególnych klientów

Ponadto moduł te
przeglądanie hi
czynności z p
operatorów
innych. P
i sporza
wielo
anali
rozl

rejestrator czasu pracy

Rejestrator Czasu Pracy

z czasu pracy
n czynności
ów, zleceń
anych prac

OPTIC NERVES....
OPTIC NERVES....
OPTIC NERVES....
OPTIC NERVES....
OPTIC NERVES....
ENOUGH
THROUGH THE OPTIC NERVES...

Freizeitraum

Eingang Passage

Andreas Maldei (GER) www.myspace.com/andimacht

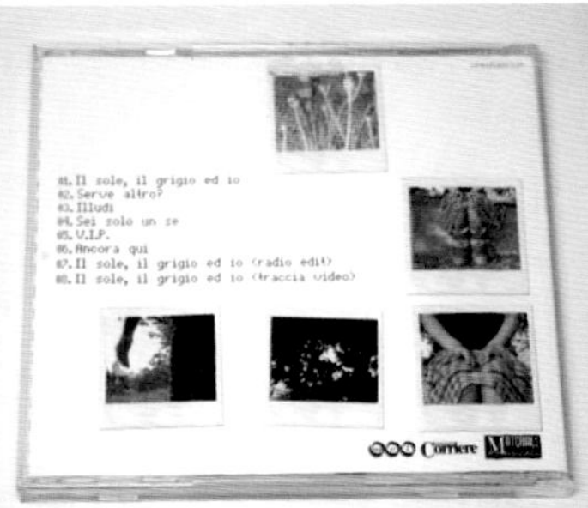

Giovanni Ricchi (ITA) www.minimalsonic.net

sentence
dominion on evil

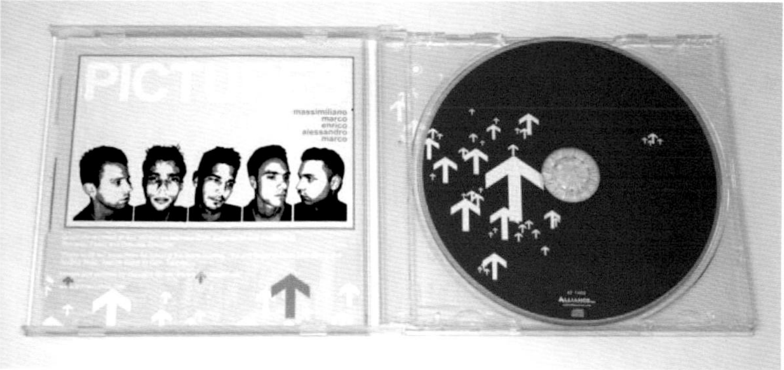

VON
AUSSER
HALB DER
LC 09546

ZWANGSVORSTELLUNG
Von ausserhalb der Schachtel
01.Botschaftsverweis
Eine glorreiche Zeit.15
02.Fremdartig Klang
Schlaflieder.14
03.Aufgrund dunkler Vermutung
Sicher Sein.13
04.Aus dem Augen aus dem Kreis
Fragwürdig.12
05.Dein Skit
Vogel frei.11
06.Rapextern
Bewusstlosigkeit.10
07.MutterKind
Tagschatten.09
08.Jemand
LC 09546
hundert10prozent
WWW.ZWANGSVORSTELLUNG.COM

Lukas Michalski (GER) www.hundert10prozent.de

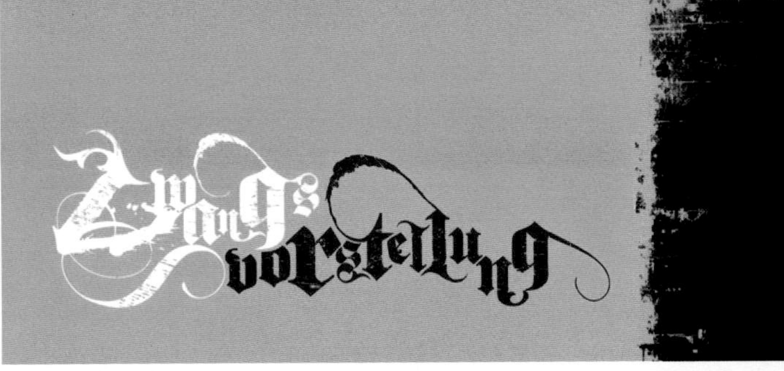

BOTSCHAFTSVERWEIS
Botschaftsbeweis

Gesuc

FREMDARTIG KLANG
„Ausgesperrt von **aussen** ist die Welt so klein
doch von **innen** ausgesperrt
wird die Wahrheit zum **Feind**"

Ergeben meiner Müdigk
sowie der Träume
der Möglichkeiten drei
drei
TA

AUFGRUND DUNKLER VERMUTUNG
Glänzende Scheisse für jedermann

VOGEL FREI

DEIN SKIT

Wer kann sich über **Freiheit** beklagen?
Und größere **Freiheit** erträumen?
Ohne seine **Freiheit** zu nutze

AUS DEN AUGEN AUS DEM KREIS
aus Zeiten der Betroffenheit

FRAGWÜRDIG

Wenn ich nachdenke, stell

der

Frag´ dich.

RAPEXTERN
„...aufgrund der Niveaupflicht"

MUTTER KIND

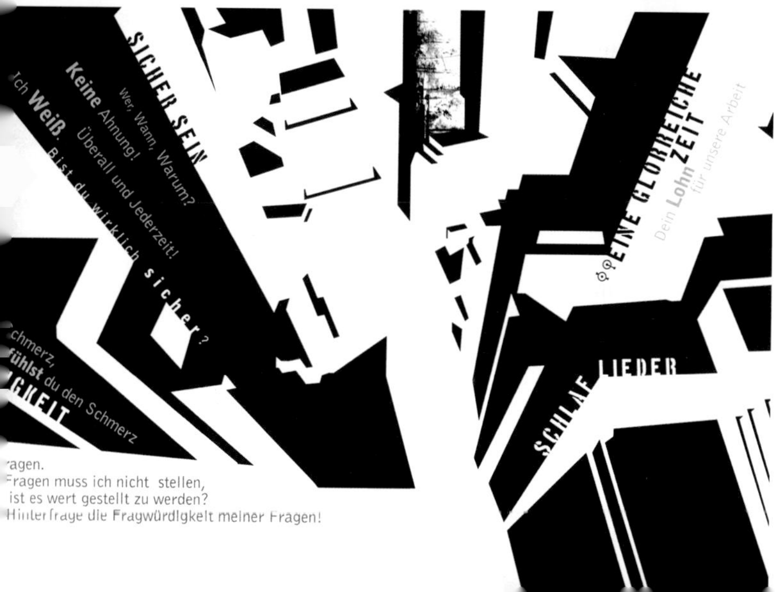

SICHER SEIN

Wer, Wann, Warum?

Keine Ahnung!

Überall und Jederzeit!

Ich **Weiß**. Bist du wirklich sicher?

chmerz,
fühlst du den Schmerz

GKEIT

ragen.
Fragen muss ich nicht stellen,
ist es wert gestellt zu werden?
Hinterfrage die Fragwürdigkeit meiner Fragen!

EINE GLORREICHE ZEIT

Dein **Lohn** für unsere Arbeit

SCHLAF LIEDER

NO AUTHORITY
DON'T LOSE HEART
LEECH
RECORDS

Mario Schmidt (GER) www.webalive.de

recently I decided to care less
about these bad emotions – oh yes it hurts
but then again after few more days it's gone
(I can) remember so many things that
brought me down to my knees
but now it's gone – everything passes by

recently I decided to care less because it's summertime
pain fades away and everyone has a smile on the face
look at this, some girls are wearing belly-tops and short skirts
but no underwear – yes we love the summertime

recently I decided to care less because it's party time
oh yes life rules – and everyone feels really great inside
as I am back by myself – knowing
we will take this feeling with(in) us – whole life long
in the end we are truly free

you're looking so fine
don't you want to be mine

together we should be at someone's mercy
the unpredictable will come true, just let it flow

WANT TO BE MINE?

LIFE ON STAGE

wake up in the morning – as I
how can anything just be so god damn bright, it was darkest night
what's the time right now, oh no, it's 3 o'clock in the afternoon – it happen

what the hell was going on, we broke the fish and Michael's gla
this party was so great and thanks for truth and the music and all those new friends

we're always too late, check the sound on the stage – we got to hurry up and then
now that we are playin' live – together (we're) one (just) recognize – No Autho

party will last all night – yeah we rock the
how can anything just feel so god damn right, this is my time, (with) good
what's the time right now, oh no, it's 5 o'clock in the morning, it happe

yeah you know me Papa Fava, always on the run fr
steady present on the mic – droppin' rhym
takin' ya breath away
I am crossing every border – want to se
Papa Mylow always s
all of a sudden – one day – m
but I keep it going on – I kno
my destiny's k

TURNIN'

I can't understand your thoughts – I just can't realize your words
we could be together – anything could happen not just the worst
but the darkness ends the day – just as lonely as I stay
and you could call the feeling loneliness when no one's left just me

but I'm happy – just as anyone could be
when my gullet's wet and everything is turning that I see
when the ceiling seems to fall right down on me
and nobody's left to pick me up, when I go down the drain

below my eyes – everything keeps turnin' that I see

and I don't understand – why you live your life that way
enjoying half the things and bitterness is covering your way
and I don't understand your decision yet to stay
clean and reasonable – worthiness in question anyway

ONE MORE SONG

one more song, for those who want to hear one
much more fun, for those who want to have some
one more beer for me and I will drop my pants
and the room is spinnin' around and around, but I hear
one more beer for me now

one thing's for sure, let's have fun now

BALANCE

she points to the sky – it is darkest night
they (the stars) are so far away
but anyway they are beautiful her
sparkling eyes – reflections of the stars
are tellin' so much about her dreams
he is thinking (while he looks into her eyes)

there is so much more in this world
than we can see with our eyes
some of us do know some secrets
others are blind to see
the reality but they seem to be so satisfied, too

just to affect the quality of your life
there is so much experience needed
just to be able to ... open your mind now

just face the extremes of our everyday world
just face the truth and then afterwards
you can head for balance

she points to the sky – it is daylight now
no one can see the stars
but anyway they are so real her
sparkling eyes – no need to see stars
(they) are telling stories of true belief
he is thinking

there is so much more in this world
you can see belief in her eyes
some of us will fight those demons (inside)
others won't change anything – wrong reality
but they seem to be satisfied too

SIMPLE SOLUTION

everyday it's harder to convince yourself
to get away from this confusion
but there is always a simple solution – you don't know
make a deeper breath and see the starting sign
you're in too deep in this aggression
(you) set (up) a smile without expression – you should go

overcome your doubts another chapter starts
be yourself without permission
take a chance on this transition – so let go
deep inside your soul you know you fall apart
but every end's a new beginning
just believe in doing the right thing – why don't you
'cause you don't know (that)

there's a simple solution
a key to solve all problems you got in your life
just need to realize there's a way to live again
it's up to you to dream on or to be satisfied
just open up your eyes

(it's) time to get away from this absorbing force.
feed the fire – keep it burnin'
once you start there's no returning – don't say no
soon again you'll be the one who's standing tall
rise above destructive feeling
you're the master pulling your strings – come on, go
you have to know

QUE

what is the most important thing in your life, what do you think is wo
what's the sense of every new day, why is there so much pain if we all are
what about your soul, do you really own one, do you need to believe
just to be sure that your soul wi

live for one big aim and for this moment – means reaching yo

what's your highest high and your lowest low, what do you think about
what's the meaning of your life, why so much learning matter if we all just want
what about the truth, do you really have friends, do you need to fo
just to be sure that you're good enoug

why is there so much love on earth while we are goin' to break near
is it belief that keeps you alive or maybe your friend, your child
will you ever arrive at your inner home, could you imagine to liv

because your destiny is written by your mind, everyday new possibilities and your heart s
do you take the chances everyday just to fulfill your dreams, don't you forget to
but if you do then m

HEAD IN HA

one thing about w
and you are sitting

one thing about b
and you're sitting

and it's always a
so make your ch
because every si

one thing about
and you're sitti

take one look

one thing abo
and maybe th

the lights seem to get darker but the truth is getting through – through you now, to beware – there is no need to anymore
the end is coming closer and the time is running out, take your time and take care, it's all that's left right now

I can't stop to think about it, doesn't matter what you do – there's no way no cure, I got to let go

the lights are fading away, truth is now part of you – you're truly yourself – to disguise – there is no need to any more
the end is really close now endless love is all you feel, I'll love you – forever – we'll meet again soon

I dreamt tonight that the end is near and I pretended to support but then close to the end I felt that I – I couldn't let go
I cried all the tears of my life in one minute as it came to the end

LIGHTS

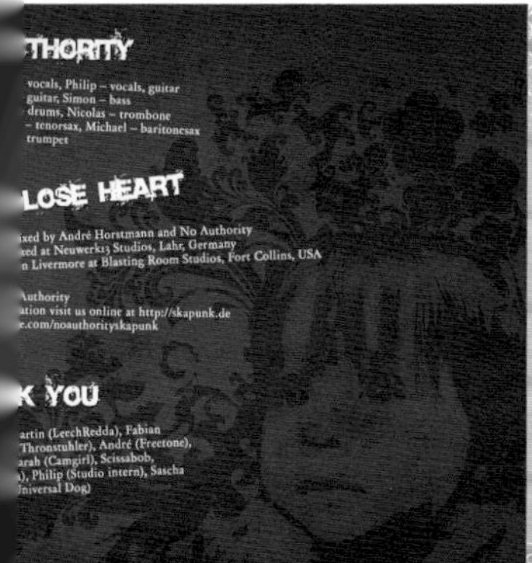

THORITY
vocals, Philip – vocals, guitar
guitar, Simon – bass
drums, Nicolas – trombone
– tenorsax, Michael – baritonesax
trumpet
LOSE HEART
ixed by André Horstmann and No Authority
xed at Neuwerk13 Studios, Lahr, Germany
n Livermore at Blasting Room Studios, Fort Collins, USA
Authority
ation visit us online at http://skapunk.de
e.com/noauthorityskapunk
K YOU
artin (LeechRedda), Fabian
Thronstuhler), André (Freetone),
arah (Camgirl), Scissabob,
), Philip (Studio intern), Sascha
Universal Dog)

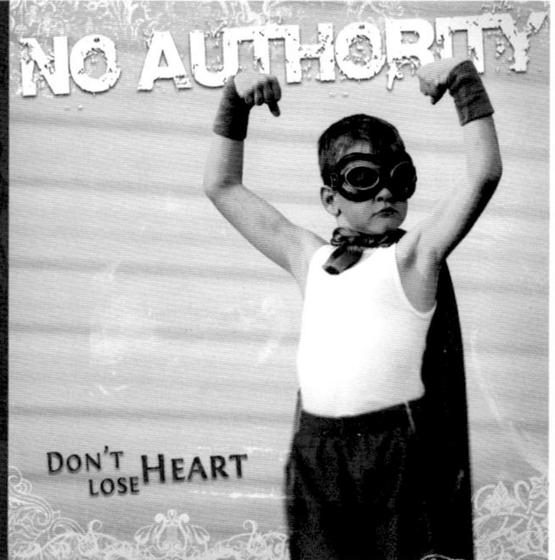

NO AUTHORITY
DON'T LOSE HEART

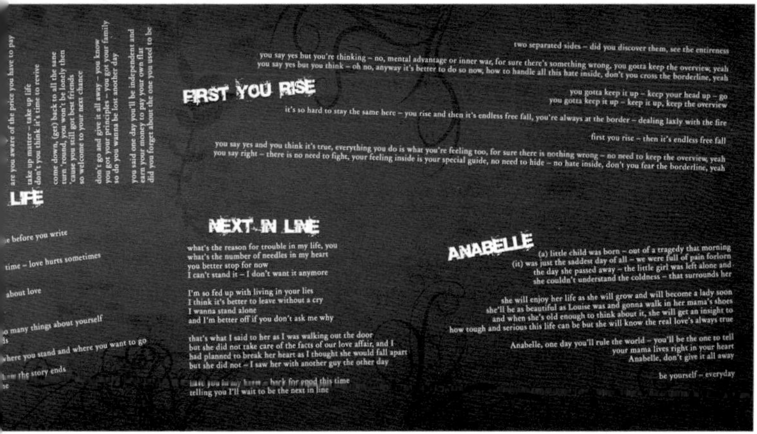

are you aware of the price you have to pay

take up matter – take up life
don't you think it's time to revive

come down, (get) back to all the sane
turn 'round, you won't be lonely then
'cause you still got best friends
so welcome to your next chance

don't go and give it all away – you know
you got your principles – you got your family
so do you wanna be lost another day

you said one day you'll be independent and
earn your money to pay your own flat
did you forget about the one you used to be

LIFE

e before you write

time – love hurts sometimes

about love

o many things about yourself
ds

where you stand and where you want to go

w the story ends
ne

FIRST YOU RISE

two separated sides – did you discover them, see the entireness

you say yes but you're thinking – no, mental advantage or inner war, for sure there's something wrong, you gotta keep the overview, yeah
you say yes but you think – oh no, anyway it's better to do so now, how to handle all this hate inside, don't you cross the borderline, yeah

you gotta keep it up – keep your head up – go
you gotta keep it up – keep it up, keep the overview

it's so hard to stay the same here – you rise and then it's endless free fall, you're always at the border – dealing laxly with the fire

first you rise – then it's endless free fall

you say yes and you think it's true, everything you do is what you're feeling too, for sure there is nothing wrong – no need to keep the overview, yeah
you say right – there is no need to fight, your feeling inside is your special guide, no need to hide – no hate inside, don't you fear the borderline, yeah

NEXT IN LINE

what's the reason for trouble in my life, you
what's the number of needles in my heart
you better stop for now
I can't stand it – I don't want it anymore

I'm so fed up with living in your lies
I think it's better to leave without a cry
I wanna stand alone
and I'm better off if you don't ask me why

that's what I said to her as I was walking out the door
but she did not take care of the facts of our love affair, and I
had planned to break her heart as I thought she would fall apart
but she did not – I saw her with another guy the other day

... back for good this time
telling you I'll wait to be the next in line

ANABELLE

(a) little child was born – out of a tragedy that morning
(it) was just the saddest day of all – we were full of pain forlorn
the day she passed away – the little girl was left alone and
she couldn't understand the coldness – that surrounds her

she will enjoy her life as she will grow and will become a lady soon
she'll be as beautiful as Louise was and gonna walk in her mama's shoes
and when she's old enough to think about it, she will get an insight to
how tough and serious this life can be but she will know the real love's always true

Anabelle, one day you'll rule the world – you'll be the one to tell
your mama lives right in your heart
Anabelle, don't give it all away

be yourself – everyday

1 JE NE REGRETTE RIEN
2 NUTS IN AMSTERDAM
3 TIME TO GO
4 1POINT059463
OFFLINE FRIENDS
OFFLINE FRIENDS

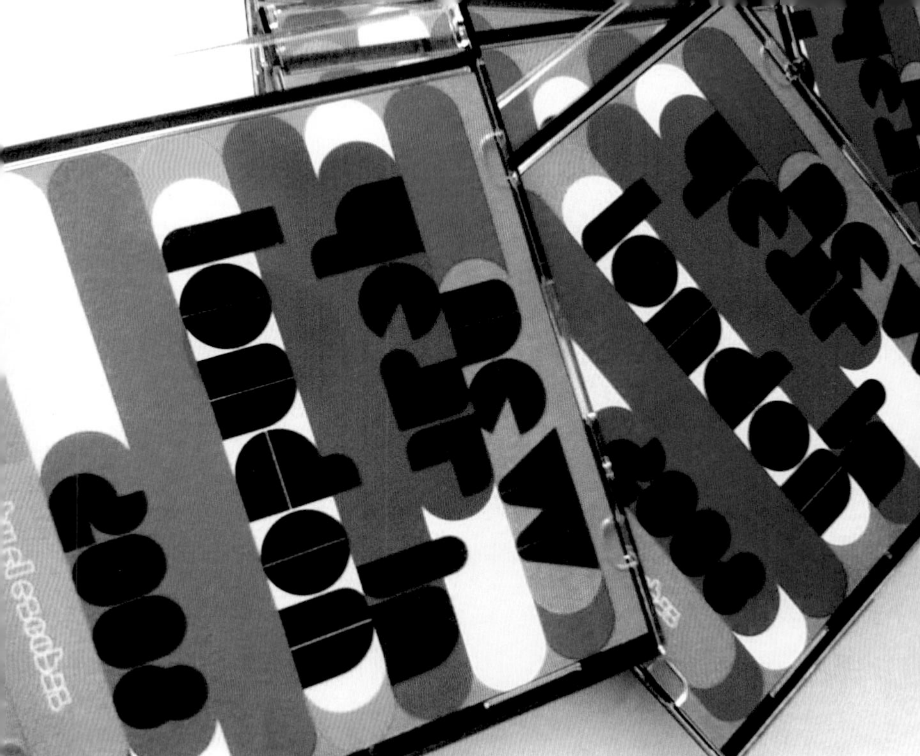

Eduardo Escobar Beckwith (MEX) www.escobas.com.mx

Rick Tonizzo (LUX) www.hookepuk.com

FF011
CHOOK//
SOUND
OF
TIME
FULL FORCE RECORDINGS 2008
WWW.FULLFORCEREC.COM

Rick Tonizzo (LUX) www.hookepuk.com

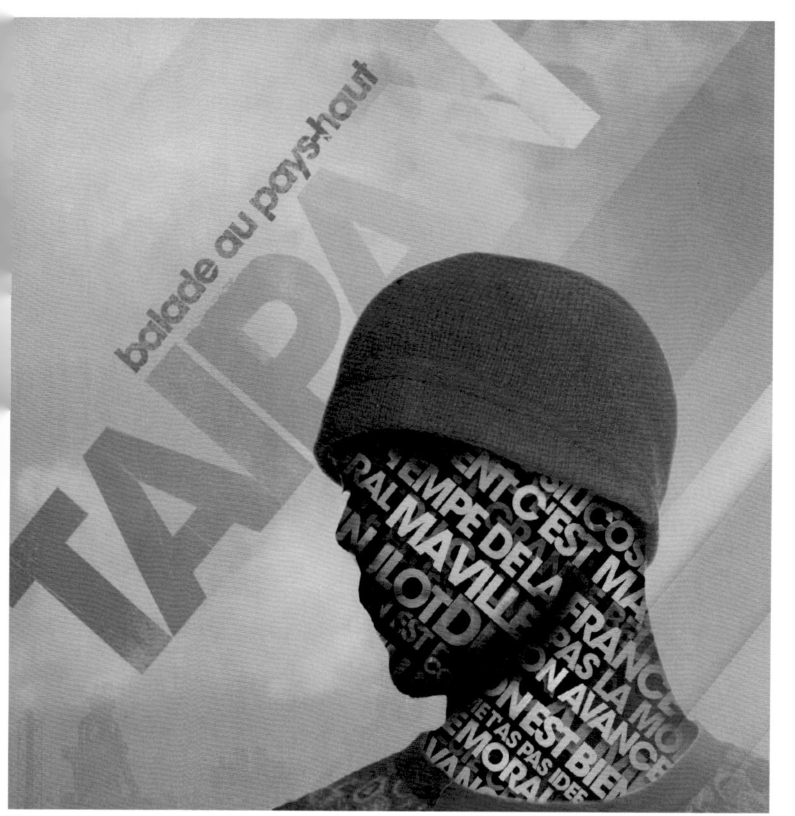
balade au pays-haut

SUCK CITY VOL.8

VOLKAN T. .... TANZ DICH TOT
TAKEN FROM THE ALBUM "SPRICH DEUTSCH ODER STIRB"
BAND: WWW.MYSPACE.COM/VOLKANT | **LABEL:** WWW.SUPERHERORECORDS.COM & WWW.RUHRMUSIC.DE

AGNOSTIC FRONT .... DEAD TO ME
TAKEN FROM THE ALBUM "WARRIORS"
BAND: WWW.AGNOSTICFRONT.COM | **LABEL:** WWW.NUCLEARBLAST.DE

IGNITE .... BLEEDING
TAKEN FROM THE ALBUM "OUR DARKEST DAYS"
BAND: WWW.IGNITEBAND.COM | **LABEL:** WWW.CENTURYMEDIA.COM

EVERYDAY DOLLARS .... SUPPLY AND DEMAND
TAKEN FROM THE ALBUM "BEFORE THE SUPPLY"
BAND: WWW.MYSPACE.COM/EVERYDAYDOLLARS | **LABEL:** WWW.SUPERHERORECORDS.COM & WWW.SWELLCREEK.DE

HEARTBREAK KID .... THROUGHOUT GENERATIONS
TAKEN FROM THE ALBUM "LIFE THRILLS"
BAND: WWW.MYSPACE.COM/HEARTBREAKKIDHC | **LABEL:** WWW.SUPERHERORECORDS.COM & WWW.SWELLCREEK.DE

ALL FOR NOTHING .... A MATTER OF CHOICE
TAKEN FROM THE ALBUM "CAN'T KILL WHAT'S INSIDE"
BAND: WWW.MYSPACE.COM/ALLFORNOTHINGNL | **LABEL:** WWW.SWELLCREEK.DE & WWW.THINGAMAJIGGER-VINYL.COM

ENDSTAND .... MEMORIES
TAKEN FROM THE ALBUM "SPARK"
BAND: WWW.MYSPACE.COM/ENDSTAND | **LABEL:** WWW.FIREINSIDEMUSIC.COM

TALK RADIO TALK .... THE WAY WE ACT
TAKEN FROM THE ALBUM "BEYOND THESE LINES"
BAND: WWW.MYSPACE.COM/TALKRADIOTALK | **LABEL:** WWW.SWELLCREEK.DE

HATEXXXEDGE .... PUT THE NEEDLE
TAKEN FROM THE ALBUM "ON FIRE"
BAND: WWW.MYSPACE.COM/HATEEDGEXXX | **LABEL:** WWW.SUPERHERORECORDS.COM & WWW.SWELLCREEK.DE

SUCK CITY VOL.8

S.S.S.P. .... PERFUME & CIGARETTES
TAKEN FROM THE ALBUM "FOR LIFE"
BAND: WWW.MYSPACE.COM/TRIPLESP | **LABEL:** WWW.SUPERHERORECORDS.COM & WWW.SWELLCREEK.DE

VINDICATOR .... KILL THE KING
TAKEN FROM THE ALBUM "ON AND ON"
BAND: WWW.VINDICATOR.DE | **LABEL:** WWW.STREETJUSTICERECORDS.DE

THE VENDETTA .... FALL & RISE
TAKEN FROM THE ALBUM "AMICI DEL NEMICI MUNDI"
BAND: WWW.MYSPACE.COM/VENDETTASCT | **LABEL:** WWW.SUPERHERORECORDS.COM

SEVEN LASTING STITCHES .... ONCE IS FOREVER
TAKEN FROM THE ALBUM "KINGSIZE"
BAND: WWW.MYSPACE.COM/SUBCRIME | **LABEL:** WWW.SUPERHERORECORDS.COM & WWW.SWELLCREEK.DE

MAY THE FORCE BE WITH YOU .... FORGET THE TRUMPETS, BRING ME THE WRECKING BALL
TAKEN FROM THE MCD "DISCO METAL YOUTH"
BAND: WWW.DISCOMETAL.DE | **LABEL:** WWW.HORRORBIZ.DE

DOOM DAY .... I WILL WALK ALONE
TAKEN FROM THE ALBUM "COUNT YOUR USELESS HOURS"
BAND: WWW.MYSPACE.COM/DOOMDAYHARDCORE | **LABEL:** WWW.SUPERHERORECORDS.COM & WWW.SWELLCREEK.DE

SPIDER CREW .... SCUMBAG
TAKEN FROM THE ALBUM "EXPECT THE UNEXPECTED"
BAND: WWW.MYSPACE.COM/SPIDERCREWMERCHANDISE | **LABEL:** WWW.SUPERHERORECORDS.COM & WWW.SWELLCREEK.DE

VIOLENCE APPROVED .... SOMEDAY
TAKEN FROM THE ALBUM "LET THE GAMES BEGIN"
BAND: WWW.MYSPACE.COM/VIOLENCEAPPROVED | **LABEL:** WWW.MYSPACE.COM/VINYLJUNKIERECORDS

SUPPORTED BY DVS

THINGA MAJIGGER

© + ℗ 2008 THINGAMAJIGGER   WWW.THINGAMAJIGGER-VINYL.COM   WWW.DESIGNBYDIGITALINK.COM

SWSHT 004 | LIMITED EDITION OF 300 COPIES

* VINYL ONLY BONUS TRACKS
ALL OTHER TRACKS TAKEN FROM SUCK CITY VOL.8 2XCD | UNDER LICENSE FR

BADER AND DE GROOT'S
VOL.8
LIMITED
EDITION
SUCK CITY
FEATURING AGNOSTIC FRONT, IGNITE,
EVERYDAY DOLLARS, SPIDER CREW,
DOOM DAY, S.S.S.P. ... AND MANY MORE!

Rick Tonizzo [LUX] www.hookepuk.com

Philipp Lampert (AUT) www.phla.at

REVISTA DE
INTERVENÇÃO E
CULTURA
CULTURA
DE MARCAS:
A CONSEQUÊNCIA DIRECTA
DA GLOBALIZAÇÃO E
DO CONSUMISMO
#0
6 EUROS

Pedro Campiche (POR) www.flickr.com/photos/corle1

Roberto Philipp (GER) www.geschmacksverteiler.de

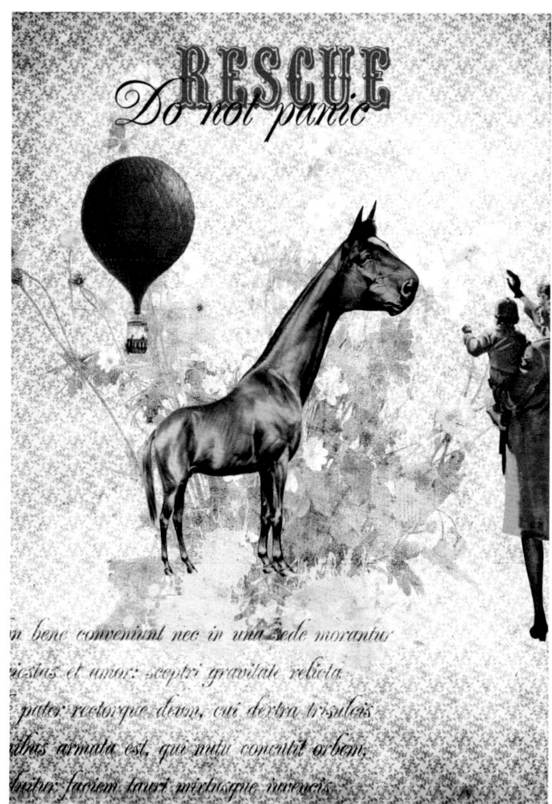
RESCUE
Do not panic
n bene conveniunt nec in una sede morantur
iestas et amor: sceptri gravitate relicta
pater rectorque deum, cui dextra trisulcis
ibus armata est, qui nutu concutit orbem,
duitur faciem tauri mixtusque iuvencis

Alexander Otto (GER) www.diftnorm.com

12.04.2008 klub erdbeermund

house techno electro
arteqcue records, karlsruhe
arteqcue records, magdeburg
florian hucker
thelager / studio23, ravensburg
plattentasche, karlsruhe
klub erdbeermund - baumeisterstr. 54, 76137 karlsruhe - www.arteqcue.de

theLager // diePartyParty
www.thelager.de
official BA-Party WM05 theLager
euro 3,-
TheDudes
(theLager Residents, Stuttgart)
Flo Hucker
(theLager, UniqueSounds, Tsch!, Karlsruhe)
visuals by Multimeedchen (Stuttgart)
02.11.2006 Bacchus Ravensburg
21:00 Uhr specials: wodka+energy (aka discoschorle): 2,50 Euro

die macht der nacht
01.10.05 in der stadtmitte
Rocken

das lineup
paradisco
(ghetto disco – karlsruhe)
+ special guest: tsch!
knut sindermann
(plus+ – pforzheim)
eintritt: 4 euro
01.10.
in der stadtmitte

Florian Hucker [GER] www.thelager.de

US
UNIQUE
SOUNDS
14.10.2006
STADTMITTE KARLSRUHE

UNIQUE SOUNDS SPEZIAL
M. TELEMANN - GLÜCK IS MY FUTURE E.P. - RELEASEPARTY
M. TELEMANN
(Wasabi Recordings, Unique Sounds, Karlsruhe)
BIANCA
(Moodlounge, Playground, Karlsruhe)
FLORIAN HUCKER
(theLager, Unique Sounds, Ravensburg)
RENIAR
(Bad Brothers, Ghetto Disco, Karlsruhe)
FLORIAN KUNZE
(Studio23, Karlsruhe)
14.10.2006
STADTMITTE Baumeisterstr. 1, Karlsruhe
www.unique-sounds.de www.mtelemann.de www.diestadtmitte.de
UNIQUE

UNIQUE SOUNDS
10.02.2007 - Die Stadtmitte
www.m.telemann.de.vu www.die-stadtmitte.de www.unique-sounds.de

Unique Sounds proudly presents
M.Telemann
(Wasabi Records, Karlsruhe)
Florian Hucker
(theLager, areyounuts?, Ravensburg)
Reniar
(Evil Empire, Ghetto Disco, Karlsruhe)
Christian Plath
(Evil Empire, Karlsruhe)
Start: 21:00 Uhr · Die Stadtmitte · Baumeisterstr. 1, Karlsruhe

Florian Hucker (GER) www.thelager.de

DISPU
ist eine köstliche
Form der Niederlage
Die gerade Linie ist in ihrer Kraft der Kurve immer überlegen.
The power of the straight line is always superior to the curve.
The straight line is godless and immoral.
OLLOW
NSTRUC
OMMT.

+ LIEBE

Jamie Oliver Aspinall (SUI) www.schnuppe.ch

Jamie Oliver Aspinall (SUI) www.schnuppe.ch

BLUMEN
IM BAUCH
EIN THEATER
VARIOCLUB OLTEN
5. OKTOBER 2007
FREIEGRUPPE

Katja Witt (GER) www.schnuppenalarm.de

WEITER
WEITER
... UM NICHT
DENEN IHR SPIEL
ZU SPIELEN

NOW
Call me
I'm your personal guardian angel

Katja Witt (GER) www.schnuppenalarm.de

REQUE

 Julian Rentzsch (GER) www.julianrentzsch.de

Drew Rios [USA]

Christian Flaccus (GER) www.schoeneneuekinder.de

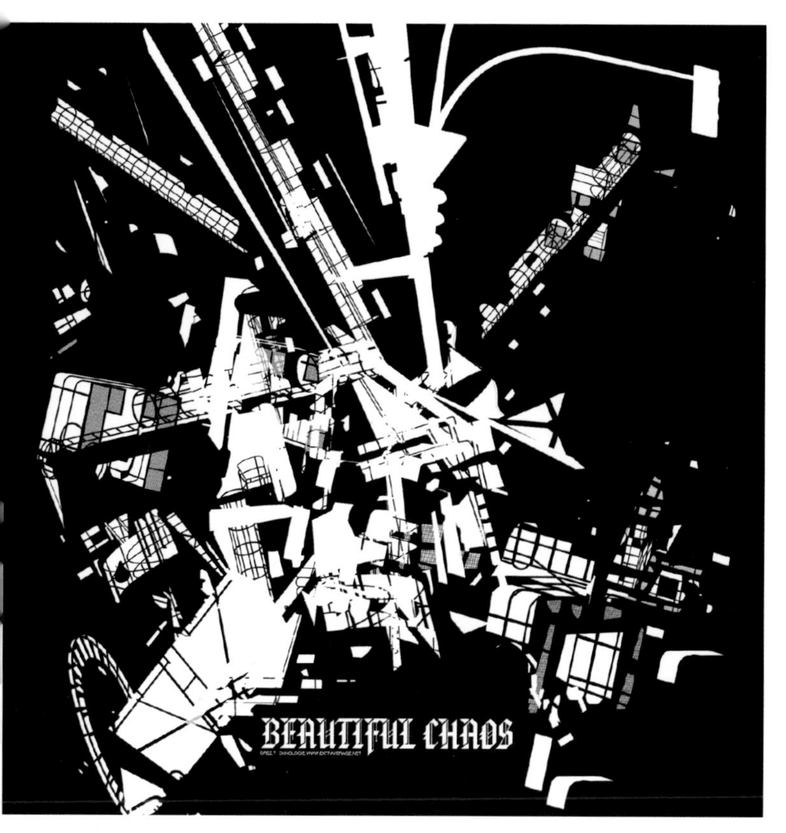

Karoly Kiralyfalvi (HUN) www.extraverage.net

SIMPLICITY
extraverage
tribute
sublime
BIGUPYOURCHEST
ROBOTAPE
KOMPYUTERWELT
ILLOGIK
anger guard
DIFERENTECHNICS
100PERCENTFRIENDSHIP
EXTRAVERAGE GRAPHICS
WORLDWIDE CONNECTIONS
VORTEX
WITNESS
BRINGIN THE TROUBLE
BRINGIN THE BASS
burn
rinse
HUMAN TECHNOLOGIK
RoboSaint
etica
ergoesoutofstyle
ruudawak

SUBLIME
ONE FOR THE TROUBLE
NINE FOR THE HARD TIMES
ANGER GUARD | CLEARSKYZ | HUMAN TECHNOLOGIK | KOMPYUTERWELT | KORREKT KRAFT

Karoly Kiralyfalvi [HUN] www.extraverage.net

TRUST. WWW.EXTRAVERAGE.NET 2007.
TRUST

Karoly Kiralyfalvi (HUN) www.extraverage.net

DESIGN
WITH
LOVE
DESIGN
IN LOVE

Pablo Alfieri (ARG) www.pabloalfieri.com

Pablo Alfieri (ARG) www.pabloalfieri.com

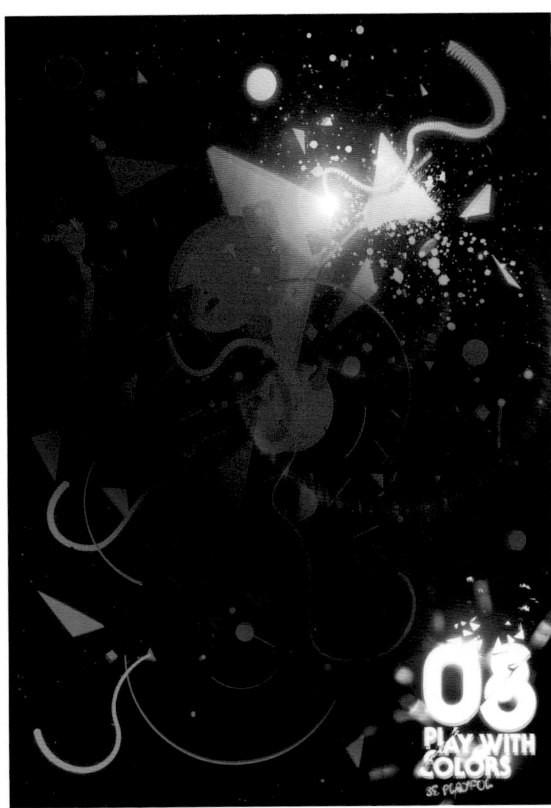

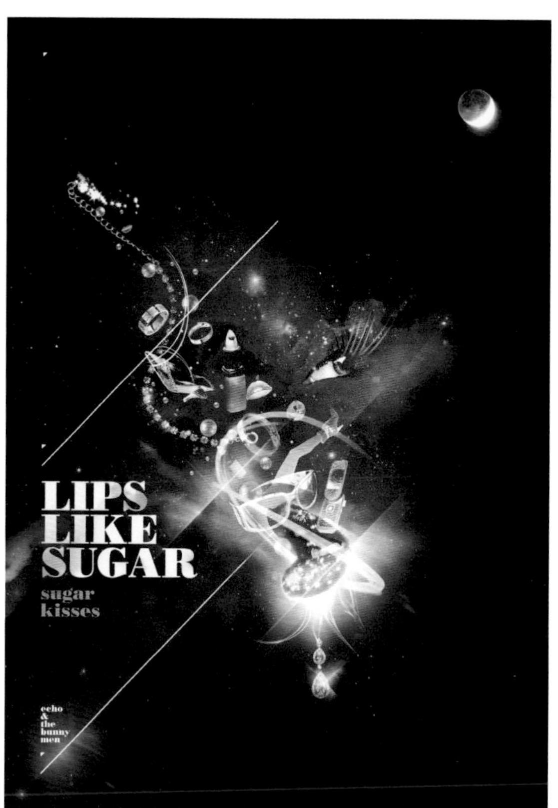
LIPS
LIKE
SUGAR
sugar
kisses
echo
&
the
bunny
men

PLAY
WITH
SHAPES

THINK
CREATE
AND
ENJOY

Lilo Krebernik (AUT) www.0717.at

SIXXA
CLOTHING FOR TOMBOYS

Roberto Chessa (GER) www.stilfreund.de

how to pimp your scooter

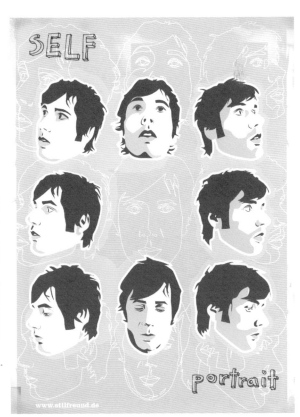

Roberto Chessa (GER) www.stilfreund.de

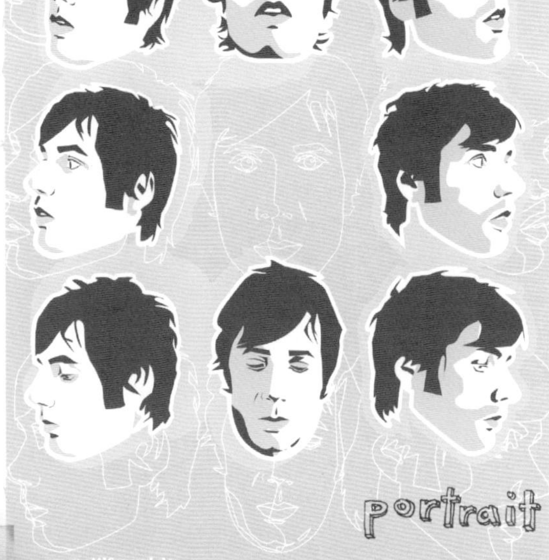

KOMM IN UNSERE
KLEINE WELT
23.06.07
ab 22.00 Uhr
im »Willie's«
Fürstenbergstr. 32a
Responsible for your
delightful entertainment:
HAL & Professor Ping
designed by stil

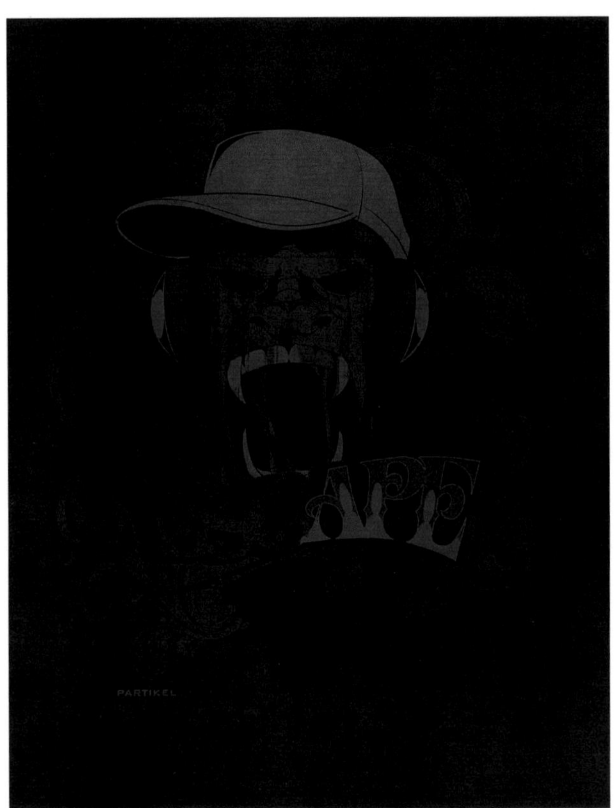
APE
PARTIKEL

Heath Killen (AUS) www.illuminationink.com

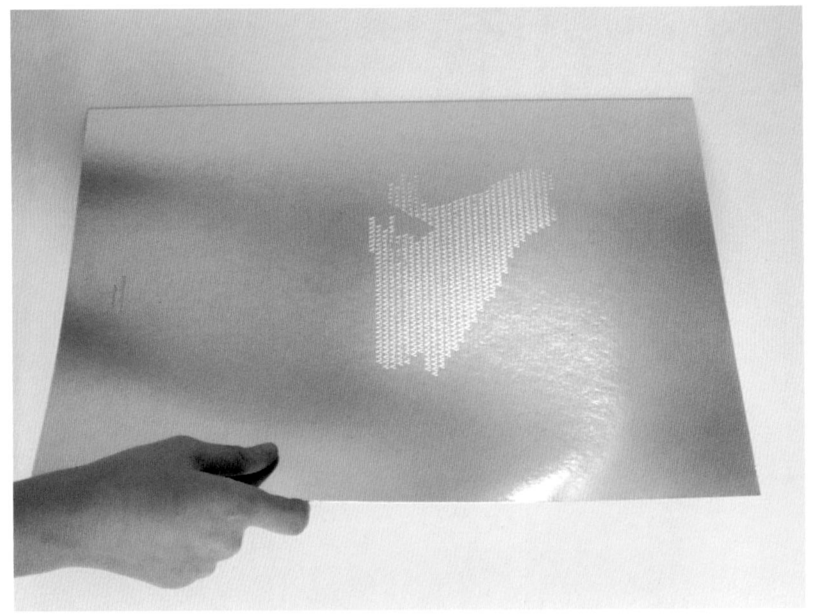

GLOBAL
EXCESS

KATE
MOSS
HORROR
VACUI
AMY
WINEHOUSE
HORROR
VACUI

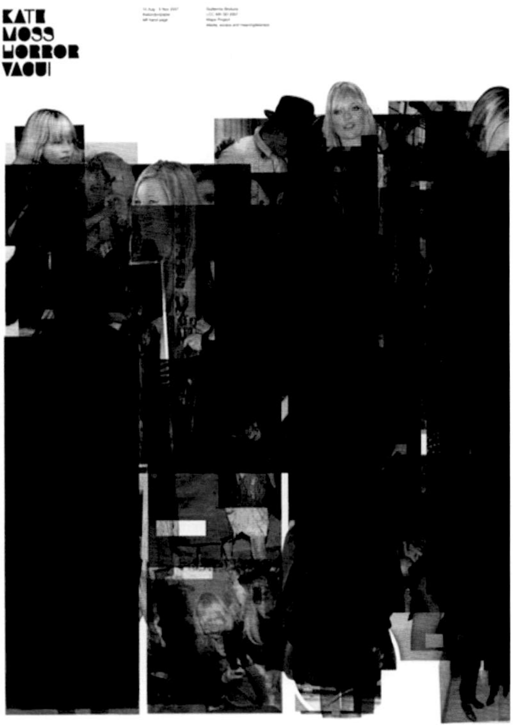

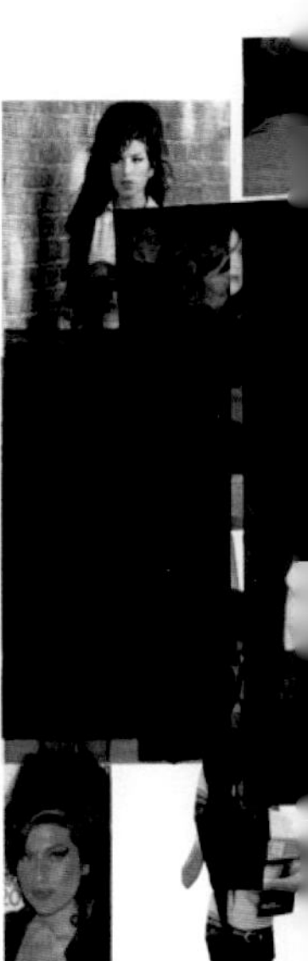

BRITNEY SPEARS HORROR VACUI

Jeff Poitiers (LUX) www.spitshiny.com

Edmond Yang (NOR) www.yangmedia.com

Edmond Yang (NOR) www.yangmedia.com

Dorota Bogucki (GER) www.boghukey.com

Matilda
it was a beautiful afternoon
the plane from Rome was delayed... again
„i'll be late, honey" said the voice on the phone... again
she felt like having a walk
the garden was blooming
„where the hell are our fucking flamingos"
she said to herself walking barefoot on the grass

Miss Prozac

best grades in high school
drama classes
editor of the school newspaper
leader of the girl's association „les femmes liberte"
queen of the prom
few drinks too much
he was really cute and the night was so warm
we're gonna have a baby, baby
honey... you're so tired... I'll get you some eggs on bacon
we're gonna be fine, just fine
hopeless Miss Prozac

Kate

Kate loves things
she adores her fashionable outfit
she is crazy about her XVII century cabinet
she is passionate about her posh jewellery
but most of all, she is desperately in love with her sunglasses.

DirtyJewel
Jewel thinks she is dirty
she thinks she's always been
she likes to talk dirty when she is alone
and she likes to peep
she would like to date older guy
someday

Dorota Bogucki (GER) www.boghukey.com

Clarks
ORIGINALS
STREET
SOMERSET
SINCE 1950

Turner Duckworth (GBR) www.turnerduckworth.com

wash me
microfiber sponge
Pamper your paintwork with a smooth and sudsy wash
Great for polishing and dusting too
Touch me, I'm soft
vroom

dry me
cham-pad
Dry and buff the easy way
All natural, genuine chamois leather
Handy, thirsty and speedy
vroom

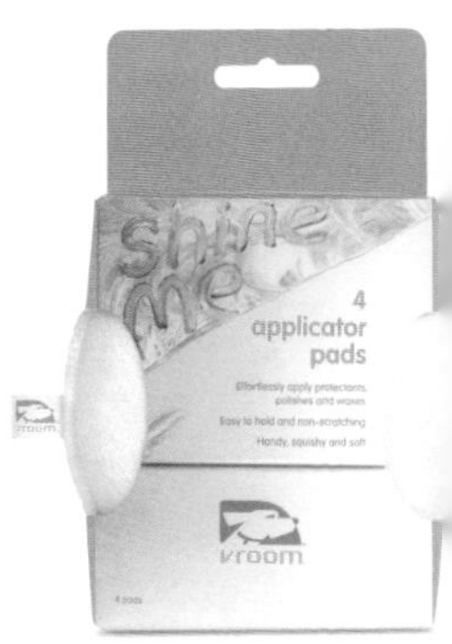
shine me
4 applicator pads
Effortlessly apply protectants, polishes and waxes
Easy to hold and non-scratching
Handy, squishy and soft
vroom
4 pads

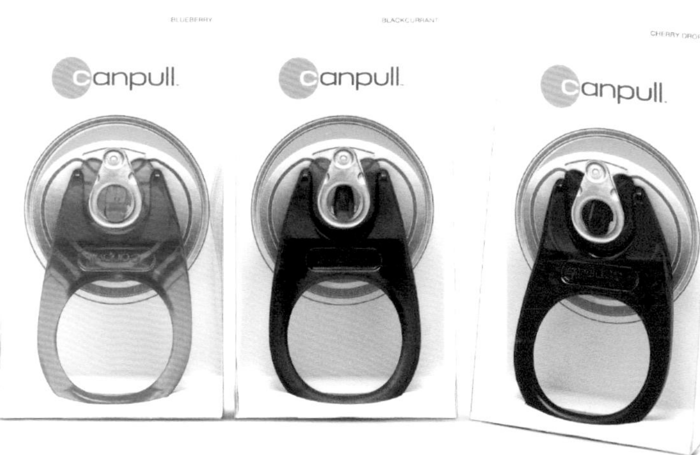

Turner Duckworth (GBR) www.turnerduckworth.com

FACE AND
BODY WASH™
NATURALLY ACTIVE INGREDIENTS
ALOE VERA, PATCHOULI, BERGAMOT AND VETIVER
Clean and fresh
NATURALLY ACTIVE
MEN'S SKINCARE
200ml ℮ 6.7 fl.oz
SENSITIVE SHAVE
CREAM™
NATURALLY ACTIVE INGREDIENTS
SHAVE GRASS, CLARY SAGE AND EUCALYPTUS
Close and smooth
NATURALLY ACTIVE
MEN'S SKINCARE
100ml ℮ 3.3 fl.oz
AFTER-SHAVING
MOISTURISER™
NATURALLY ACTIVE INGREDIENTS
SELF-HEAL, BORAGE AND NATURAL VITAMIN E
Calms and soothes
NATURALLY ACTIVE
MEN'S SKINCARE
50ml ℮ 1.6 fl.oz

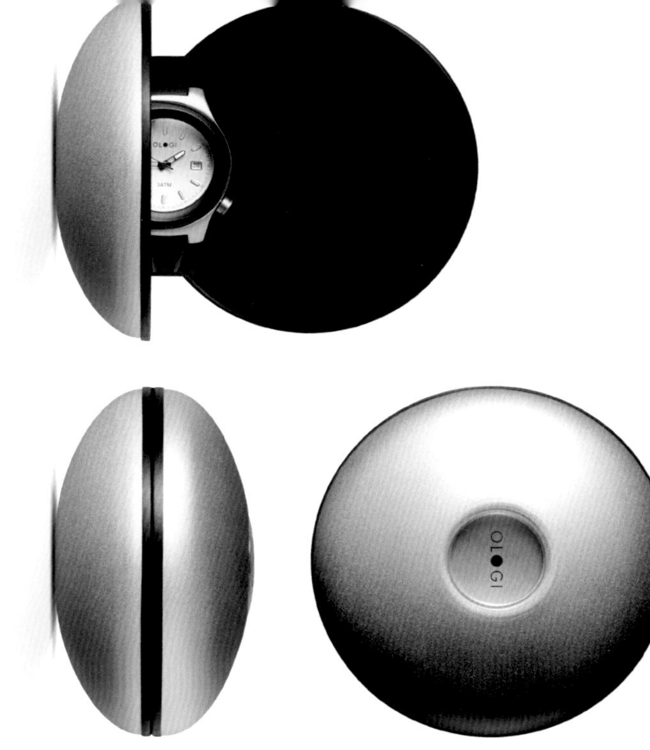

 Turner Duckworth (GBR) www.turnerduckworth.com

(Lepus californicus)
Oakville Grocery

Oakville Grocery
SINCE 1881
OAKVILLE ~ HEALDSBURG ~ SAN FRANCISCO ~ PALO ALTO
Oakville Grocery
SINCE 1881

1881
Oakville Grocery
SINCE 1881

all natural
pop
sea salt
rice chips
think popped!
parmesan
potato chi
think popped!
never fried. never bake
salsa
corn chips
think popped!
sea salt
corn chips
think popped!
never fried. never bake
NET WT 3.25 OZ (92g)
barbe
potato
think popped
never fried.

chips
chips
chips
chips

Turner Duckworth (GBR) www.turnerduckworth.com

NEAL'S YARD
COVENT GARDEN
REMEDIES
GERANIUM & ORANGE MASSAGE
MADE IN ENGLAND

NEAL'S YARD
COVENT GARDEN
REMEDIES
ELDERFOWER CLEANSING
FOR OILY AND PROBLEM SKIN
MADE IN ENGLAND

NEAL'S YARD
COVENT GARDEN
REMEDIES
BABY BATH
A MILD BATHTIME CLEANSER AND SHAMPOO
MADE IN ENGLAND

Turner Duckworth (GBR) www.turnerduckworth.com

BRAINS
SA
PREMIUM CASK BEER
BRAINS
ORIGINAL CASK
BRAINS
BITTER
BRAINS
DARK

BELAZU
SPECIAL RESERVE AGED
BALSAMIC VINEGAR
BELAZU
EXTRA VIRGIN
LIGURIAN TAGGIASCA
OLIVE OIL
A CLASSIC ITALIAN OIL
WITH A DELICATE SWEET
FLAVOUR AND A HINT OF
PEPPER ON THE FINISH

BELAZU
EXTRA VIRGIN OLIVE OIL
PREMIER CHOIX

BELAZU
UNFILTERED
EARLY HARVEST
ARBEQUINA
Extra Virgin Olive Oil
PRODUCT OF SPAIN
1 litre

 Michael Fetz (GER) www.fetzdesign.com

Eduardo Escobar Beckwith (MEX) www.escobas.com.mx

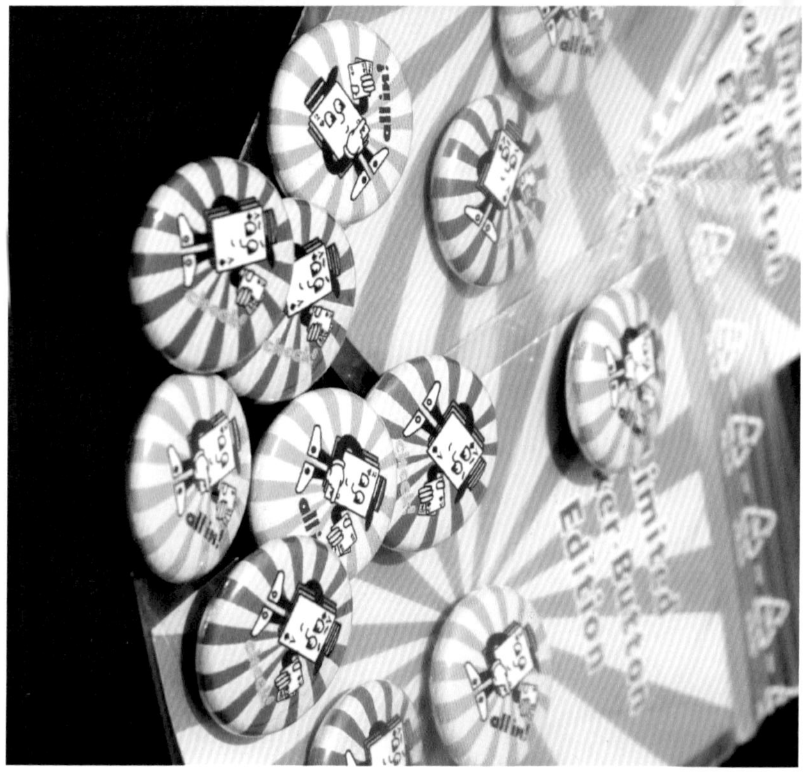

 Miriam Klobes (GER) www.mk-kommunikationsdesign.de

Bell [POL] www.flickr.com/cheer_up_bell

bell

Bell (POL) www.flickr.com/cheer_up_bell

ciah-ciah (POL) www.ciahciah.com

ciah-ciah (POL) www.ciahciah.com

I
Kiss

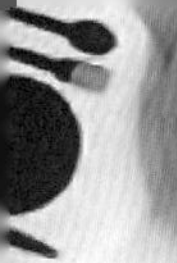

Mira (ITA) www. lovepics.it

FOR
YOU
Love
is
Life
Love
is
Life

Mira [ITA] www.lovepics.it

Ruth Biniwersi [GER] www.bei-ruth.com

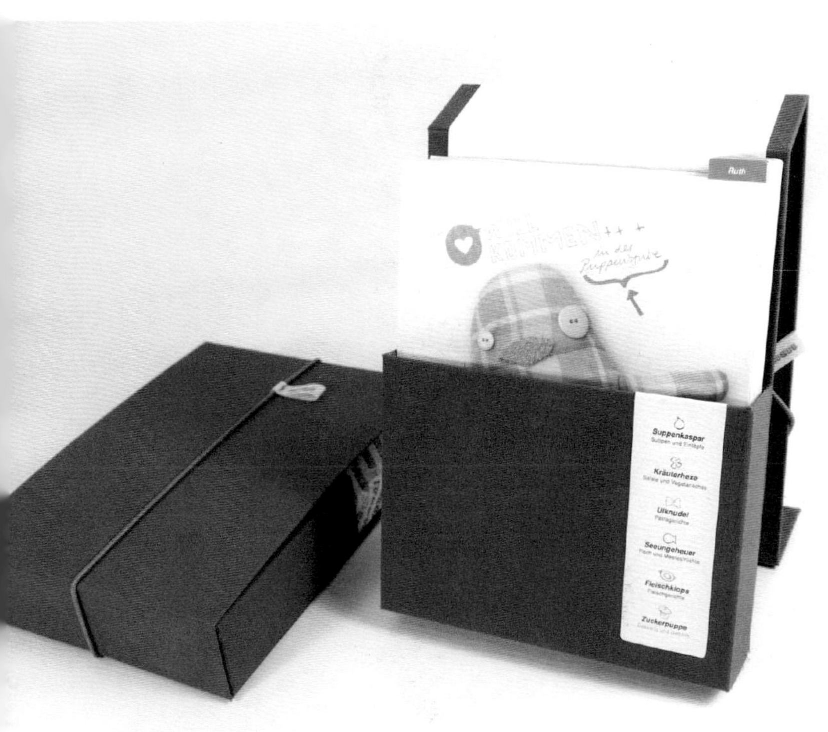
Ruth
Suppenkaspar
Kräuterhexe
Ulknudel
Seeungeheuer
Fleischklops
Zuckerpuppe

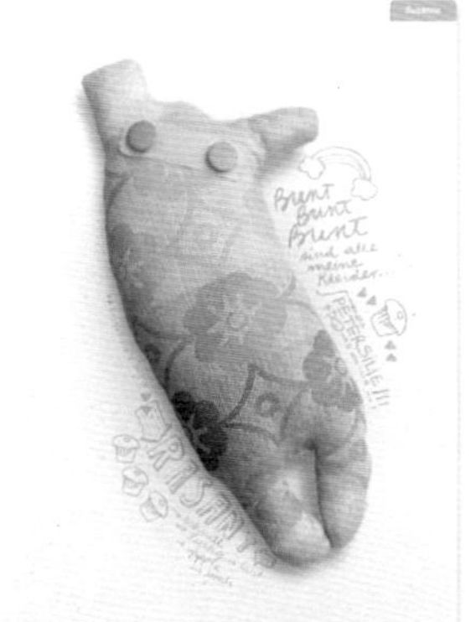

Ruth Biniwersi (GER) www.bei-ruth.com

***
Wo sind die
TOASTIES
der
[FLEISSIGE]*
ohne Fleiß
keinen
Preis

Ruth Biniwersi (GER) www.bei-ruth.com

Adam Arber (GBR) www.roadkilltoys.com

Ruth Biniwersi (GER) www.bei-ruth.com

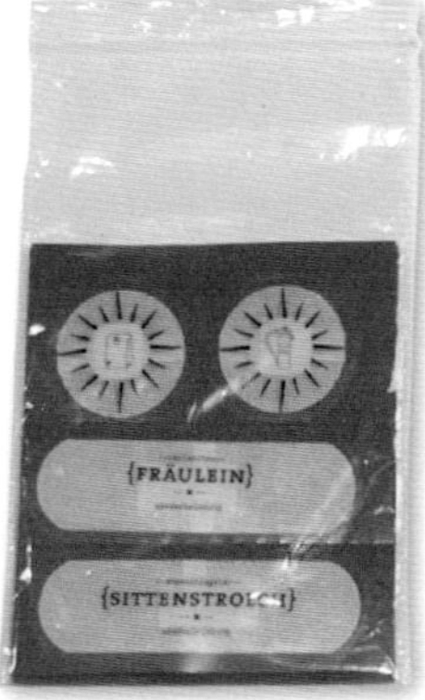

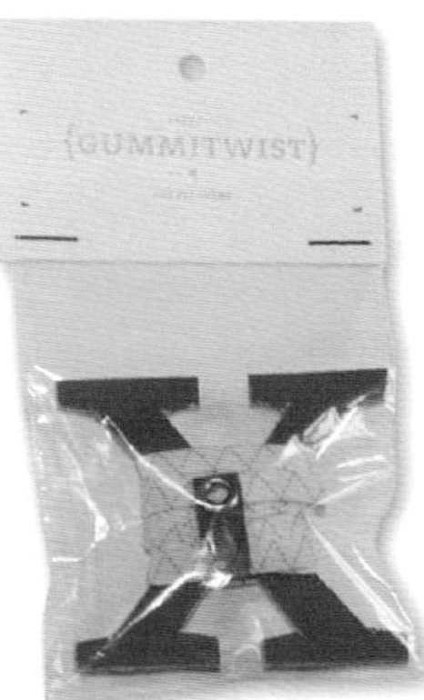

EMP Pfisterer (GER) www.empp.de

Mira [ITA] www.lovepics.it

morning
thursday friday saturday

lovely morning
wednesday thursday friday

Sandra Marchionna (GER) www. klimashirts.spreadshirt.net

EISBÄRKILLER

GRILLSAISON

WASSERSCHUTZPOLIZEI

KLIMAFLEISCH

KONSUMIDIOT

KONSUMIDIOT

GRILLSAISON

KLIMAFLEISCH

Der globale Viehbestand verursacht 18% aller Treibhausgas-Emissionen. **Setzen Sie ein Zeichen!** Kaufen Sie seltener Fleisch – und wenn, am besten Bioprodukte. Unterstützen Sie diese Kampagne mit Ihrer Beteiligung!

Sehr geehrter Herr Minister,

angeregt durch die Kampagne: **Zeichen setzen!** gegen den Klimawandel bitte ich Sie, Verantwortung für den Klimaschutz zu übernehmen. Fördern Sie die finanzielle Unterstützung der Bauern bei der Umstellung auf Biolandbau und sorgen Sie für eine Kennzeichnungspflicht bei Produkten aus Massentierhaltung.

Gehen Sie mit gutem Beispiel vorran und **setzen Sie ein Zeichen für Deutschland.**

Mit freundlichen Grüßen

Name

Datum, Unterschrift

An den

Minister
Horst Seehofer
BMELV
Wilhelmstraße 54

10117 Berlin

ciah-ciah [POL] www.ciahciah.com

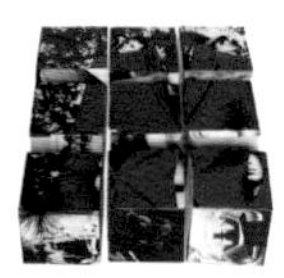

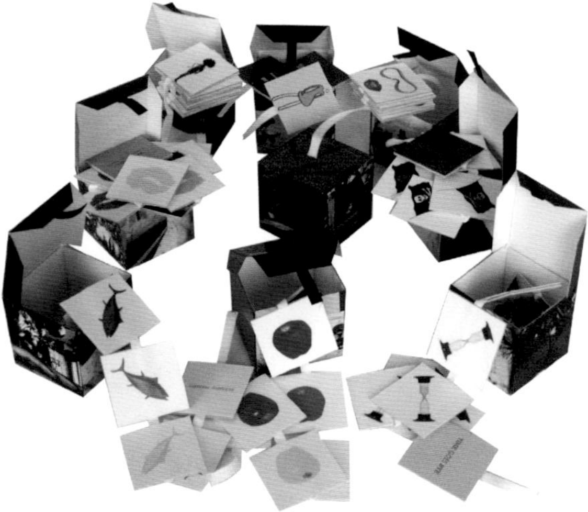

Dorota Bogucki (POL) www.boghukey.com

Kevin J. Furst (USA) www.kevinfurstdesign.com

Who
Know's
What
The
Future
Holds?

Lara Allport & Simon Barrett (AUS) www.thenationalgrid.com.au

Dorota Bogucki (POL) www.boghukey.com

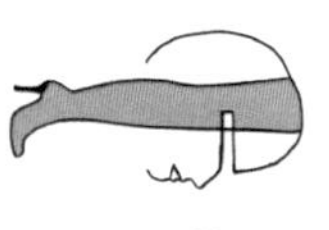

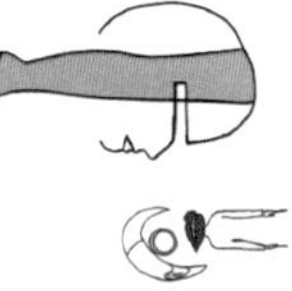

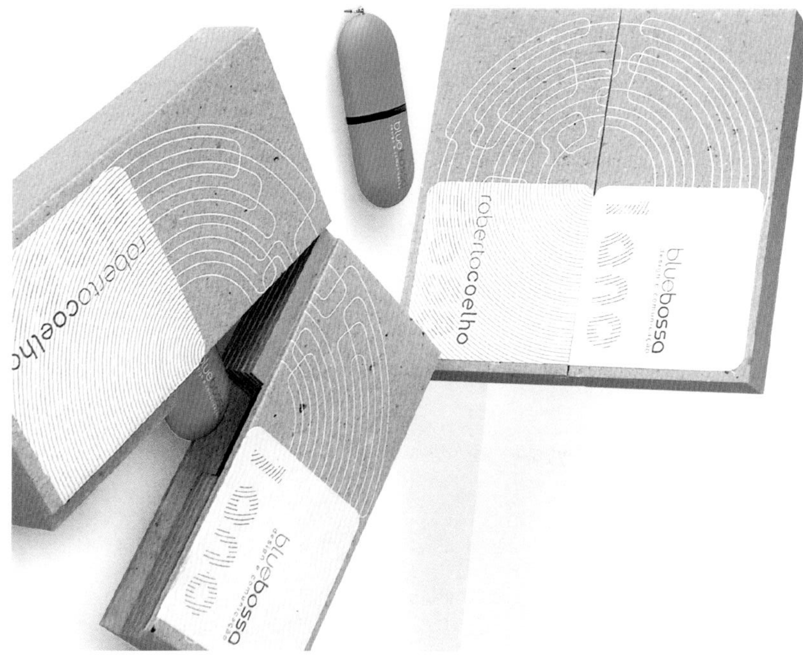

 Evandro Martins (BRA) www.bluebossa.art.br

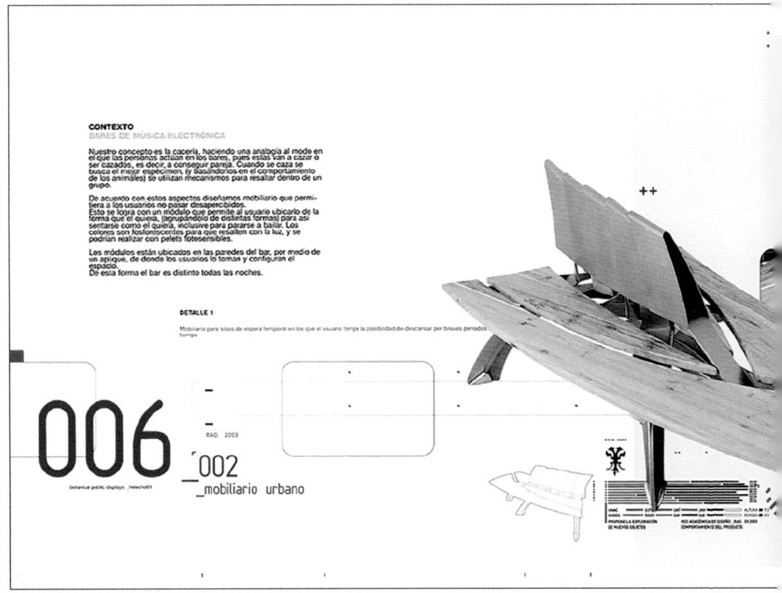
CONTEXTO
BARES DE MÚSICA ELECTRÓNICA
Nuestro concepto es la cacería, haciendo una analogía al modo en el que las personas actúan en los bares, pues estas van a cazar o ser cazados, es decir, a conseguir pareja. Cuando se caza se busca el mejor espécimen, (y basándonos en el comportamiento de los animales) se utilizan mecanismos para resaltar dentro de un grupo.
De acuerdo con estos aspectos diseñamos mobiliario que permitiera a los usuarios no pasar desapercibidos.
Esto se logra con un módulo que permite al usuario ubicarlo de la forma que el quiera, (agrupándolo de distintas formas) para así sentarse como el quiera, inclusive para pararse a bailar. Los colores son fosforescentes para que resalten con la luz, y se podrían realizar con pelets fotosensibles.
Los módulos están ubicados en las paredes del bar, por medio de un apique, de donde los usuarios lo toman y configuran el espacio.
De esta forma el bar es distinto todas las noches.
DETALLE 1
RAD. 2003
006
_002
_mobiliario urbano
++

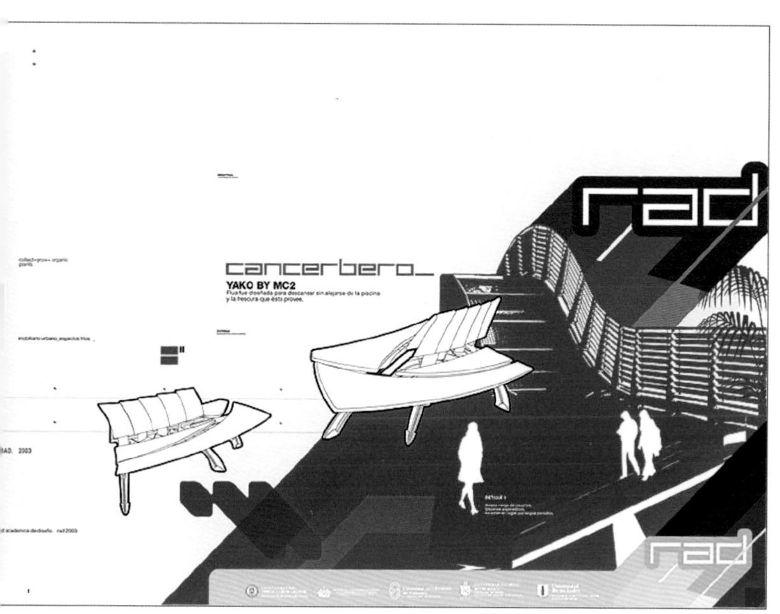
rad
collect+grow+ organic
parts
cancerbero_
YAKO BY MC2
Flua fue diseñada para descansar sin alejarse de la piscina
y la frescura que ésta provee.
mobiliario-urbano_espacios fríos _
RAD. 2003
d academica dediseño. rad 2003
rad

Jorge Restrepo (COL) www.wonksite.com

amaru_
AMARU BY MC2
Flua fue diseñada para descansar sin alejarse de la piscina
y la frescura que ésta provee.
botanical public displays
rad
rad

006 _002
_mobiliario urbano

CONTEXTO
BARES DE MÚSICA ELECTRÓNICA

Nuestro concepto es la caceria, haciendo una analogía al modo en el que las personas actúan en los bares, pues estas van a cazar o ser cazados, es decir, a conseguir pareja. Cuando se caza se busca el mejor especimen, (y basándonos en el comportamiento de los animales) se utilizan mecanismos para resaltar dentro de un grupo.

De acuerdo con estos aspectos diseñamos mobiliario que permitiera a los usuarios no pasar desapercibidos.
Esto se logra con un módulo que permite al usuario ubicarlo de la forma que el quiera, (agrupándolo de distintas formas) para así sentarse como el quiera, inclusive para pararse a bailar. Los colores son fosforescentes para que resalten con la luz, y se podrían realizar con pelets fotosensibles.

Los módulos están ubicados en las paredes del bar, por medio de un aplique, de donde los usuarios lo toman y configuran el espacio.
De esta forma el bar es distinto todas las noches..

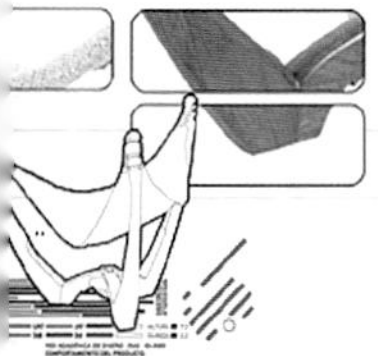

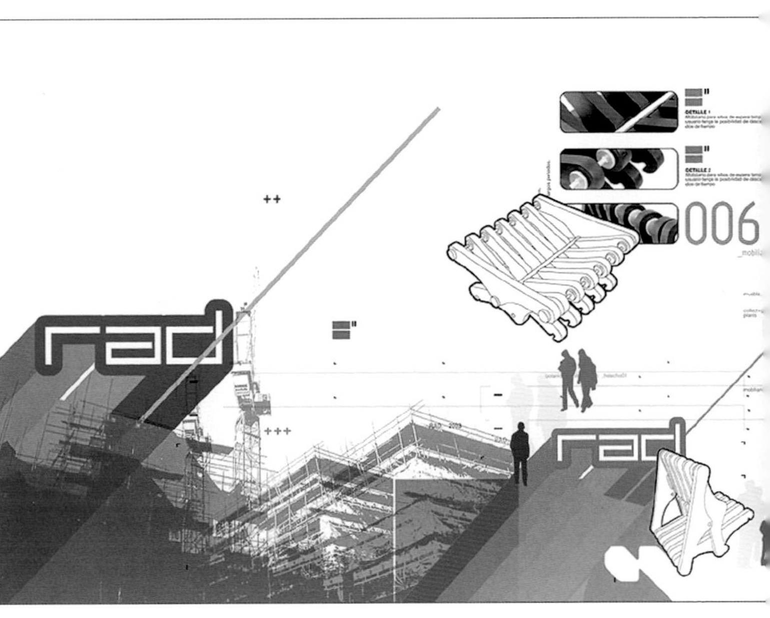

rad
++
+++
DETALLE 1
DETALLE 2
006
rad

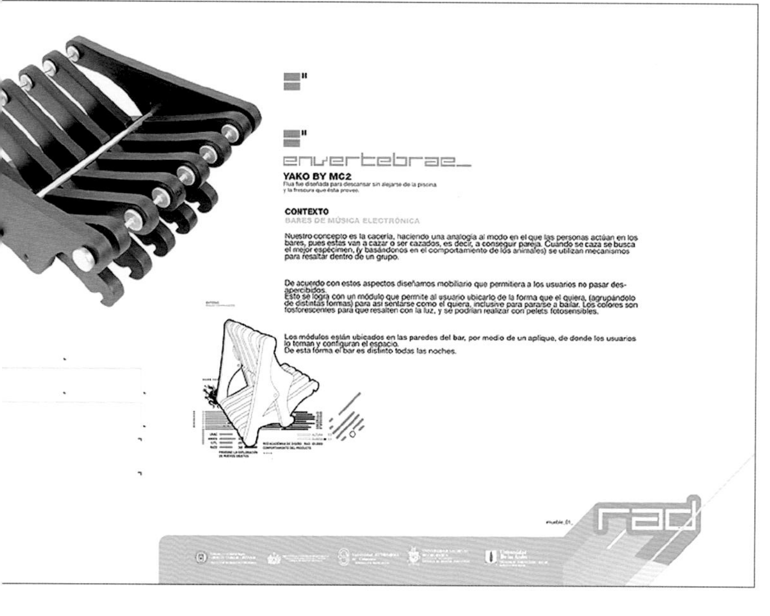
envertebrae_
YAKO BY MC2
Flua fue diseñada para descansar sin alejarse de la piscina
y la frescura que ésta provee.
CONTEXTO
BARES DE MÚSICA ELECTRÓNICA
Nuestro concepto es la cacería, haciendo una analogía al modo en el que las personas actúan en los bares, pues estas van a cazar o ser cazados, es decir, a conseguir pareja. Cuando se caza se busca el mejor espécimen, (y basándonos en el comportamiento de los animales) se utilizan mecanismos para resaltar dentro de un grupo.
De acuerdo con estos aspectos diseñamos mobiliario que permitiera a los usuarios no pasar desapercibidos.
Esto se logra con un módulo que permite al usuario ubicarlo de la forma que el quiera, (agrupándolo de distintas formas) para así sentarse como el quiera, inclusive para pararse a bailar. Los colores son fosforescentes para que resalten con la luz, y se podrían realizar con pelets fotosensibles.
Los módulos están ubicados en las paredes del bar, por medio de un aplique, de donde los usuarios lo toman y configuran el espacio.
De esta forma el bar es distinto todas las noches.
mueble_01_
rad

Emil Bertell [FIN] www. fenotype.com

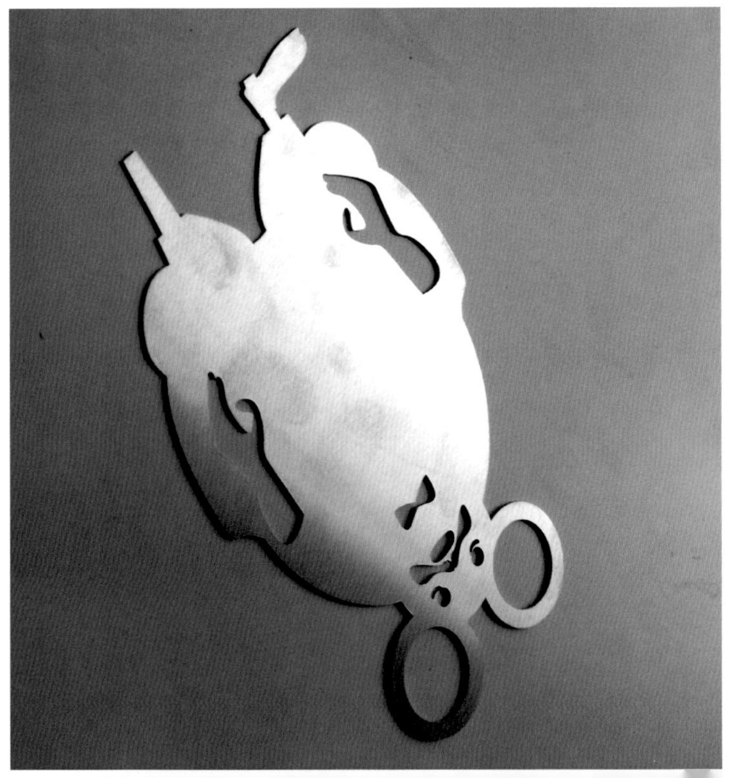

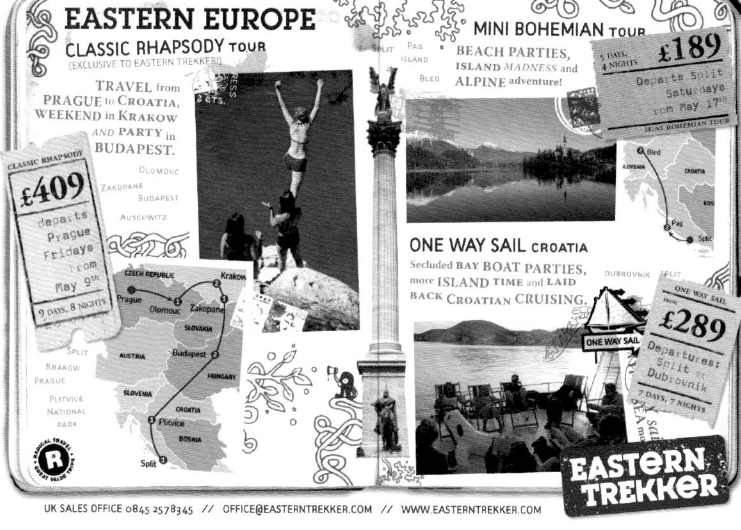

EASTERN EUROPE
CLASSIC RHAPSODY TOUR
(EXCLUSIVE TO EASTERN TREKKER!)
TRAVEL from PRAGUE to CROATIA, WEEKEND in KRAKOW AND PARTY in BUDAPEST.
CLASSIC RHAPSODY
£409
departs Prague Fridays from May 9th
9 DAYS, 8 NIGHTS
OLOMOUC
ZAKOPANE
BUDAPEST
AUSCHWITZ
CZECH REPUBLIC
Krakow
Prague
Olomouc
Zakopane
SLOVAKIA
AUSTRIA
Budapest
HUNGARY
SLOVENIA
CROATIA
Plitvice
BOSNIA
Split
SPLIT
KRAKOW
PRAGUE
PLITVICE NATIONAL PARK
RADICAL TRAVEL GREAT VALUE TRIPS
MINI BOHEMIAN TOUR
SPLIT
PAG ISLAND
BLED
BEACH PARTIES, ISLAND MADNESS and ALPINE adventure!
5 DAYS, 4 NIGHTS
£189
Departs Split Saturdays from May 17th
MINI BOHEMIAN TOUR
Bled
SLOVENIA
CROATIA
Pag
Split
ONE WAY SAIL CROATIA
Secluded BAY BOAT PARTIES, more ISLAND TIME and LAID BACK CROATIAN CRUISING.
DUBROVNIK
SPLIT
ONE WAY SAIL
ONE WAY SAIL
£289
Departures: Split or Dubrovnik
7 DAYS, 7 NIGHTS
EASTERN TREKKER
UK SALES OFFICE 0845 2578345 // OFFICE@EASTERNTREKKER.COM // WWW.EASTERNTREKKER.COM

Lilo Krebernik (AUT) www.0717.at

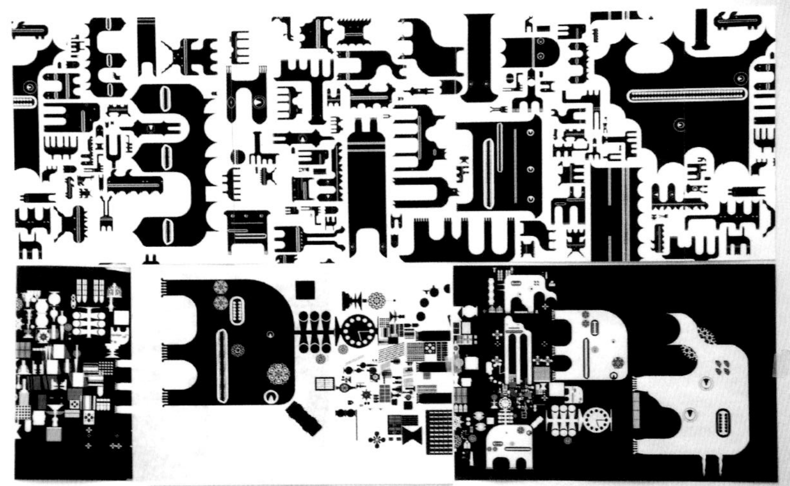

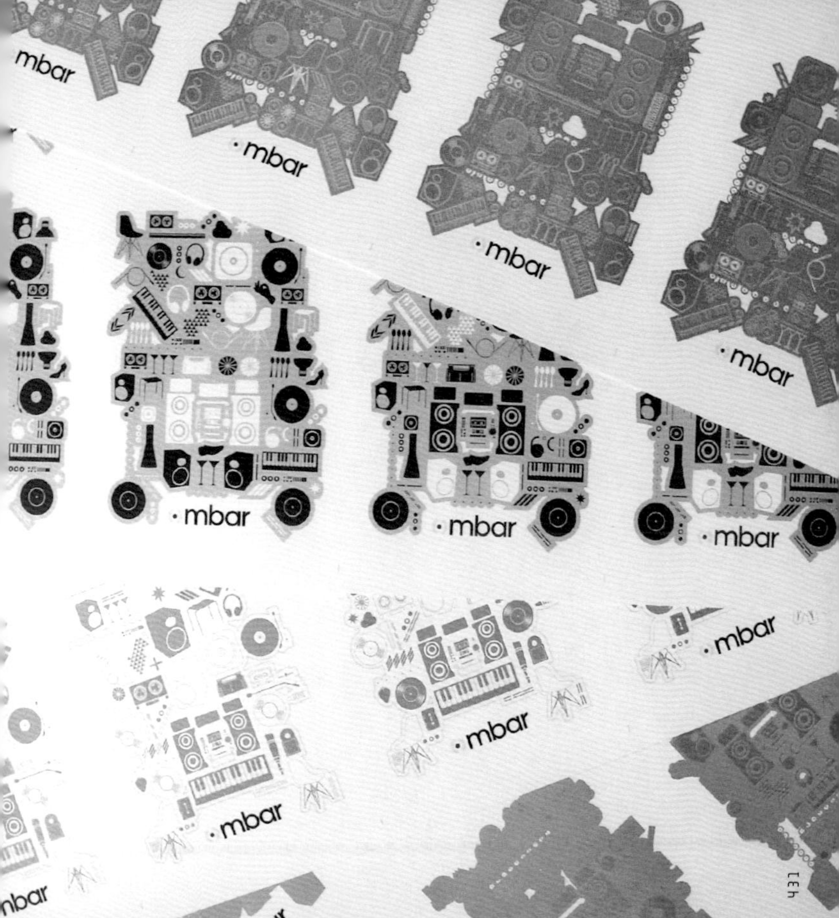
mbar
mbar
mbar
mbar
mbar
mbar
mbar
mbar
mbar
mbar
mbar

Kulturruine Spirit e.V.
Vampires Paradise
19. Februar 2005
Gothic + Mittelalter + Darkwave

KULTURRUINE
76131 KARLSRUHE

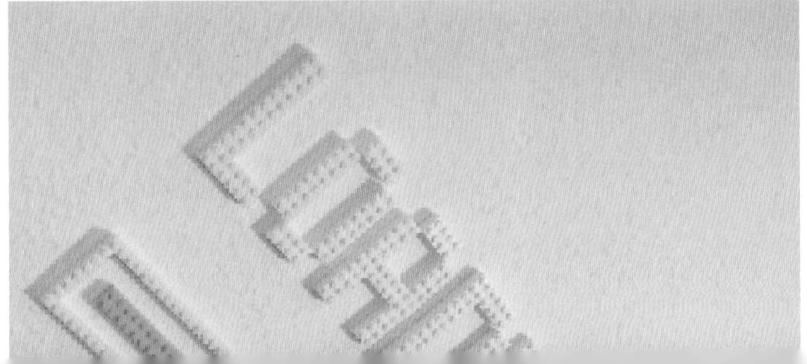

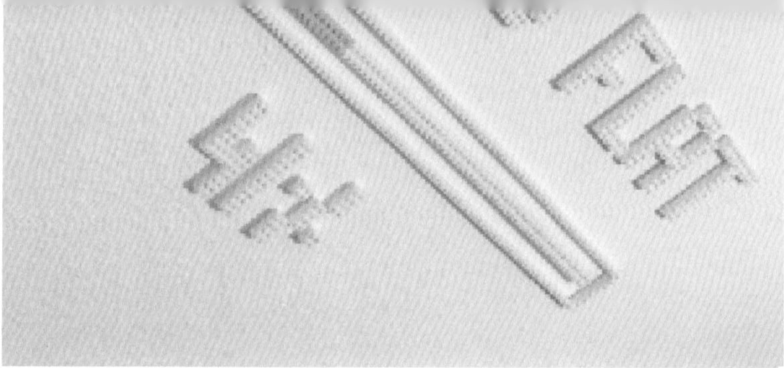

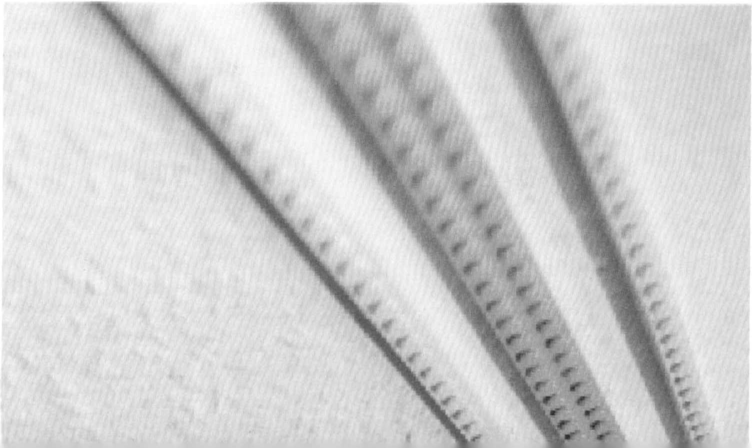

Katharina Putick [GER] www.dakapu.com

BIT
SHIT

7
N
STICK
STOFF

Diana de Sousa Matoso (GBR) www.dsway.co.uk

WALK A WAY

Sima Niroumand (GER) www. meinfreundistdj.de

MEIN
FREUND
IST
DJ

Annabelle Fiset [CAN] www.annabellefiset.com

Florian Jakober (SUI) www.floriangrafik.ch

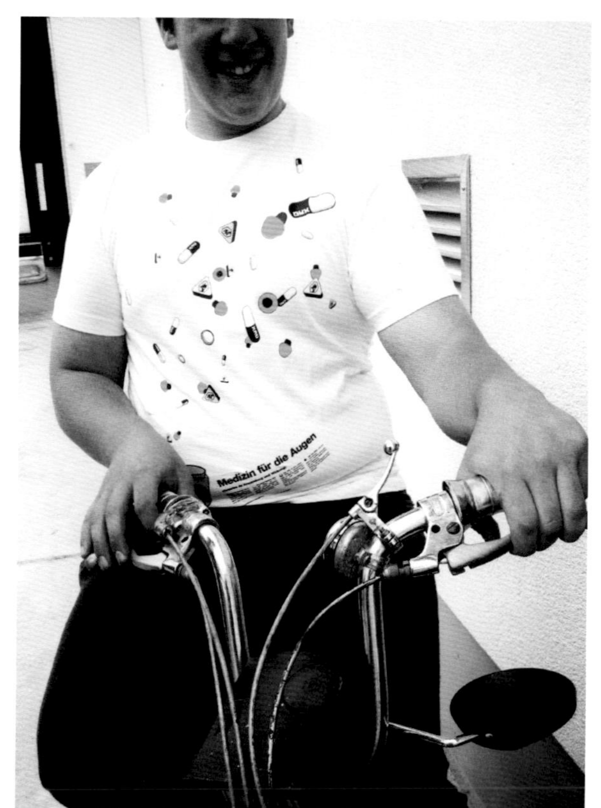
Medizin für die Augen

Sandro Hasieber (GER)

escoba's
escoba's

Eduardo Escobar Beckwith [MEX] www.escobas.com.mx

escobas

Susanne Dunkel (GER) www.susannedunkel.com

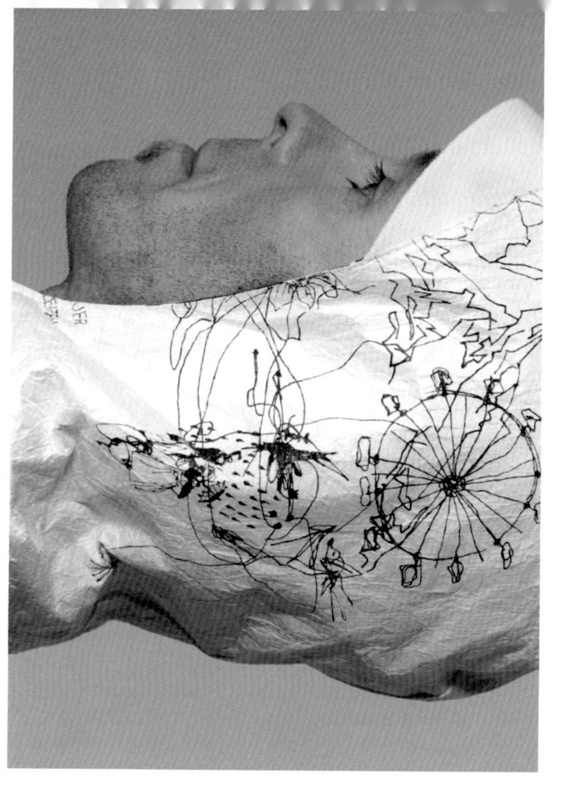

Wenn
Du denkst
es geht nicht mehr
kommt von
irgendwo ein
Lichtlein her

Herz
allen
gut
1855

Herz
allen

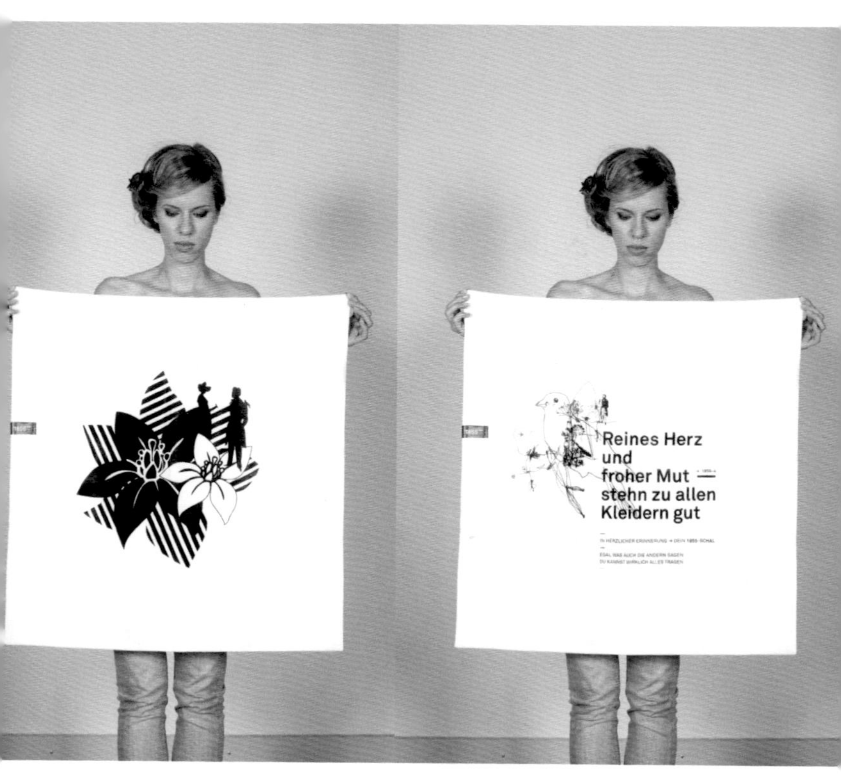
Reines Herz
und
froher Mut
stehn zu allen
Kleidern gut
IN HERZLICHER ERINNERUNG → DEIN 1855-SCHAL
EGAL WAS AUCH DIE ANDERN SAGEN
DU KANNST WIRKLICH ALLES TRAGEN

Herz

Mut —
allen
gut

Schau — dort spaziert Herr Biedermeier
und seine Frau, den Sohn am Arm.
Sein Tritt ist sachte wie auf Eier —
sein Wahlspruch: Weder kalt noch warm.

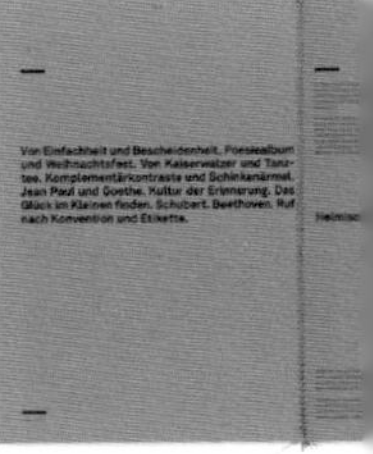
Von Einfachheit und Bescheidenheit. Poesiealbum und Weihnachtsfest. Von Kaiserwalzer und Tanztee. Komplementärkontraste und Schinkenärmel. Jean Paul und Goethe. Kultur der Erinnerung. Das Glück im Kleinen finden. Schubert. Beethoven. Ruf nach Konvention und Etikette.

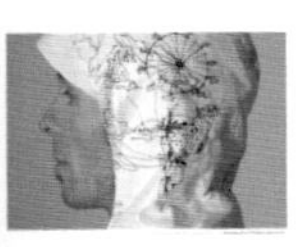

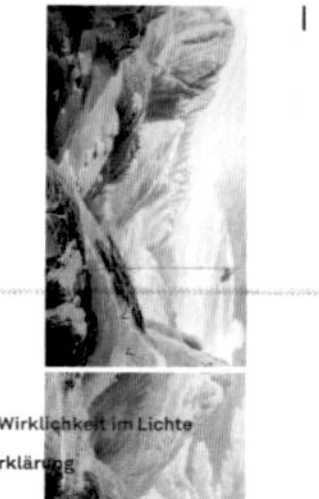
Die reine Wirklichkeit im Lichte
—
milder Verklärung

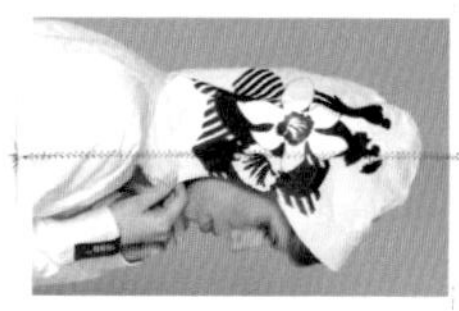

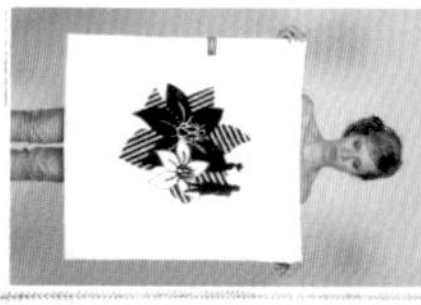

Reines Herz
und
froher Mut
stehn zu allen
Kleidern gut

Reines
und
froher
stehn z
Kleider

18. fílmfēštivął ćőtťbūŝ
Festival des osteuropäischen Films
Festival of East European Cinema

19. fílmfēštivął ćőtťbūŝ
Festival des osteuropäischen Films
Festival of East European Cinema

18. fílmfēštivął ćőtťbūŝ
Festival des osteuropäischen Films
Festival of East European Cinema
Nikon
Sixt
Kodak
Canon
DHL
FedEx
Bionade

19. fílmfēštivął ćőtťbūŝ
Festival des osteuropäischen Films
Festival of East European Cinema
Nikon
Sixt
Kodak
Canon
DHL
FedEx
Bionade

Hochschule
Ostwestfalen-Lippe
University of
Applied Sciences

Hochschule
OWL

DO NOT ENTER !
submag
NON ENTRARE
NELLA COMMUNITY
WWW.SUBMAG.IT
(POTRESTI NON RIUSCIRE AD USCIRNE)
SUBMAG è un marchio di subdued_www.subdued.it

DO NOT ENTER !
submag
NON ENTRARE
NELLA COMMUNITY
WWW.SUBMAG.IT
(POTRESTI NON RIUSCIRE AD USCIRNE)
SUBMAG è un marchio di subdued_www.subdued.it

Diana Schondelmaier (GER)

zwei
zwei
zweimalzwei
schloß
noten

knopf
musik

Osal8
Joe Nader
Musician. Producer. Promoter. Omnidigital DJ.
Integrated Entertainment
Integrated Entertainment

MATRIX &
FUTUREBOUND

Heiko Gimbel (GER) www.formgrad.de

1 MACHE IMMER DEN ERSTEN SCHRITT VOR DEM ZWEITEN
2 KOORDINIERE DEINE AKTIVITÄTEN, DENKE VORAUS
3 RÜCKSCHRITTE GEHÖREN DAZU – LASS DICH NICHT ENTMUTIGEN
4 NEUE MÖGLICHKEITEN STEHEN OFFEN
WIR NUTZEN DIE MÖGLICHKEITEN!
AM 28. JULI UM 15.00 UHR WERDEN WIR „KIRCHLICH"
HEIRATEN UND IM ANSCHLUSS DARAN UNSERE
TOCHTER HELEN KATHARINA TAUFEN
Diesen besonderen Tag möchten wir mit unseren Freunden
und Verwandten im Wagner's Hof in Undenheim feiern.
Dazu laden wir Euch herzlich ein.
Eins ist übrigens doch klar:
Wer nicht absagt, der ist da! Absagen bitte bis spätestens 30. April unter Tel. 06152 · 84438

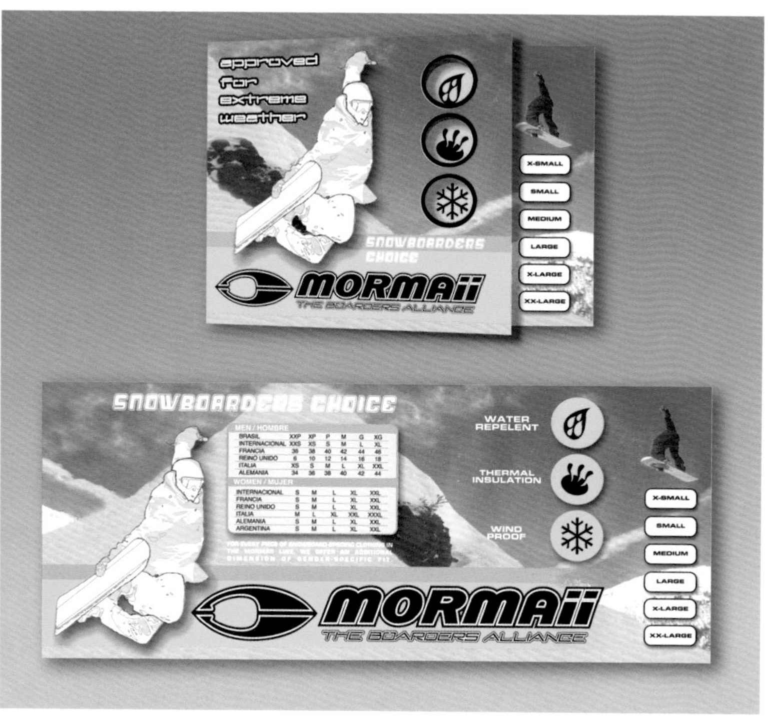

Sergio Skarek (ARG) www.skarek.com.ar

Sarah Ferrari (GBR) www.sarahferrari.com

LEA
DING

PERIÓDICO UNIVERSITARIO MARCA REGISTRADA

01/08

DICIEMBRE DE 2008

www. marcaregistrada.com

EL SALÓN DE OP GRÁFICAS Y LOS PRECURSORES DEL DISEÑO

LA IMAGEN DEL PAÍS

Por: Jessica Sánchez

Este año OP Gráfi cas decidió abrir el Concurso de Diseño Gráfi co para mayores de 26 años, como búsqueda de nuevos talentos, que no por su edad, sino por su reconocimiento artístico, enriquecieran el IV Salón OP Gráfi cas, que se ha venido realizando desde 1983. En aquel entonces tuvo como invitado al maestro David Consuegra, quien este año es homenajeado en este salón, como reconocimiento a su enseñanza y trayectoria, las cuales trajeron como benefi cio grandes avances en esta disciplina para el país.

El concurso contó, como en los salones anteriores, con el apoyo del Museo de Arte Moderno de Bogotá (MAMBO), donde fueron exhibidas las obras y se llevó a cabo la premiación el 12 de septiembre de 2007. Profesionales en el área, con gran reconocimiento en el país, fueron seleccionados "románticamente" como jurados: Martha Granados, Maripaz Jaramillo, Carlos Duque, César Cifuentes, Christian Schrader, Decano del Programa de Publicidad de la Tadeo, y Dicken Castro, quien fue decano del Programa de Diseño de Interiores, también de nuestra Universidad.

La acogida que tuvo el concurso fue grande y se contó con la participación de un sinnúmero de tadeístas, de los cuales muchos fueron seleccionados y pudieron exhibir sus obras en el Salón. Entre ellos estuvo el premiado con el tercer puesto: Alberto Villa, egresado del Programa de Diseño Industrial del 82 y quien más adelante fue profesor de la Tadeo por algún tiempo. Su afiche inspirado en Escher, reflejaba la temática del concurso, "Colombia positiva", de una forma bastante particular: cuadros de diferentes colores, los cuales se convertían en palomas que se besaban y delimitaban el mapa de Colombia y, en una esquina, una paloma blanca representando aquel anhelo de un pueblo en su búsqueda por la paz. Eso es Colombia, aquella diversidad de colores que tiene un mismo sueño.

Otros escogieron caminos diferentes para representar a Colombia: Juan Carlos Baena, ganador del concurso, utilizó elementos propios de la identidad, ya posicionados, como el sombrero "vueltiao", el café, motivos precolombinos, entre otros, dándole cierta profundidad al afiche, al tiempo que fundía letras entre líneas y objetos. Mientras, el segundo puesto, María Isabel Cabarcas, se inclinó por trazos y líneas caprichosas de colores básicos, que parecen plasmar de forma etérea una orquídea. Diferentes puntos de vista y diversidad se encontraron en esta convocatoria, de alto nivel por el reconocimiento de sus jurados y la trayectoria del evento, el cual ha venido realizando esta labor social en pro del desarrollo e investigación de esta especialidad, que no tiene aún mucha promoción y apoyo en el país. OP Gráfi cas quiso romper con el esquema de convocatorias sólo para los muy jóvenes. Alberto Villa, nuestro tercer puesto, comentó al respecto: "Me pregunto si es que existe, en general, la creencia de que después de los treinta ya no se tienen ideas". Se tienen muchas ideas, por supuesto, y más posibilidades de explorar campos diferentes, alejados ya las tendencias y las modas. Pero con continuidad, pues como afi rmó José Fernando Isaza, Rector de la Universidad: "Hay cosas que se deben hacer antes de los 24, aparte de divertirse, y una de ellas es realizar un proyecto serio", eso crea hábitos en la búsqueda de conocimiento que con el paso de los años se manifi esta en trabajos de calidad, como los que se vieron en este concurso.

Sin embargo, una última inquietud debe sembrar una refl exión para los que vienen: las herramientas digitales deben proveer facilidades en la ejecución de trabajos, pero la máquina jamás poDrá diseñar en lugar del profesional. De ahí la importancia del boceto en papel. "Nunca los trazos digitales van a ser mejores que los que se realizan a mano", reitera Villa. Entonces, las tendencias informáticas en todos los campos del diseño, que se manejan en la actualidad, parecen más preocupadas por la imagen que por su propio contenido. "Sí, había afi ches muy bonitos, pero sin contenido, vacíos y que no dejaban ningún tipo de mensaje en el espectador", señaló Schrader.

Los medios digitales son simplemente una herramienta. La funcionalidad de cualquier producto debe basarse en su contenido, aquel mensaje que sea de provecho para la sociedad. Hace falta preguntar a las generaciones de hoy en día, y a unas cuantas que ya han venido pasando, ¿qué hay detrás de la imagen? ®

OBRAS QUE FUERON PRESENTADAS POR LOS TADEÍSTAS EN EL IV SALÓN DE OP GRÁFICAS

PENSAR LA IMAGEN

Por: Jorge Restrepo

La temática con la que se convocó a la elaboración de los carteles fue "Colombia Positiva", un llamado a reconocer los valores que alientan el país. Concursaron 42 tadeístas, con un porcentaje del 27% en la participación general, el más alto por institución. OP Gráficas es una de las empresas más reconocidas del sector gráfi co en Colombia. Está cumpliendo 40 años de participación en el ámbito comercial de la publicidad, la fotografía y el diseño, pero, además, a través de iniciativas como los salones de diseño, anuarios de publicidad y, más recientemente, su Calendario OP Gráficas ha buscado apoyar y promover el desarrollo de estas disciplinas en el país. La cuarta versión del Salón op Gráficas es su manera de celebrar eso 40 años de vida

¿ESTAS SEGURO?

UN LUGAR PROTEGIDO EN LA TADEO

Por: Carlos Rojas

La seguridad que hoy tenemos en la Universidad y sus alrededores está orientada por la Dirección de Recursos Académicos y Administrativos, en cabeza de Juan Sastoque, y es el resultado de un arduo trabajo que se ha venido realizando desde hace muchos años, cuando se adoptaron algunas estrategias, que fueron determinantes para que la Jorge Tadeo no tuviera que trasladarse a otro sector de la ciudad.

La primera de las estrategias fue la adquisición de predios de uso comercial y residencial, en los que se supervisores, corredores de seguridad y escuaDrón motorizado,los cuales están ubicados estratégicamente y hacen recorridos permanentes que brindan seguridad a los estudiantes y transeúntes las 24 horas del día y los 365 días del año. Todos estos anillos están conformados por guardias de una de las mejores compañías de vigilancia privada (algunos acompañados con perros adiestrados).

La tercera estrategia es el apoyo logístico, brindado por los recursos tecnológicos como radioteléfo- de utilizar marcando el 4444, desde cualquier acceso telefónico dentro de la universidad, esta línea permite reportar cualquier eventualidad o acción sospechosa.

Aparte de las estrategias de seguridad que se crearon para la Universidad, también se hizo un convenio con otras universidades e instituciones, el cual permite un mayor cubrimiento de vigilancia en el sector. En este convenio también está involucrada la Policía Nacional, que se reúne con los directores de seguridad de las universidades del centro para hacer responsables de la calidad de la seguridad. De acuerdo con los balances realizados por la Dirección de Recursos Humanos y Administrativos, la mayoría de los robos reportados no fueron producto de la confrontación o uso de arma blanca: fueron por descuido, por no denunciar irregularidades o por dar "papaya", como se dice popularmente. Por tanto, las recomendaciones básicas que contribuyen a que todos seamos partícipes de nuestra seguridad son: no incurrir en el grave error de tomar bebidas alcohólicas hasta altas horas de la

DISEÑADORES GRAFICOS EN HONG KONG

> Jorge Restrepo >>

Colombia Passion Exhibition es un proyecto que nace de Jorge Restrepo el cual nos cuenta: "Un día una amiga [Monica Reyes], me dio el contacto de Jimmy Chan el CEO de NewWebPick magazine, a partir de ese momento empecé a venderle la idea de hacer un especial sobre Colombia aprovechando que ellos en cada edición invitan a un país, tiempo mas tarde Jimmy me propone la idea de hacer una con diseñadores colombianos" El problema de selección fue sencillo, inicialmente se convocaron amigos y conocidos de Jorge, los cuales tienen un trabajo muy bueno. También se recibieron trabajos de ilustradores en flickr, o con trabajos subidos en internet, tratando de buscar un equilibrio entre los diseñadores mas reconocidos y gente joven que está proponiendo cosas.

La labor de NWP por apoyar el diseño colombiano es grande, los medios, la gente, los diseñadores, muchos alrededor de las piezas, con buenos comentarios. Pero cuando se le pregunta a Jorge que piensa del diseño colombiano experimental , responde: "Por la misma razón que se le llama experimental, es decir la gente los considera experimentos y no piezas finales que puedan ser vendidas a clientes. En mi caso particular, si bien es cierto empecé con piezas experimentales que se exponían en ciertos ámbitos, también experimentales, poco a poco fui creyendo que ese diseño podría ser "vendible". Creo que no imaginamos que dichos experimentos, pueden ser valorados por clientes y los clientes no se acostumbran por ende, a recibir dichos trabajos. Es un círculo vicioso sin fin."

+Entrevista+

1- Cómo y cúando surgio la idea de COLOMBIA PASSION + HONG KONG EXHIBITION POSTER?

Un día una amiga [Monica Reyes], me dio el contacto de Jimmy Chan el CEO de NewWebPick magazine, a partir de ese momento empecé a venderle la idea de hacer un especial sobre Colombia aprovechando que ellos en cada edición invitan a un país.

Un dái Jimmy me propuso la idea de hacer una exposición con diseñadores colombianos, y si estaba dispuesto a ayudarle, de inmediato me puse en la tarea de convocar la gente.

2- Cómo fue el proceso de selección de diseñadores y piezas?

Realmente fue sencillo, inicialmente convoqué a amigos y conocidos los cuales considero que su trabajo es muy bueno. También recibí trabajos de gente en flickr, o con trabajos subidos en Internet, traté de buscar un equilibrio entre los diseñadores mas reconocidos y gente joven que está proponiendo cosas.

3- Quienes fueron seleccionados [ver lista]

4- Cómo fue recibida la muestra en Honk Kong?

Muy bien, realmente la labor de NWP por apoyar el diseño colombiano es grande, los medios, la gente, los diseñadores, muchos alrededor de las piezas, con buenos comentarios.

5- Cómo se ve el diseño colombiano en el exterior, q nos hace falta y a q nivel estamos con el resto del mundo?

Yo creo que como la selección Colombia, nos falta fogueo, es decir poder participar en exposiciones, revistas, libros, alrededor del mundo. Yo siento que tenemos un buen nivel, pero los diseñadores e ilustradores, sienten mucho miedo en exponer las piezas públicamente, en un mercado internacional, y se quedan en los computadores y cajones de sus estudios. Falta mas que nada, valor en mostrar sus trabajos.

6- Porqué cree que en el caso de colombia el diseño experimental se queda en piezas individuales del autor, o en el mejor caso, piezas promocionales de eventos donde el target son diseñadores y no sale a un nivel más comercial?

Por la misma razón que se le llama experimental, es decir la gente los considera experimentos y no piezas finales que puedan ser vendidas a clientes. En mi caso particular, si bien es cierto empecé con piezas experimentales que se exponían en ciertos ámbitos, también experimentales, poco a poco fui creyendo que ese diseño podría ser "vendible". Creo que no imaginamos que dichos experimentos, pueden ser valorados por clientes y los clientes no se acostumbran por ende, a recibir dichos trabajos. Es un círculo vicioso sin fin.

7- Existe más apoyo e interes hacia el diseño gráfico novedoso y experimental allá [el resto del mundo] que acá [colombia, latino-america]?

La respuesta es SI, para los de "allá" el diseño experimental no existe o si existe realmente es experimental, no el que nosotros consideramos así. Por ende se convierte en diseño comercial.

+Perfil+

LEO ESPINOSA

Leo Espinosa desempacó maletas en Bogotá durante unos días. Actualmente está radicado en Estados Unidos. La Galería Colombiana de Diseño lo recibió con brazos abiertos y ojos bien atentos. En el viaje visual de sus poderosas imágenes, le confesó a los asistentes de su charla, su interés en retomar el mundo de los cómics. Su trabajo inició dos décadas atrás, como director de arte de Leo Burnett y BBDO. En 1993, se trasladó a New York e inició una interesante carrera como ilustrador. No para Innita, ilustrador y amigo, le comentó a proyectodiseño lo siguiente: "Leo aún asombra con su fluidez. Tiene un manejo vectorial impecable y fascinó al público con esta nueva etapa colorida y familiar. Puede decirse que se encuentra en una era post-powerpuff girls en combinación con el Godzilla japonés y el Tintín viajero, en un escenario muy a los Jetsonics de Hanna-Barbera. Su concepto tiene una alta dósis de humor nada infantil". En la actualidad, Espinosa vive en Cambridge e invitó a los ilustradores colombianos a seguir creyendo en su trabajo, porque el talento ya lo tienen. **www.studioespinosa.com**

NUMA

NUMA Studio es un estudio creativo y agencia de producción parte de Numa Project Ltd., que ofrece soluciones en comunicación visual, diseño web, diseño gráfico, fotografía, ilustración, branding, identidad corporativa y dirección de arte. Creada por Andrés Rodríguez y Diana Trujillo Neme, NUMA Studio cuenta con un equipo de profesionales en diferentes paises, y se especializa en los sectores moda, diseño, belleza, luxury goods, marcas premium, lifestyle y servicios exclusivos.

Nuestro equipo ha creado exitosas estrategias, campañas y piezas creativas para marcas de moda, accesorios, diseñadores, fotógrafos, agencias de modelos, galerías de diseño y decoración, perfumes, cosméticos, gadgets tecnológicos, cafés, restaurantes, hoteles, agencias de viajes, firmas de arquitectura e interiorismo y publicaciones especializadas.Desde 1999 hemos desarrollado projectos y campañas para marcas en España, Estados Unidos, Argentina, Colombia y otras ciudades, que requiren un altísimo nivel visual y conceptual acorde con sus grupos objetivos de alto poder adquisitivo y un consumidor cada vez más global y con un avanzado sentido de la estética. **www.numaproject.com**

KAL

Carlos Andres Lopez, "Kal", es colombiano. Nació en Bogotá en 1975. Estudió Diseñador gráfico de la Universidad Jorge Tadeo Lozano, donde se ha desempeñado como profesor de cátedra en ilustración, ilustración digital y taller de diseño, dedicado a la ilustración editorial desde hace más 6 años, su trabajo ha sido publicado en periódicos y revistas como El Espectador, Credencial, Malpensante y Número. Además de ser profesor en diferentes universidades mantiene activa su labor como ilustrador desarrollando imágenes y piezas gráficas para empresas como Skandia, Bayer, Luxus, Inif, Frito Lay, J.W., Thompson, Fondo de Prevención Vial, Secretaria de Gobierno, entre otros.

Trabaja también como diseñador gráfico ra. y publicista independiente. Ha expuesto individual y colectivamente sus trabajos de ilustración y pintura en Colombia, y en agosto de 2004 participó en la Exposition de Jeunes Artistes Colombiens, en París, Francia. "Los siete mejores cuentos escandinavos", publicado por Editorial Norma, es el primer libro infantil que ilustro. **www.quadra404.com**

"un cartel de lujo"

+ Catalina Estrada + Rodez + Jorge Restrepo + Carlos Roldán + Marcela Restrepo + Kal + Monica Naranjo + Popular de Lujo + Juan Diaz + Wilson Borja + Pilar Berrio + Juan Esteban Duque + Diego Contreras + Camilo Maecha + Ruben Romero + Metralla Gráfica + Typozon + Diego Melo + Lorena Álvarez + Eduardo Peña + Kontra + Álex Sarmiento + Mauricio Vásquez + Randy Mora + Paula Montenegro + Yurika + David Ñañez + Nicolás Ortega +

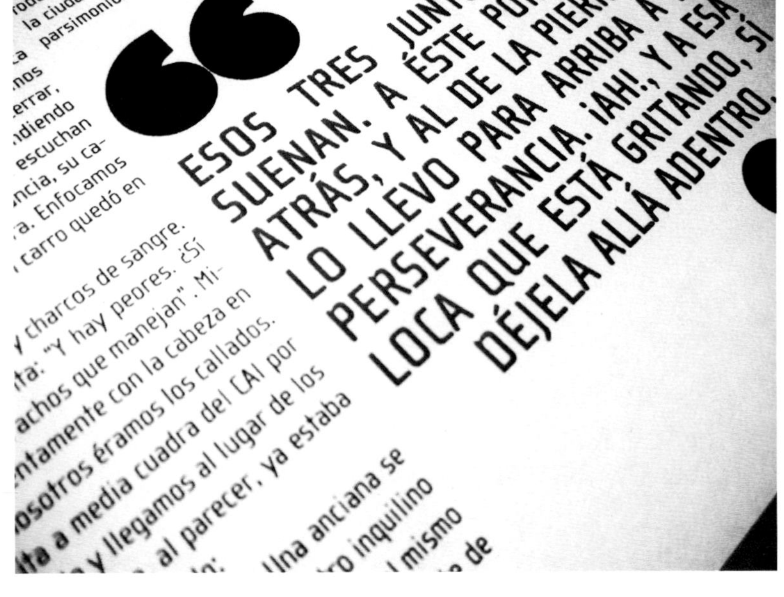

la ciudad
parsimoniosa y
escuchan
Enfocamos
carro quedó en
charcos de sangre.
"Y hay peores. ¿Sí
que manejan". Mi-
con la cabeza en
éramos los callados.
a media cuadra del CAI por
y llegamos al lugar de los
al parecer, ya estaba
Una anciana se
inquilino
mismo
ESOS TRES
SUENAN. A ÉSTE
ATRÁS, Y AL DE LA PIERNA
LO LLEVO PARA ARRIBA A LA
PERSEVERANCIA. ¡AH!, Y A ESA
LOCA QUE ESTÁ GRITANDO, SÍ
DÉJELA ALLÁ ADENTRO.

NOSOTROS
DICIEMBRE
ESPINOSA
MARCA REGISTRADA
04/08
HONG KONG
QUÉ HACER CON EL TIEMPO LIBRE Y LAS GANAS.
Muchos desconocen qué hay en el séptimo piso del módulo siete. Otros han estado cerca de éste, porque es el camino des- de el ascensor hacia la terraza de oma o porque se sentaron o acostaron a descansar en los sofás del fondo del corredor. Los que son gomosos de la música, el cine, la danza y otras manifes- taciones de este tipo, ya deben estar anticipando a qué me
un principio, los talleres que se ofrecían se podían contar con los dedos de la mano, pero después fueron aumentando, en concor- dancia con los intereses de los jóvenes. Actualmente se ofrecen treinta y ocho opciones
ESOS TRES JUNTOS SUENAN. A ÉSTE PÓ ATRÁS, Y AL DE LA PI LO LLEVO PARA ARRI PERSEVERANCIA. GRITA LOCA QUE ESTÁ ALLÁ ADENT

and reveal
esigners
o life.
DE-
SIGN
„Mich würde ja mal interessieren, ob das ‚de-' vor dem ‚-sign' eigentlich eine Negativvorsilbe ist, die so etwas wie das deutsche ‚ent-' bedeutet. de-sign gleich entzeichnen, oder entstellen."
AUS EINER UMFRAGE ZUM THEMA „FREMD-/SELBSTBILD"
SIGN Verantwortungsbewusstes Design
Eine kartographische Definitionsskizze
BE-
WUSST
Anregungen für eine verantwortungsbewusstere Designpraxis

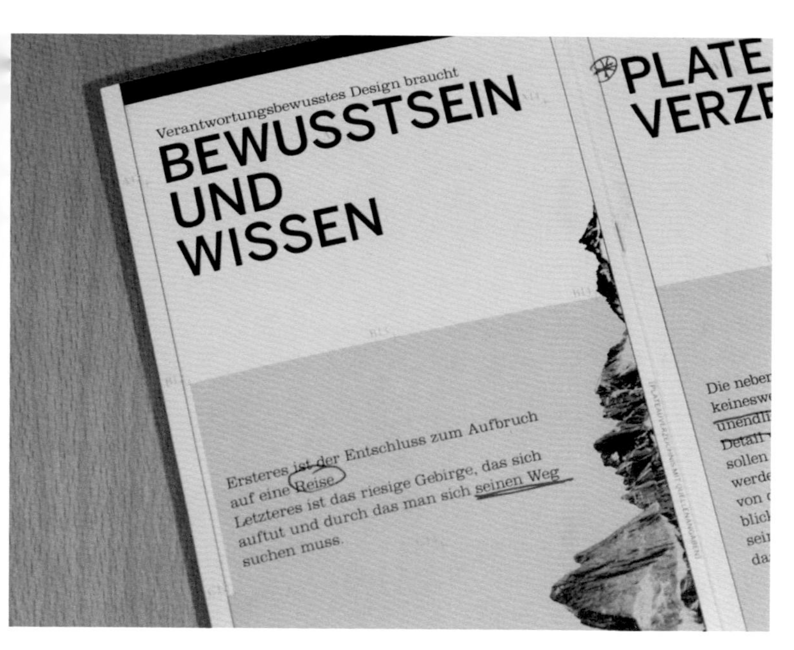
Verantwortungsbewusstes Design braucht
BEWUSSTSEIN
UND
WISSEN
Ersteres ist der Entschluss zum Aufbruch
auf eine Reise.
Letzteres ist das riesige Gebirge, das sich
auftut und durch das man sich seinen Weg
suchen muss.
PLATE
VERZE

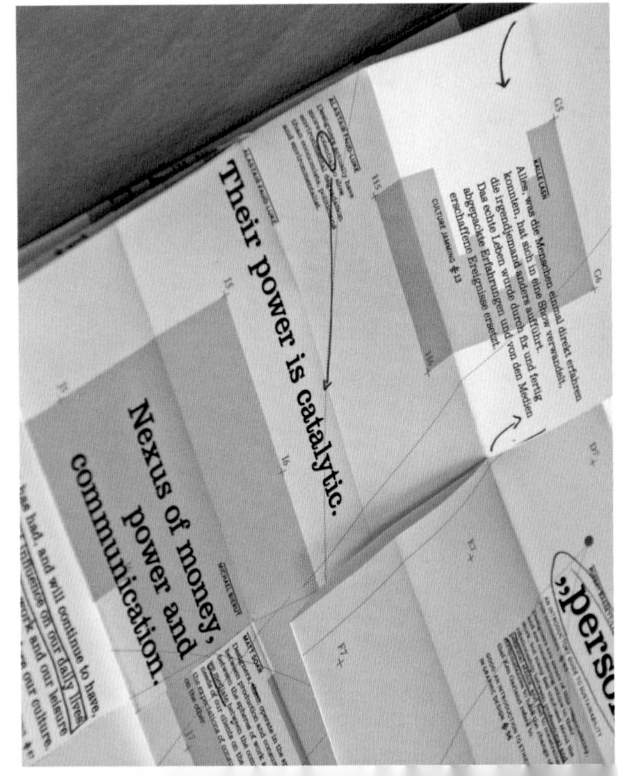
KALLE LASN
Alles, was die Menschen einmal direkt erfahren konnten, hat sich in eine Show verwandelt, die irgendjemand anders aufführt. Das echte Leben wurde durch fix und fertig abgepackte Erfahrungen und von den Medien erschaffene Ereignisse ersetzt.
CULTURE JAMMING 13
„perso
ALASTAIR FAUD-LUKE
Their power is catalytic.
MICHAEL BIERUT
Nexus of money, power and communication.
MATT SOAR
has had, and will continue to have, influence on our daily lives work and our leisure our culture.

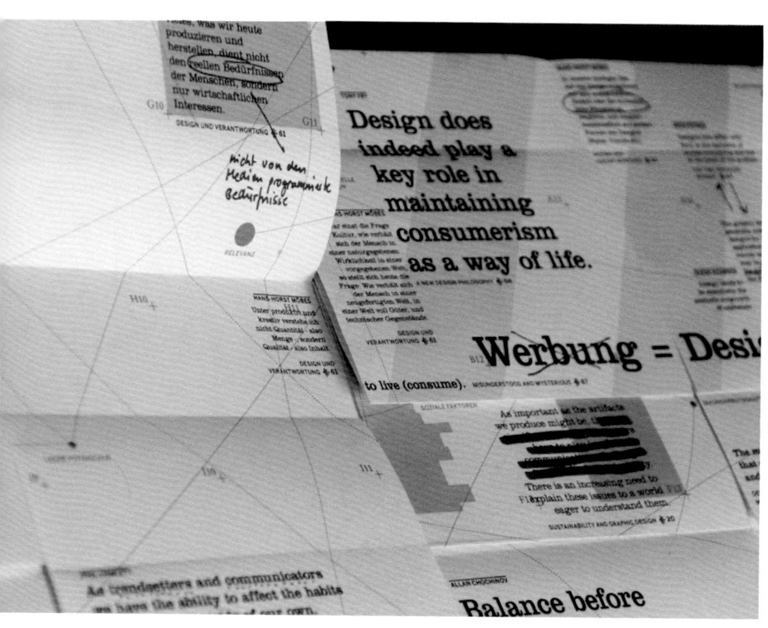

was wir heute
produzieren und
herstellen, dient nicht
den reellen Bedürfnissen
der Menschen, sondern
nur wirtschaftlichen
Interessen.
DESIGN UND VERANTWORTUNG 61
Design does indeed play a key role in maintaining consumerism as a way of life.
A NEW DESIGN PHILOSOPHY 54
HANS HORST MÖBES
Unter produktiv und kreativ verstehe ich nicht Quantität – also Menge – sondern Qualität – also Inhalt.
DESIGN UND VERANTWORTUNG 61
Werbung = Desi
to live (consume).
MISUNDERSTOOD AND MYSTERIOUS 67
As important as the artifacts we produce might be,
There is an increasing need to explain these issues to a world eager to understand them.
SUSTAINABILITY AND GRAPHIC DESIGN 20
ALLAN CHOCHINOV
Balance before
As trendsetters and communicators we have the ability to affect the habits

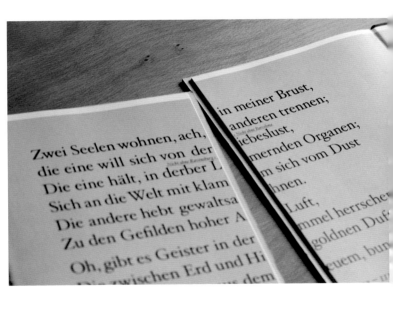

Zwei Seelen wohnen, ach,
die eine will sich von der
Die eine hält, in derber L
Sich an die Welt mit klam
Die andere hebt gewaltsa
Zu den Gefilden hoher A
Oh, gibt es Geister in der
Die zwischen Erd und Hi
in meiner Brust,
anderen trennen;
iebeslust,
mernden Organen;
m sich vom Dust
hnen.
Luft,
mmel herrsche
goldnen Duf
euem, bun

Status
Quo
vadis?

BACON CARAVAN CREEK

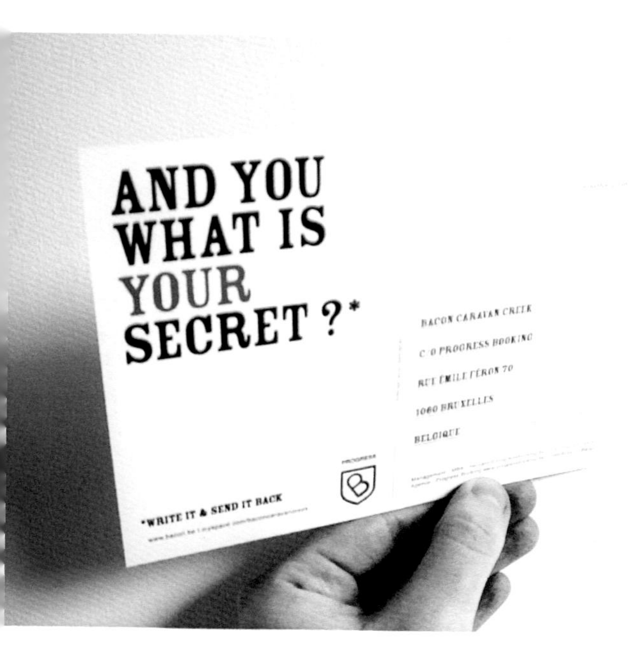
AND YOU
WHAT IS
YOUR
SECRET ?*
BACON CARAVAN CREEK
C/O PROGRESS BOOKING
RUE ÉMILE FÉRON 70
1060 BRUXELLES
BELGIQUE
*WRITE IT & SEND IT BACK

Presented by Analog Africa
AFRICAN SCREAM CONTEST
MOUSSAOUIPHON
ORCHESTRE
PICOBY BAND

 Petra Schröder + Dirk von Manteuffel (GER) www.sosumi.net

ប្រយ័ត្នគ្រាប់មីន!!

Wir laden *Euch* ganz herzlich dazu ein.

Plan!

Standesamtliche Trauung 11:30
im Küsterhaus Schwanewede
(gleich neben der schönen alten Dorfkirche)

anschließend Kaffee und Kuchen,
oder Herzhaftes, dann ein Ausflug in die landschaftliche Idylle vor Ort

abendliches Schlemmen
(unter freiem Himmel, wenn das Wetter mitmacht – wovon wir ausgehen!)

Wo?

im hohen Norden
Auf dem Vorberg 44,
28790 Schwanewede
da, wo Anne herkommt

Wann?

am Samstag, den 23.08.2008

Wie?

Na, es wird doch geheiratet!
Aber Ihr sollt Euch wohl fühlen.
Und sicherheitshalber ein Paar bequeme Schuhe mitbringen, wir sind schließlich auf dem Land.

Was?

In unsere enge Bude geht kaum noch was rein.
Geldgeschenke wären uns daher am liebsten.

Weiteres

Für Fragen
Benedikt:
Tel. 0931–28 64 36
Eva:

... Wir freuen uns sehr auf Euch!

Eva Zechel (GER) www.exmono.de

 Birgit Groismaier (AUT) www.erwinbauer.com

Carl Valentin GmbH
Neckarstraße 78-82
D-78056 Villingen-Schwenningen

Firmensitz und Geschäftsleitung:
Überlingen / Bodensee

Telefon ++49 (0) 77 20 / 97 12-0
Telefax ++49 (0) 77 20 / 99 49 87-1

E-Mail: info@valentin-carl.de
Internet: www.valentin-carl.de

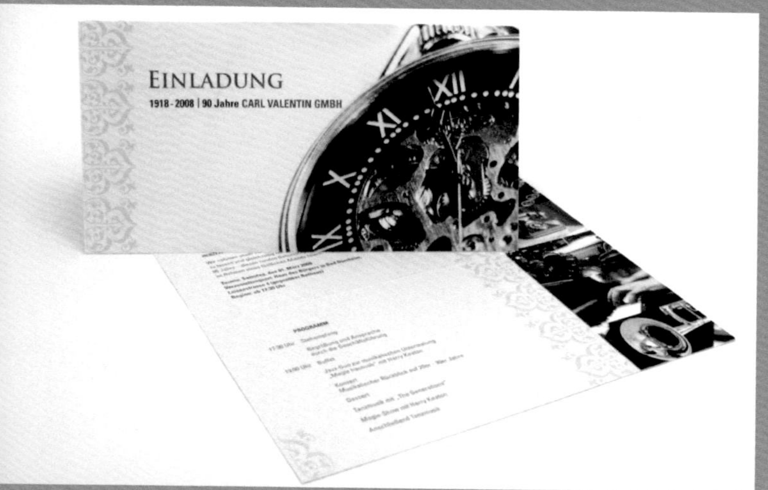
EINLADUNG
1918 - 2008 | 90 Jahre CARL VALENTIN GMBH

Diana Schondelmaier (GER)

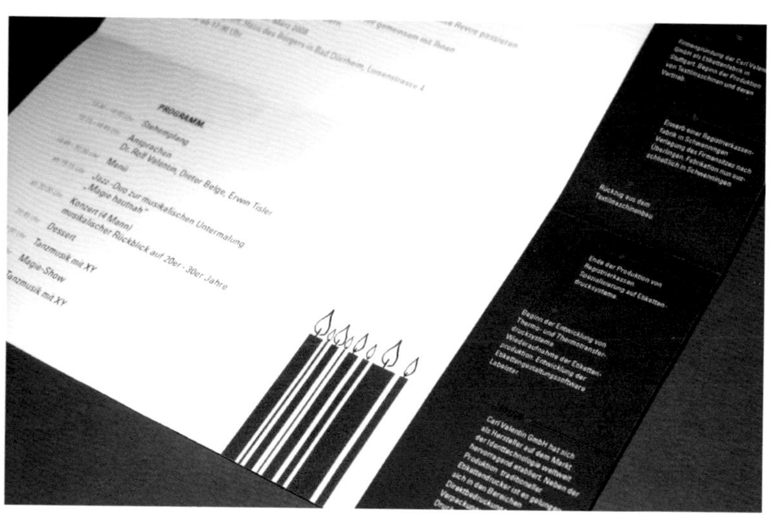
PROGRAMM
Stehempfang
Ansprachen
Dr. Rolf Valentin, Dieter Beige, Erwin Tisler
Menü
Jazz-Duo zur musikalischen Untermalung
„Magie hautnah"
Konzert (4 Mann)
musikalischer Rückblick auf 20er - 30er Jahre
Dessert
Tanzmusik mit XY
Magie-Show
Tanzmusik mit XY
Rückzug aus dem Textilmaschinenbau
Ende der Produktion von Registrierkassen
Carl Valentin GmbH hat sich als Hersteller auf dem Markt der Identtechnologie weltweit hervorragend etabliert.

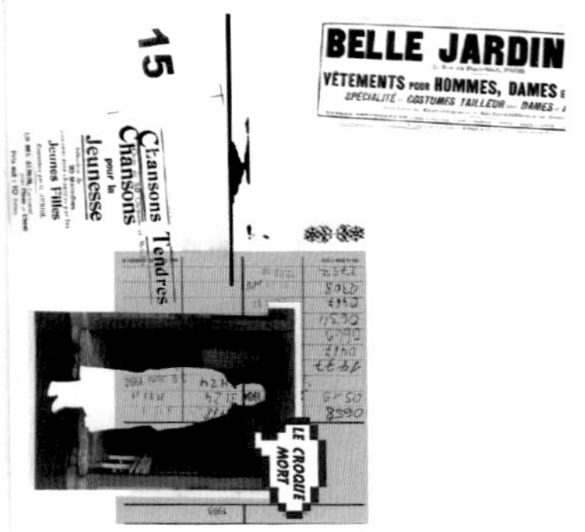
BELLE JARDIN
VÊTEMENTS POUR HOMMES, DAMES
SPÉCIALITÉ - COSTUMES TAILLEUR - DAMES
15
Chansons Tendres
Chansons
pour la
Jeunesse
Jeunes Filles
LE CROQUE MORT

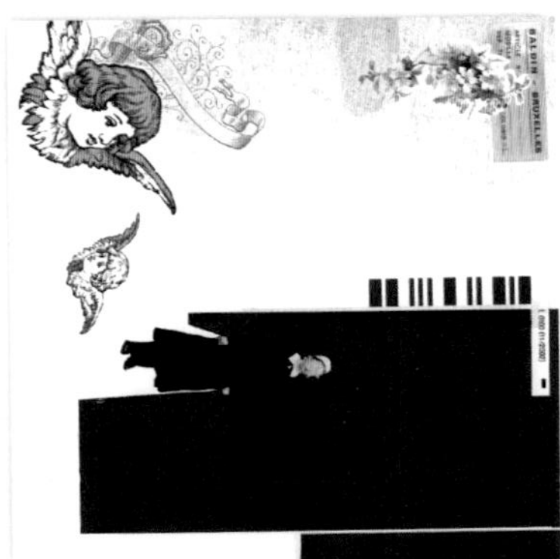
BALDIN - BRUXELLES

Tutto
è più facile!
Die Platte bleibt für Nachbestellungen aufbewahrt.
Platten Nr.

Bob says !!!

Stefan Weyer (GER) www.stefan-weyer.com

PAN
ICCL
UB

P A N I C C L U B

INDIE POST P
BECAUSE THE MUSIC THAT THE
UNK NEW WA
Y CONSTANTLY PLAY IT SAYS N
VE ELECTRO
OTHING TO ME ABOUT MY LIFE

Stefan Weyer [GER] www.stefan-weyer.com

06.06.2008

0606
2008

PRODUKTION AM DOM

EINTRITT 2.50€ 3.00€
FLYER ~~FLYER~~

beyond
designtreff
beyondrisør
NASJONALT DESIGNTREFF
12. OG 13. JUNI 2008
WWW.BEYONDRISOR.NO

beyondrisør
12. og 13. juni 2008
treff

stiller støy

/Forord

One of the complaints I often come across in reference to Norwegian design is that it is overshadowed somewhat by its Scandinavian neighbours. When the world thinks of Scandinavian design it thinks of Arne Jacobsen, IKEA and Alvar Aalto. In other words: Denmark, Sweden and Finland.

Norway doesn't have a famous design figurehead. There's nobody for the young designers to look up to. Apparently Norway has no design history or reputation to trade on.

Funnily enough, however, this is exactly the same reason why Norwegian design is so exciting right now.

Through my work over the last three years as curator of 100% Norway, two things have become very apparent:

- firstly, the quality of design in Norway – across all disciplines – is improving at an impressive rate. The ball has been set rolling with what seems to be an unstoppable momentum.
- Secondly, I can confirm that the international markets are definitely, without a doubt, very interested in Norwegian design.

The crucial thing to understand here is that it's not because it's Norwegian in any contrived aesthetic or clichéd fashion. Nor even because it might possess that timeless Scandinavian chic we all love and know so well. In fact, all international design eyes are on the talent currently emerging from this country for one simple reason: because it's really, really good.

Norway has recently released an explosion of new world-class talent on the international design scene. The impressive line-up of designers involved in **BeyondRisør** is proof of this.

Industry – whether Norwegian or otherwise – needs to sit up and take notice, and – as we can see from this exhibition, it is happily beginning to do so.

Indeed the very existence of **BeyondRisør** is indicative of an exciting, creative, collaborative and proactive climate for design in Norway. Starting here, this is a place where – with open minds and far-reaching ambition – there is great potential for the future.

Henrietta Thompson, design and architecture editor and writer, and curator for the exhibition 100% Norway in London

side 4 – 5

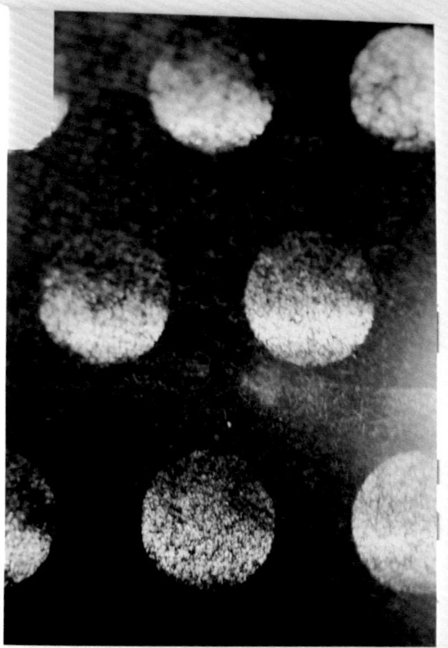

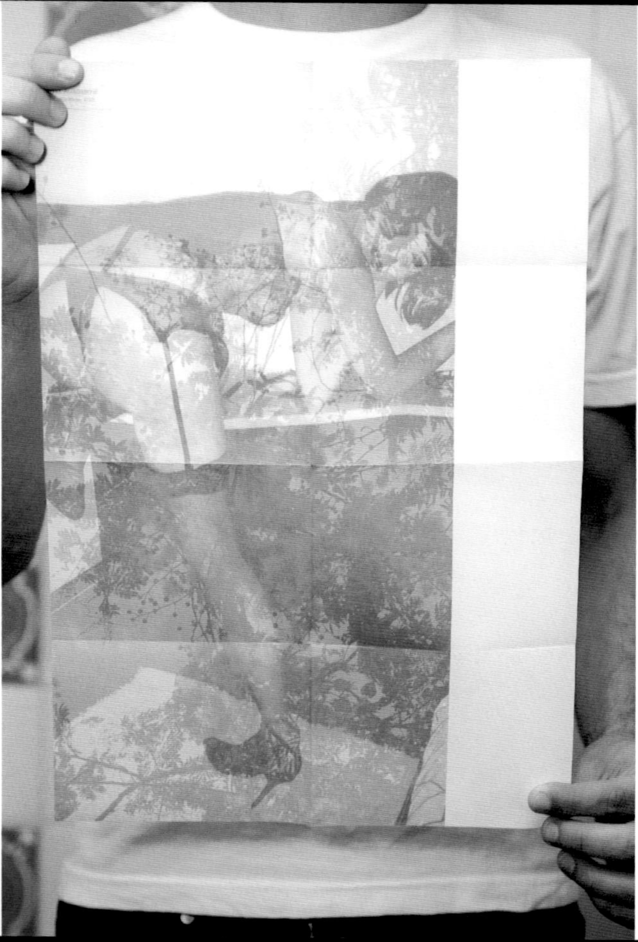

V.ROM
MEZANINO
INAUGURAÇÃO
STOP PLAY MOON
EXPOSIÇÃO
MEZANINO DA V.ROM
MOTEL BEGA
MOTEL BLINDADO
MOTEL BEGA
EXPOSIÇÃO INDIVIDUAL DE PAULO BEGA
Fotografias, colagens, música e objetos
Jackson Araújo
fotosfera
Heineken
ONE

Lucas Rampazzo [BRA] www.flickr.com/photos/lucasrampazzo

MEZANINO
MOTEL
BEGA

V.ROM
MEZANINO
MOTEL
BEGA

Isabelle Gehrmann (GER) www.ahdaad.com

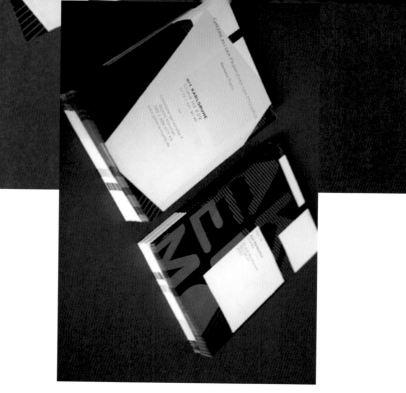

Winner
of the
Gunn Report
for Media
Four
Consecutive
Years
For more information please contact
debra.isaacson@omd.com
0207 908 3516
www.omd.com
OMD

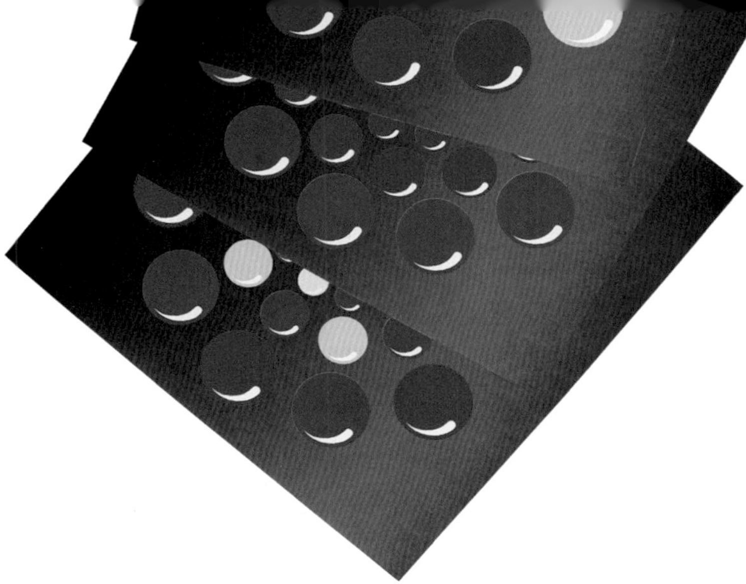

Mark Richardson (GBR) www.superfried.com

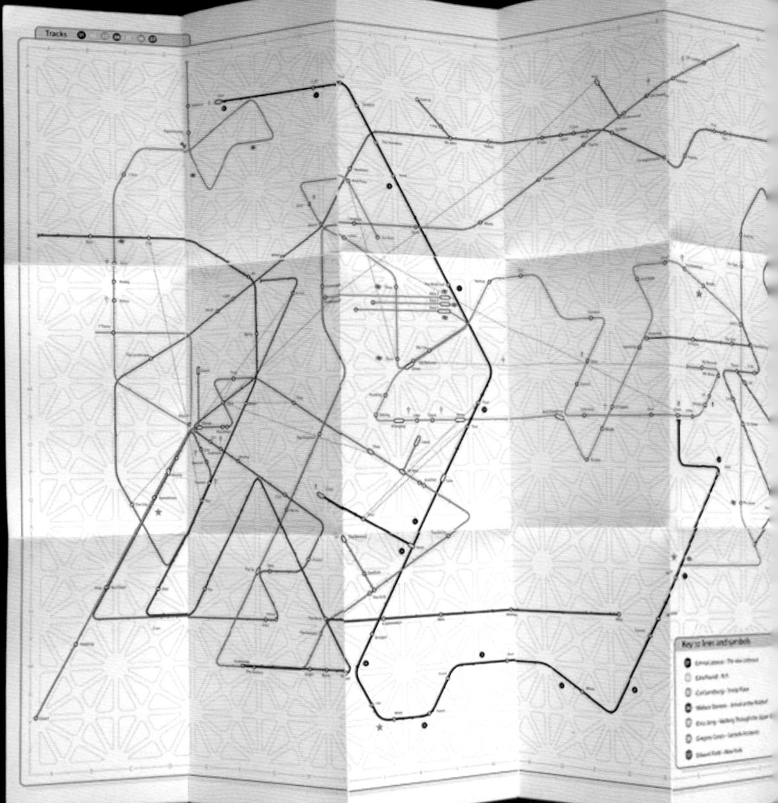
Tracks
Key to lines and symbols

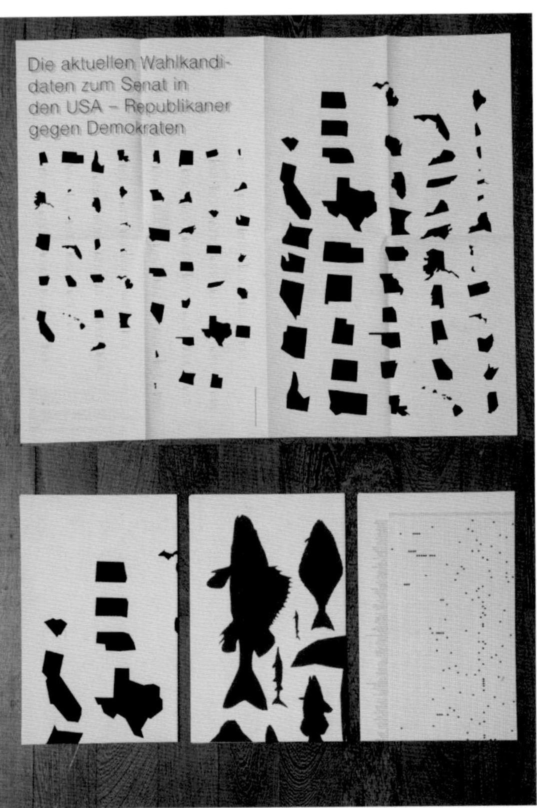
Die aktuellen Wahlkandi-
daten zum Senat in
den USA – Republikaner
gegen Demokraten

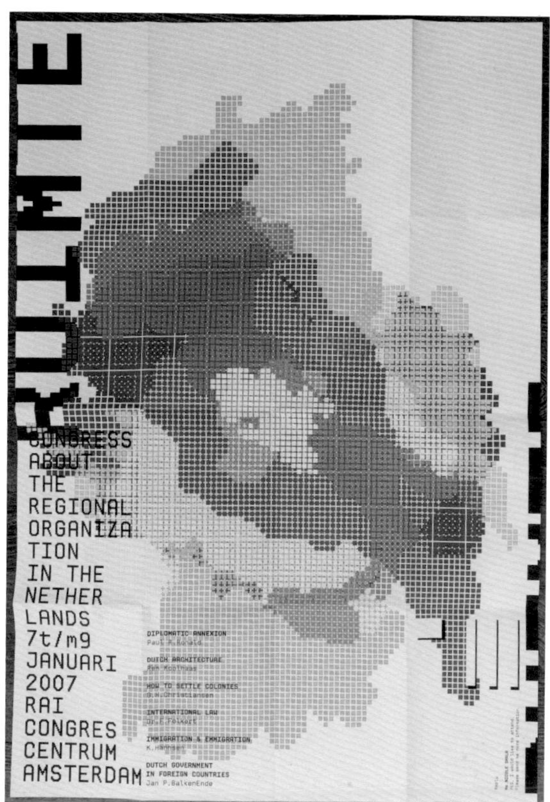
RUIMTE
CONGRESS
ABOUT
THE
REGIONAL
ORGANIZA
TION
IN THE
NETHER
LANDS
7t/m9
JANUARI
2007
RAI
CONGRES
CENTRUM
AMSTERDAM
DIPLOMATIC ANNEXION
DUTCH ARCHITECTURE
HOW TO SETTLE COLONIES
INTERNATIONAL LAW
IMMIGRATION & EMMIGRATION
DUTCH GOVERNMENT
IN FOREIGN COUNTRIES
Jan P.BalkenEnde

knickelkopp™
yvonne frieß
liebigstraße 11a · 45145 essen
tel +49.201.2881673
mail@knickelkopp.de
www.knickelkopp.de

Lara Allport & Simon Barrett (AUS) www.thenationalgrid.com.au

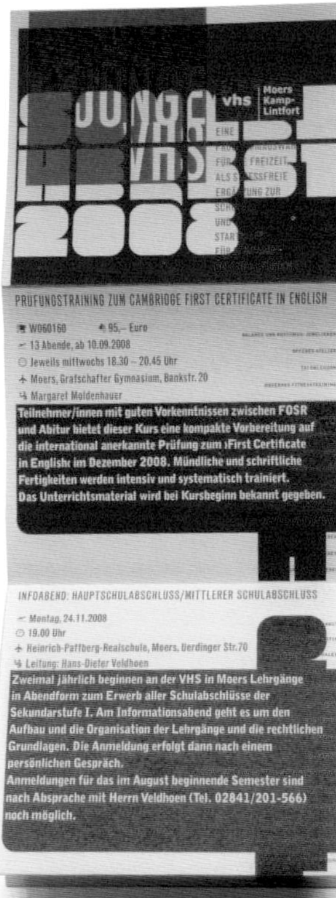
vhs
Moers Kamp-Lintfort
2008
PRÜFUNGSTRAINING ZUM CAMBRIDGE FIRST CERTIFICATE IN ENGLISH
W060160 95,– Euro
13 Abende, ab 10.09.2008
Jeweils mittwochs 18.30 – 20.45 Uhr
Moers, Grafschafter Gymnasium, Bankstr. 20
Margaret Moldenhauer
Teilnehmer/innen mit guten Vorkenntnissen zwischen FOSR und Abitur bietet dieser Kurs eine kompakte Vorbereitung auf die international anerkannte Prüfung zum ›First Certificate in English‹ im Dezember 2008. Mündliche und schriftliche Fertigkeiten werden intensiv und systematisch trainiert. Das Unterrichtsmaterial wird bei Kursbeginn bekannt gegeben.
INFOABEND: HAUPTSCHULABSCHLUSS/MITTLERER SCHULABSCHLUSS
Montag, 24.11.2008
19.00 Uhr
Heinrich-Pattberg-Realschule, Moers, Uerdinger Str. 70
Leitung: Hans-Dieter Veldhoen
Zweimal jährlich beginnen an der VHS in Moers Lehrgänge in Abendform zum Erwerb aller Schulabschlüsse der Sekundarstufe I. Am Informationsabend geht es um den Aufbau und die Organisation der Lehrgänge und die rechtlichen Grundlagen. Die Anmeldung erfolgt dann nach einem persönlichen Gespräch.
Anmeldungen für das im August beginnende Semester sind nach Absprache mit Herrn Veldhoen (Tel. 02841/201-566) noch möglich.

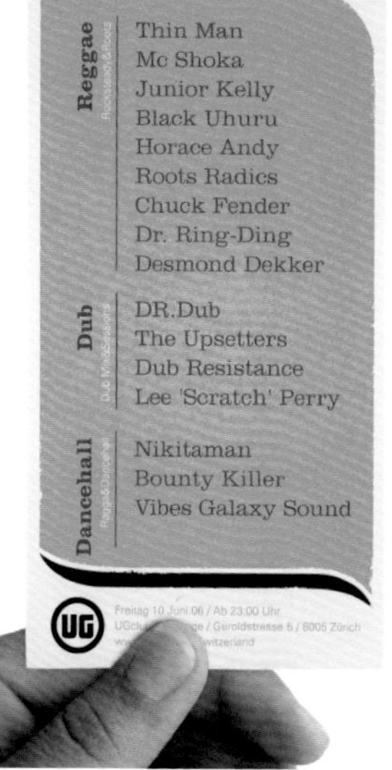

Reggae
Thin Man
Mc Shoka
Junior Kelly
Black Uhuru
Horace Andy
Roots Radics
Chuck Fender
Dr. Ring-Ding
Desmond Dekker
Dub
DR.Dub
The Upsetters
Dub Resistance
Lee 'Scratch' Perry
Dancehall
Nikitaman
Bounty Killer
Vibes Galaxy Sound
UG
Freitag 10 Juni 06 / Ab 23.00 Uhr

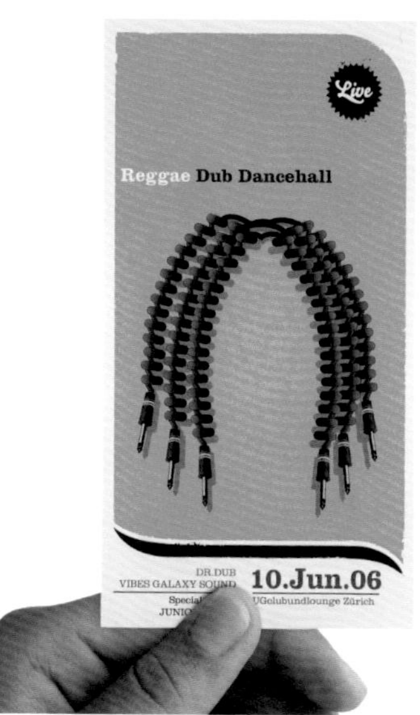

Live
Reggae Dub Dancehall
DR.DUB
VIBES GALAXY SOUND
10.Jun.06
UGclubundlounge Zürich

Rico Maier (SUI) www.ricomaier.ch

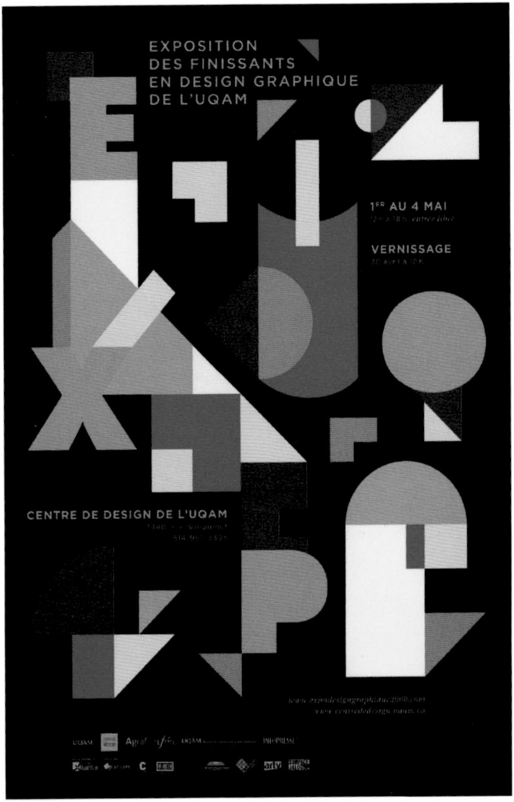

Audree Lapierre (CAN) www.audreelapierre.com

EXPOSITION
DES FINISSANTS
EN DESIGN GRAPHIQUE
DE L'UQAM

1ER AU 4 MAI

VERNISSAGE

CENTRE DE DESIGN DE L'UQAM

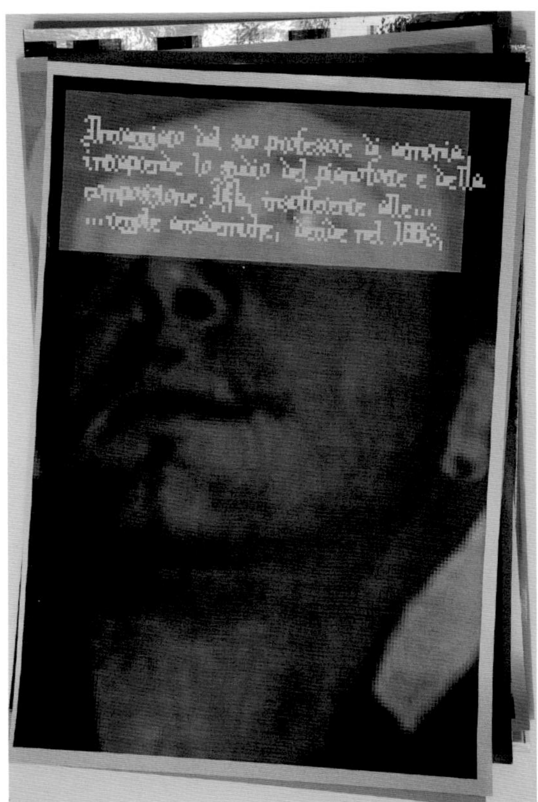

 Miriam Klobes (GER) www.mk-kommunikationsdesign.de

sommerintensiv
23. – 29.07.2007

Tanzworkshops im Studio 11
mit internationalen Dozenten

Manipulationen verschiedene körpe Hierdurch besteht die Möglichkeit, hältnis von Innen und Aussen, in Eigeninitiative oder Geschehen la Sensation und Ausdruck, Erzählung den. Das Ziel ist dabei weniger d bestimmten Stiles sondern vielmeh unterschiedlicher Werkzeuge für e und Weise des Tanzens.

„Dance is nothing more than focus, actions, relaxation an

Nicolas Delamotte Legra studierte Tanz am Conse de Rouen (FR), an der A Mac Innes (FR), an der Cannes Rosella Hightowe Dansacademie (NL). Er tanzte bei C Krizstina De Châtel (NL), The Nat Greece (GR) und in verschiedenen P u.a. mit Het Nationale Ballet (NL) reografen Bruno Listopad (P), Mart (USA), Nannine Linning (NL), den M (USA) und Jorge Isaac (Venezuela) Laure Delamotte Legrand (FR). In K und Benjamin Petitjean etablierte

MorphoDidius, mit welchem er von 2002 bis 2005 in Holland arbeitete. Seit 1998 choreografiert er zeitweise für Tanz und Theater. Desweiteren unterichtete er Amateure als auch professionelle Tänzer und Schauspieler in Frankreich, Belgien, Holland und Griechenland. ---

Feldenkrais® und Zeitgenössischer Tanz (Release based) --- Susanne Mueller Nelson (CH)

--- Der Unterricht beginnt mit einer Feldenkrais®Lektion, dessen Thema im restlichen Unterricht miteinbezogen wird. Danach folgt eine Bodensequenz, in welcher der Gebrauch des Bodens für Rollen und Stützelemente untersucht wird. Das Warm up im Stehen fokussiert auf die Wahrnehmung von Bewegung und Atmung. Dabei interessieren die Art, wie Zentrum und Peripherie zusammenarbeiten und das Spiel mit Gleichgewicht und Ungleichgewicht. Insgesamt baut der Unterricht aufeinander auf: von einfachen bis hin zu komplexen, dynamischen Bewegungen. Die abschliessende, choreografische Sequenz ermöglicht schliesslich das Bewusstwerden von Präsenz, Bezug zum Raum, den anderen und der Musik.

Susanne Mueller Nelson, geboren 1963, Tänzerin, Choreografin, Bewegungs- und Tanzpädagogin für Zeitgenössischen Tanz und Improvisation, Feldenkrais Practitioner®; Ausbildung in der CH, Montpellier (F) und New York. Stipendium der Otto Tschumi Stiftung.

onmedia
OMD

probe
omg research news
contact me
Talent Pool
Aivars Avontinš
Research Director OMG Latvia
Aviar's team has won two national Curling titles and in December will represent Latvia in the European Curling Championship for 3rd time. His goal is to represent Latvia in the Olympic Games.
contents
Snapshots
The Living Room
PHD London
OMG tools fan club
Google Earth
Research Germany
00
02
03
05
I've been in my

Charlie Hoffmann & Nicole Skala (GER) www.charlie-hoffmann.de, www.nicoleskala.de

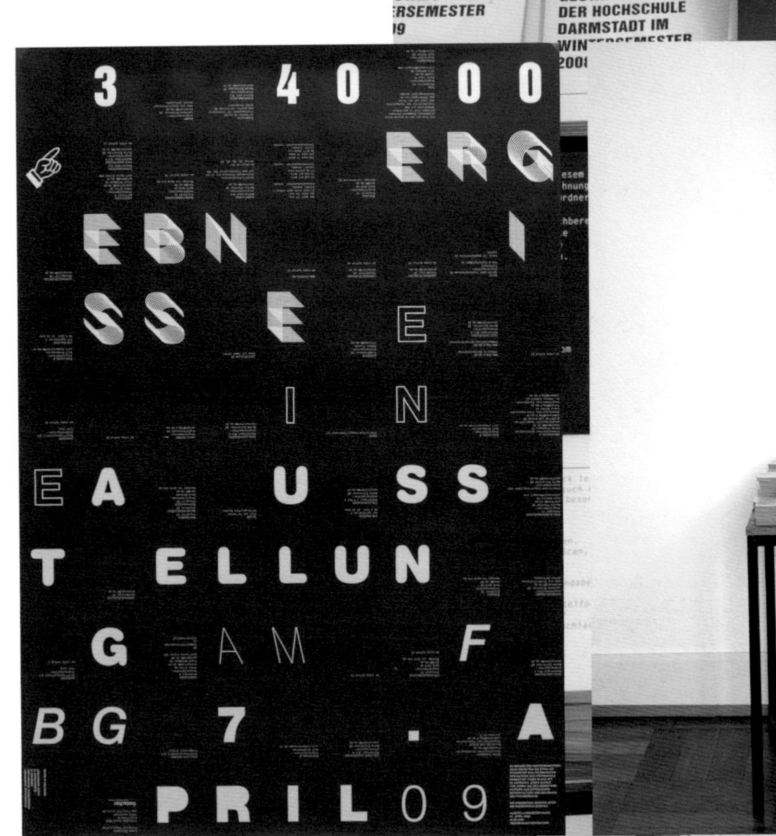

DARMSTADT IM
WINTERSEMESTER
2008/09
Le coq est mort,
le coq est mort,
Il ne pleura plus
cocodi, cocoda,
Cocococococococodi, cocoda.
The cock is dead,
the cock is dead,
He will never cry
cocodi, cocoda,
Cocococococococodi, cocoda.
85 AUFRUFE
AN DIE STUDENTEN
DES FACHBEREICHS
GESTALTUNG
DER HOCHSCHULE
DARMSTADT IM
WINTERSEMESTER
2008/09
40 00 ERGEBNISSE EINES AUSSTELLUNG AM F 7. APRIL 09
85 AUFRUFE
AN DIE STUDENTEN
DES FACHBEREICHS
11
13:00 Uhr Kanon singen im Foyer.
»Der Hahn ist tot«. Wahlweise in
deutsch, englisch oder französisch.
20/10/08
Farb-Laserdrucker
Medienlabor ML1-4
Ansprechpartner:
Bernd Östreicher BÖ
oestreicher@h-da.de
61
Mach um 9:30 Uhr ein Foto. Drucke
es an einem Farb-Laserdrucker
im Format Din-A4 aus und hänge es
ins Treppenhaus des Altbaus.
12/01/09
85 AUFRUFE
3
05
Denke darüber nach, weshalb du
an dieser Hochschule bist; weshalb
du Designer sein möchtest. Halte
deine Gedanken fest. Bewahre die
Aufzeichnung auf und sieh sie dir
85 AUFRUFE
AN DIE STUDENTEN
DES FACHBEREICHS
GESTALTUNG
DER HOCHSCHULE
DARMSTADT IM
DES FACHBEREICHS
GESTALTUNG

POINT OF YOU 12.–16. JULI
STEPHANIE MARINA LIEBSCHER
KRISTIN LOSCHERT
EILEEN JERICHEN
MARKUS FITTLER

POINT
OF
YOU
12.–16.
JULI

h_da

Diplomarbeiten des Sommersemesters 2006 | Industriedesign & Kommunikationsdesign
Vernissage & Diplomverleihung 14. Juli, 18 Uhr | Ausstellung 12.–16. Juli, 11–18 Uhr
Hochschule Darmstadt | University of Applied Sciences | FB Gestaltung | Olbrichweg 10, 64287 Darmstadt

Sebastian Rühl (GER) www.varietegraphique.de

...AND CAN I TAKE A PICTURE, PLEASE?

INTERVIEWS & PICTURES OF (ALMOST) EVERY STAR★

WWW.OLIVERTANSON.COM

REACHING THE STARS

Sebastian Rühl (GER) www.varietegraphique.de

INTERVIEWS & PICTURES OF (ALMOST) EVERY STAR*
WWW.OLIVERTANSON.COM
REACHING THE STARS
...AND CAN I TAKE A PICTURE, PLEASE?

AUR
ORA
AURORA
The Artzine
AURORA
AUR-
ORA
www.aurora-collective.com
AURORA
The Artzine
AURORA
The Artzine

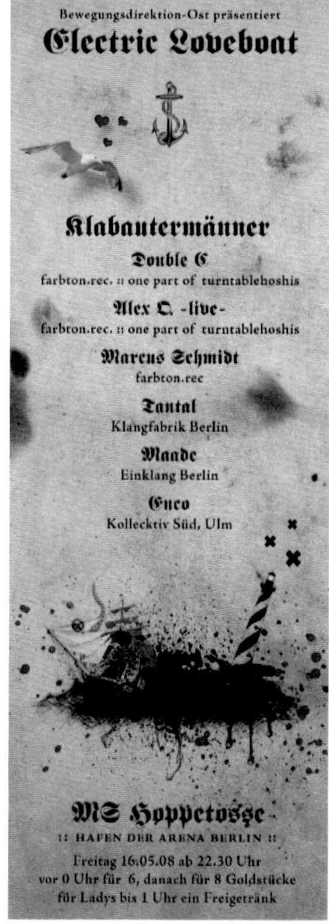

Sebastian Rühl (GER) www.varietegraphique.de

FAIRTRADE
BUSINESS FOR DEVELOPMENT
FAIRTRADE LABELLING ORGANIZATIONS INTERNATIONAL
FAIRTRADE

WHO ARE WE?
WITHOUT FAIRTRADE, WE WOULDN'T
AS BANANA PRODUCERS. THE
WE RECEIVE FOR A BOX OF
BANANAS DOES NOT
COLOMBIA
COCOA
... WHO DOES THE CERT
Certification is done by an independe
certification company, FLO-CERT GMBH.
FAIRTRADE STANDARDS EXIST FOR FOOD PRODUCTS SU
COFFEE, COCOA, HONEY, JUICES, WINE GRAPES,
DRIED FRUITS, NUTS AND SPICES, AND NO
PRODUCTS SUCH AS FLOWERS AND PLANTS, SPORTS BAL
SEED COTTON.
... HOW TO CONTACT US
FLO INTERNATIONAL E.V.
Bonner Talweg 177 || D-53129 Bonn || Germany
E-Mail info@fairtrade.net
NATIONAL LABELLING INITIATIVES
www.fairtrade.net/labelling_initiatives.html
FLO-CERT GMBH
Bonner Talweg 177

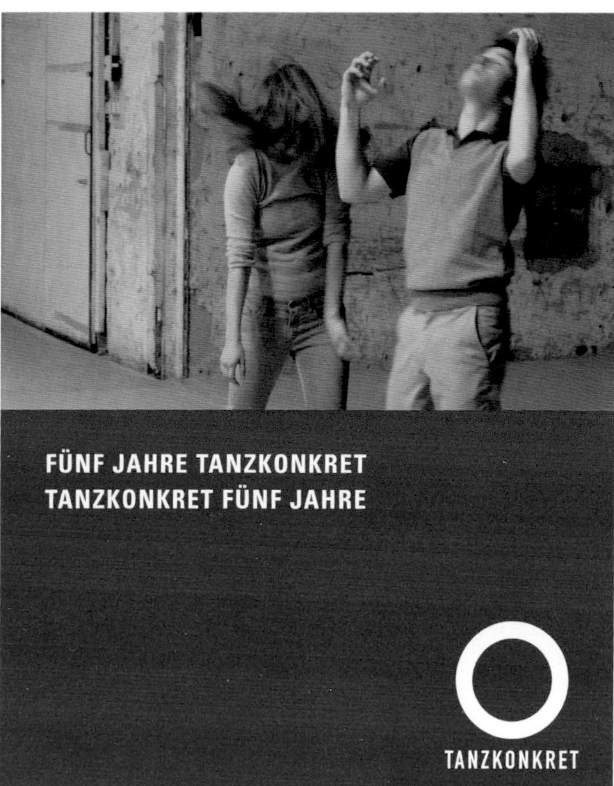

Katja M. Becker, Stephanie Podobinski (GER) www.beau-bureau.de

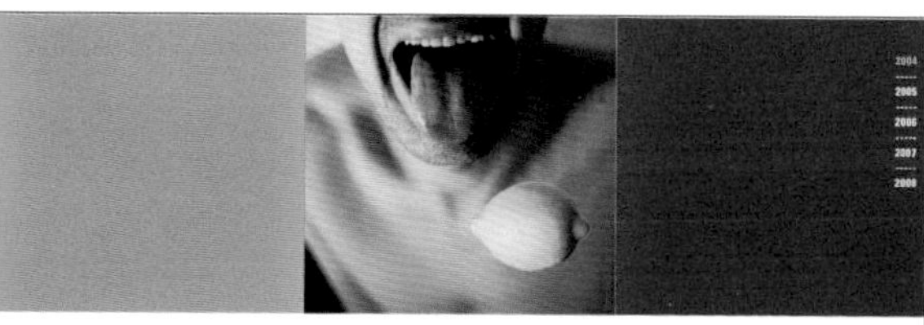

DOUBLE FEATURE: TWO FISH UND SELFISH
Eine Produktion von TANZTAGE BERLIN

0016

1 | TRIPLICATE | BERLIN
CHRISTIANE MÜLLER FORSCHT

Inszenierung: Angela Schubot | Martin Clausen
Choreographie | Tanz: Angela Schubot | Martin Clausen
Javier Aldman Morillo. Lichtdesign: Benjamin Schälike
Soundassistenz: Franziska Köhler
Produktionsbüro: Tanztage Berlin

In der heutigen Zeit sind wir fast zwanghaft bemüht, ganz wir selbst zu werden. Hier gehen die Beteiligten den Weg umgekehrt, anders als in so mancher Therapie. Sie stellen den Kollegen eigenes Material zur Kopie frei, versuchen jemand anderes zu werden, um den letzten Rest an Authentizität in sich selbst zu entdecken.

2 | UNDER | BERLIN

Solo von Javier Morillo | SELFISH

Noch normal? Eine Entdeckungsreise auf der Grenze zwischen gesundem und krankem Verhalten.

3 | FRONTIS NULLA FIDES | BERLIN
FRAU MALCHERT BESSER MISSTRAUEN

Solo von Martin Clausen

Häufig möchte man lieber andere verändern, als an sich selbst zu arbeiten. Dieser Wunsch nach Veränderung findet vielfältige Ausformungen.

TWO FISH begann im Jahr 2000 mit der Zusammenarbeit der Choreographin Angela Schubot und dem Schauspieler Martin Clausen. Schon bei der nächsten Produktion schloss sich dem Team der Spanier Javier Aldman Morillo an, der unter dem Namen SELFISH auch eigene Arbeiten entwickelt. In der Regie von Martin Clausen entstanden zwischen 2001 und 2007 mehrere Soli und Trios. Nach Studium der Kulturwissenschaften und Ausbildung zum Lehrer der F. M. Alexander Technik kam er 1998 mit „nicu and the navigators" an die Sophiensæle. Er arbeitete dort u. a. mit Lubricat, Sommer Ulrickson, Hanna Hegenscheidt und 2006 in Susanne Truckenbrodts „Peer Gynt"-Inszenierung. Angela Schubot, Mitbegründerin von TWO FISH, kuratierte 2007 das „Sixpack vs. Festival" in den Sophiensælen und zeigte dort ihr Solo „remake – inbetween the slightly different me feat. the blurry friend". 2004 erhielt sie ein „impulstanz Stipendium" im Tanzquartier Wien. Sie arbeitete u. a. mit Cora Frost, Theatercombinat Wien und Constanza Macras | Dorky Park. Mit „Triplicate" begeisterte die Gruppe bei der Tanzplattform 2004 als Trio. TWO FISH tourten in den letzten Jahren mit zahlreichen Gastspielen durch Europa und USA.

WWW.TWOFISH.INFO

ALIFE (UA) | KÖLN
Eine Produktion von silke z.resistdance in Koproduktion mit tanzhaus nrw und Commedia Futura | Eisfabrik Hannover

Konzept: Silke Z. in Kooperation mit Jan Höwel. Choreographie: Silke Z. Bühne | Licht: Jan Höwel. Tanz: Sugata Hirano | Ricardo Pereira | Morgan Nardi | Anette Bergmann | Caroline Simon. Soundkomposition: André Zimmermann. Dramaturgie: Alexandra Dederichs. Produktionsleitung: Katja Steinbach

Amok, Rausch, Trance, intensive Herausforderungen, extreme Zustände. Warum setzten Menschen ihr Leben aufs Spiel, suchen nach einem Ort des Daseins, der fernab von jeglicher Struktur und Organisation liegt oder brechen aus, auf der Suche nach einer nicht gelebten Freiheit und totaler Selbstbestimmung? Mittels Tanz, Sound und interaktivem Bühnenraum kreisen die fünf Akteure in „alife" um das Thema Lebendigkeit und deren Verlust, um die Leere und den Versuch, ihr zu entfliehen.

Silke Z. arbeitet seit mehr als fünf Jahren in NRW an eigenen Stücken, die sich durch eine inhaltliche Motivation und Klarheit der Mittel auszeichnen. Ausgebildet am European Dance Development Center (EDDC) in Arnheim und Düsseldorf erhielt sie neben dem Kölner Tanztheaterpreis den Förderpreis des Festivals Theaterzwang freier Theater NRW 2004.

Ausführliche Biographie (Siehe oben)

WWW.RESISTDANCE.COM

LIPPENBITTER – EIN TANZSPIEL FÜR 5 | KÖLN
TEIL IV DER PENTALOGIE SINNESVERSCHIEBUNG
Eine Produktion von Ilona Pászthy in Kooperation mit der Fabrik Heeder Krefeld und der kölner tanz agentur 0017

Choreographie: Ilona Pászthy. Tanz: Julia Eisele | Anat Vaadia | Wilfredo Cohen | Gianni Cuccaro. Gast: Jochen Leyrer. Dramaturgie: Barbara Fuchs. Bühnenbild: Megi. Musik: Andreas Wagner. Licht: Marco Wehrspann. Videodokumentation: Tom Meyer. Projektmanagement | PR: Ursula Plaas

Vier Geschmacksqualitäten: süß, sauer, salzig, bitter. Vier Tanzende, vier Menschen, begegnen sich. Tänzerisch spannen sie einen Bogen zwischen der zarten Sinnlichkeit des Schmeckens und radikalem Sinnesverlust, zwischen Genuss und Kompensierung, zwischen Alltäglichkeit und Absurdität. In der Konfrontation mit der Statik skulpturaler Bühnenobjekte entwickeln sie neue Formen tänzerischer Bewegungsprozesse. Unaufhörlich werfen sie ungewöhnliche Bühnen- und Körperbilder in einen Raum, der für spezifische Formen der Sinnesverschiebung steht, an der Grenze zu irreversiblem Sinnesverlust in einer von Mediatisierung und Digitalisierung geprägten Welt.

Ilona Pászthy, geb. in Hannover. Tanzausbildung in Hannover und an der Dansacademie Rotterdam. Diplom-Studium Illustration und Malerei in Hildesheim, Bielefeld und Münster. Engagements u. a. an den Bühnen Köln, bei Johann Kresnik, Tanztheater Irina Pauls, Leipzig, Kammerspiele Mainz, beim Desperate Figures Dance Theatre, Tanzensemble Maja Lex in Köln.

2008

0034

DOUBLE FEATRURE: JA JA DER JODOK UND GLAZE / GLACÉ / GLANZ (UA) I KÖLN

1 I JA JA DER JODOK
Eine Produktion des POGOensembles

Nominiert für den Kölner Tanztheaterpreis 2007

Konzept I Choreographie I Tanz: POGOensemble
mit Dilan Ercenk I Denise Temme I Tessa Temme

Thematische und zugleich akustische Grundlage ist Peter Bichsels Erzählung „Jodok lässt grüßen" aus seinen Kindergeschichten. Bichsels sprachliches Spiel, Tempo, Dynamik sowie Bildlichkeit des Erzählten übertragen sich auf das Bewegungsspiel der Akteurinnen, in deren Aktionsrahmen Gemeinschaftlichkeit zugunsten einer anonymen Lebensform aufgegeben wird. Anstelle von echten Beziehungen, treten nützliche Bindungen namenloser Objekte.

Das POGOensemble formierte sich 2001 aus dem Studienschwerpunkt Kreativität der Sporthochschule Köln. Das Ensemble arbeitet mit einer Bewegungssprache, die abseits tradierter Schultechniken anzusiedeln ist. Eine intensive und skurrile Tanzsprache bleibt aber stets Träger der Idee. „Young choreographer to watch" I Bemerkenswerter Nachwuchs (Jahrbuch ballettanz 2007), wichtigstes Theaterstück 2007 (StadtRevue Jahrescharts).

WWW.POGOENSEMBLE.DANCE-GERMANY.ORG

2 I GLAZE / GLACÉ / GLANZ I KÖLN
Eine Produktion von Rochus Aust & POGOensemble

Konzept: Rochus Aust & POGOensemble
Musik: Rochus Aust
Choreographie: POGOensemble mit Dilan Ercenk
Denise Temme I Tessa Temme

Innere Angelegenheiten waren von jeher unantastbar. Egal ob politisch, gesellschaftlich oder privat, Zutritt für Kritiker untersagt. Die akzeptierte Unantastbarkeit schützt vor allem den eigenen Raum vor unbequemen Interventionen: my home is my castle. Trotz – oder gerade wegen – aller Einmischungsverbote, werden ungeheure Energien auf den Schutz der Fassade verwendet. Egal ob politisch, gesellschaftlich oder privat, Hauptsache es glänzt nach außen. So wird der Zuckerguss der Vertuschung bald zur zweiten Identität.

Rochus Aust, geb. 1968 in Recklinghausen. Musikstudium: Staatliche Hochschule für Musik, Trossingen und Royal College of Music, London. Preisträger internationaler Wettbewerbe als Trompeter, Komponist und Bildender Künstler. Stipendien u. a. durch den DAAD und die Märkische Kulturkonferenz. Konzertreisen in über 75 Länder mit CD-Produktionen und Aufnahmen für mehr als 50 Radio- und Fernsehsender. Seit 2007 Zusammenarbeit mit dem POGOensemble (ULTIMA FERMATA I IL CIELO und PARADISO).

WWW.ROCHUSAUST.DE

POSING PROJECT B I THE ART OF SEDUCTION WIEN I ÖSTERREICH
Eine Produktion von Liquid Loft I Chris Haring

Auszeichnung: Goldener Löwe Biennale di Venezia 2007

Choreographie I Künstlerische Leitung: Chris Haring
Tanz I Choreographie: Liquid Loft mit Luke Baio I Stephanie Cumming
Alexander Gottfarb I Katharina Meves I Anna Maria Nowak
Komposition I Sound: Olim (Andreas Berger)
Dramaturgie I Licht: Thomas Jelinek
Bühnenart I künstlerische Begleitung: Aldo Giannotti
Film I Foto: Michael Loizenbauer, Produktion: Marlies Pucher

Posing Project B ist Synthese von Tanz und Installation, die das Verführungsspiel zwischen Performer, Performerinnen und Publikum thematisiert und erlebbar macht. Verführung will eine Verbindung mittels gegenseitiger Irreführung herbeiführen. Und das geht nicht ohne die Intervention einer dritten Partei – dem Pfeil des Eros. Posing Project B ist eine künstlerische Auseinandersetzung mit den Grundmustern der Kommunikation. Die Pose ist Kommunikationsmittel und Ausdruck einer Haltung. Für die Kölner Aufführung entwickelte Chris Haring eine speziell auf den ungewöhnlichen Raum der Orangerie zugeschnittene Version seiner Choreographie und lässt sich durch dessen besondere Atmosphäre inspirieren.

Chris Haring, Choreograph und Tänzer, lebt in Wien als freier, spartenübergreifender Künstler. Er arbeitete mit internationalen Compagnien wie DV 8 Physical Theatre (London), Nikolais I Louis Dance Co (USA), man act (GB), Nigel Charnock (GB), und mit Pilottanz, Willi Dorner, Tanz*Hotel u. a. 1995 gründete er das Grenztanz Festival in Castles Mühle, Österreich. In Zusammenarbeit mit dem Multimedia-Künstler und Komponisten Klaus Obermaier entwickelte und performte er die Videotanzperformances D.A.V.E. and VIVISECTOR. 2005 gründete er liquid loft mit Andreas Berger, Thomas Jelinek und Stephanie Cumming und choreographierte international erfolgreiche Stücke, unter vielen anderen Posing Project B – The Art of Seduction, das den Goldenen Löwen auf der Biennale in Venedig gewann. 0035

WWW.LIQUIDLOFT.COM

BARBARA KRAUS MACHT IHRE LIEBLINGS PERFORMANCE I WIEN I ÖSTERREICH
Eine Koproduktion von Barbara Kraus und brut Wien

Konzept I Realisation I Performance: Barbara Kraus
Inhaltliche Zusammenarbeit mit eine einer und Jack Hauser
Beratung I Raum: Paul Horn
Produktionsleitung: theater & kunst, das Schauturnier
Licht: Viktor Duran

Mit Dank an meine Schwestern, Freunde, Freundinnen und die verborgene Vielheit unserer Existenz

Katja M. Becker, Stephanie Podobinski (GER) www.beau-bureau.de

gute Laune!
MDC
4
Brülzhalde
Küssnacht
Sa 9.9. 06
22°°
Eintritt frei!
dj's
Dubstep
Rephlector
Meilenstein
Holik
maisonduchill.com

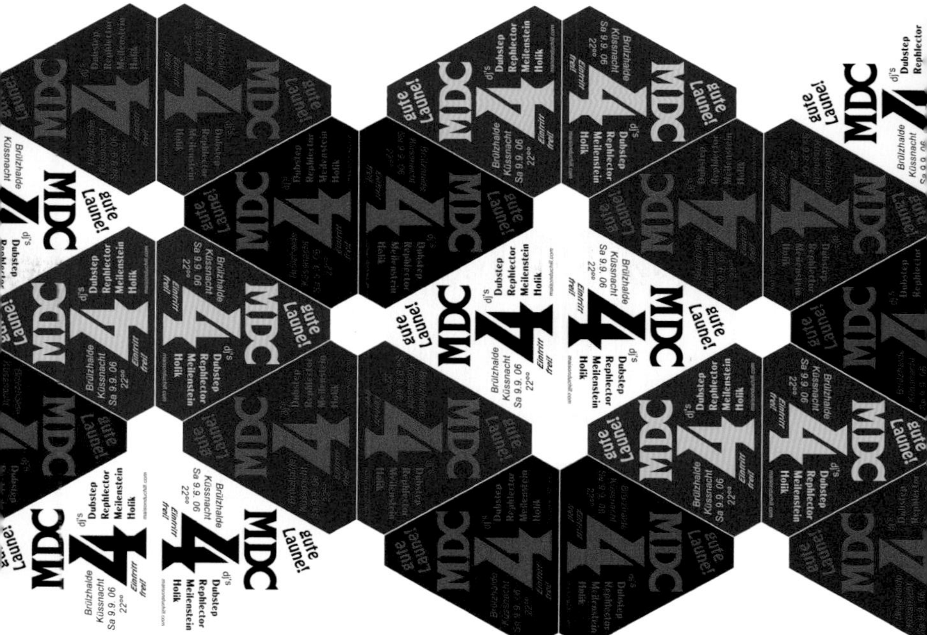

 Florian Jakober (SUI) www.floriangrafik.ch

Jamie Oliver Aspinall (SUI) www.schnuppe.ch

LOVE PARTY
FREITAG 1. JUNI 07
OLTEN SCHUETZI

DJ RUZZI
DJ NICK RASSAL
RAW SOUL ■ DEEP FUNK

EINTRITT 10.-
AB 23.00 BIS 4 UHR

WE ARE FUCKIN' SICK OF BLOODY BLACK AND WHITE ARTSY
FARTSY PALE SHIT - GIVE US A BIT OF FLESH PLEASE
BAGGED, BUFFED, MIKE'D & RIPPED
EINLADUNG

Alexander Dahlmann (GER) www.alexander-dahlmann.de

ZUM GEBURTSTAG
ALLES GUTE UND
HERZLICHEN
GLÜCKWUNSCH
RAMONA!

HERZLICHEN
GLÜCKWUNSCH
UND ALLES GUTE
ZUM GEBURTSTAG
CARMEN!

HERZLICHEN
GLÜCKWUNSCH
UND ALLES GUTE
ZUM GEBURTSTAG
CARMEN!

ZUM GEBURTSTAG
ALLES GUTE UND
HERZLICHEN
GLÜCKWUNSCH
RAMONA!

HERZLICHEN
GLÜCKWUNSCH
UND ALLES GUTE
ZUM GEBURTSTAG
CARMEN!

Heike Forbrig (GER) www.coklat.de

Marko Puclin (GER) www.puclin.com

Marko Puclin (GER) www.puclin.com

Avenue

Darkroom
Electric Avenue
Electro + House
DJ Rockabilly
DJ Myliamo
22.Juni + 06.Juli 06
Ludwigsburg

Sarah Ferrari (GBR) www.sarahferrari.com

University of Brighton Faculty of Arts and Architecture Open Days

Wednesday 6 February 2008
Wednesday 13 February 2008

Introductory Talks
The Head of the School of Arts & Communication and the Head of the School of Architecture & Design will welcome you with an introductory talk. Times for specific subject areas are indicated below. It would be helpful if visitors could arrive at least 10 minutes before the talks are due to start. Guided tours of course areas are on offer after each of the introductory talks.

10.00am & 1.30pm
- Fine Art Painting
- Critical Fine Art Practice
- Fine Art Sculpture
- Fine Art Printmaking
- Music and Visual Art
- Theatre and Visual Art
- Dance and Visual Art
- Digital Music

10.45am & 2.15pm
- Three Dimensional Design
- Wood Ceramics and Plastics
- Fashion Design with Business Studies
- Fashion Textiles Design with Business Studies
- Interior Architecture (introductory talk morning only)

11.30am & 3.00pm
- Editorial Photography
- Graphic Design
- Illustration

Visitors will be able to meet staff and students, talk to staff from our partner colleges in relation to the following HND courses:
- Music Prodution
- Art & Design (Fine Art)
- Art & Design (Crafts)
- 2D & 3D Design and Communication
- Multimedia
- Fine Art

Faculty of Arts and Architecture
Grand Parade, Brighton BN2 0JY
Telephone our mail switchboard on 01273 600900, stating the course in which you are interested, or visit our open day website: www.brighton.ac.uk/opendays

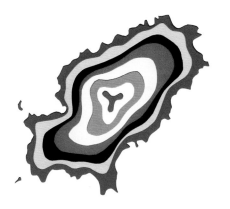

DJ's
Paul Oakenfold
Paul Van Dyk
Armin Van Buuren
Ferry Corsten
Judge Jules
Fergie
Tall Paul
Eddie Halliwell

Cream Ibiza

Saturday 28 August
Midnight - 7am

Amnesia
Ibiza

Sarah Ferrari (GBR) www.sarahferrari.com

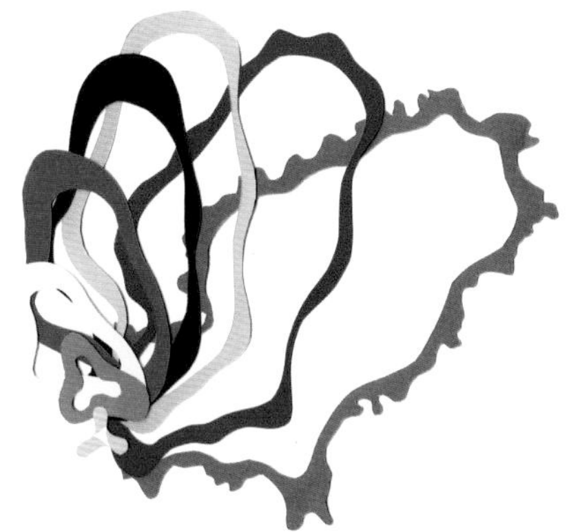

Cream Ibiza

DJ's
Paul Oakenfold
Paul Van Dyk
Armin Van Buuren
Ferry Corsten
Judge Jules
Fergie
Tall Paul
Eddie Halliwell

Cream Tickets 0870 242 7326
Ticketmaster 0870 155 0109
Ticket Bank 0170 234 5050
See Tickets 0871 220 0260

Tickets Online
www.ticketline.co.uk
www.ticketmaster.co.uk
www.ticketbank.co.uk

Saturday 28 August
Midnight - 7am

Amnesia
Ibiza

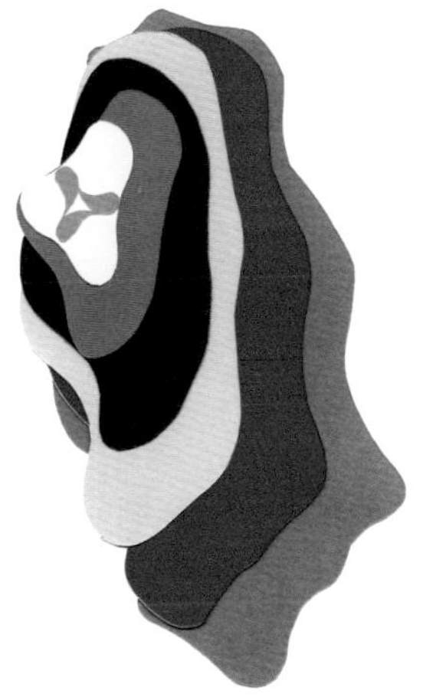

DJ's
Paul Oakenfold
Paul Van Dyk
Armin Van Buuren
Ferry Corsten
Judge Jules
Fergie
Tall Paul
Eddie Halliwell

Tickets Online
www.ticketmaster.co.uk

Saturday 28 August
Midnight - 7am

Amnesia
Ibiza

EIN
BILD
IM
KOPF
SECRET
SCHÜLER STELLEN AUS:
VERANSTALTUNGSORT
10. – 29. APRIL 2009
In Zusammenarbeit mit Initiative X und dem Museum X haben rund 100 Schüler aus 12 verschiedenen Schulen unter dem Motto „Mut" Skizzenbücher gestaltet und im Team kreative Projekte zum Thema Kunst und Design erarbeitet.
www.xxx.com
VERANSTALTUNGS
LOGO

Carina Kümpel (GER) www.carina-inside.de

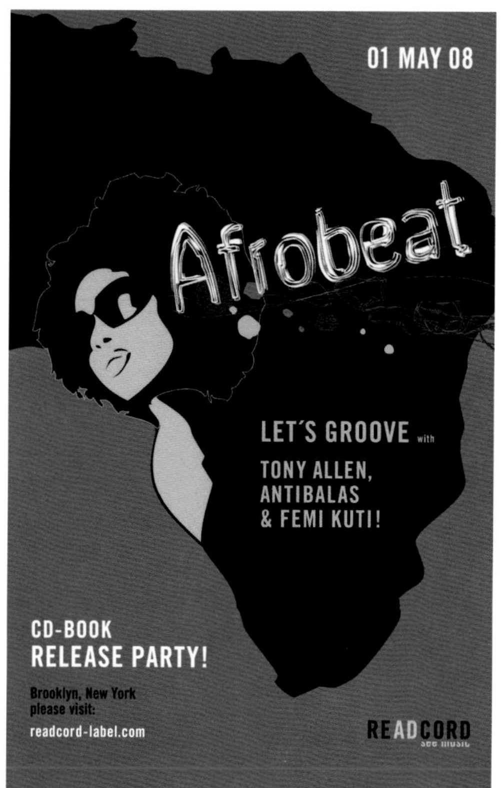
01 MAY 08
Afrobeat
LET'S GROOVE with
TONY ALLEN,
ANTIBALAS
& FEMI KUTI!
CD-BOOK
RELEASE PARTY!
Brooklyn, New York
please visit:
readcord-label.com
READCORD

Céu
A DIVINA COMÉDIA
A Glória daquele que tudo move
penetra pelo universo.

Diana de Sousa Matoso (GBR) www.dsway.co.uk

Inferno
A DIVINA COMEDIA
Deixai Toda Esperança, Vós Que Entrais!

DJ MARKY & FRIENDS.
1Xtra
BBC
DJ MARKY, ELEITO MELHOR
DJ INTERNACIONAL BBC
XTRABASS AWARDS

VIBE
DRUM&BASS
DJ MARKY, ELEITO MELHOR DJ INTERNACIONAL
BBC XTRABASS AWARDS
1Xtra
BBC

PEL
GRO
NO
MILO
Centro Cultural Batidão
R$ 10
www.peligro.com.br
www.milogarage.com
milo garage
rua minas gerais, 203
metrô consolação
Junho/2006
01/ Astronauta Pinguim
08/ Indios Eletronicos
15/ Mamelo Soundsystem
22/ Caxabaxa
29/ National

Sarah Ferrari (GBR) www.sarahferrari.com

HAZ
QUE
LA
BANDA
SIENTA GANAS
DE VOLVER
A VERTE
A TI
ENERO 10
LA FLORIDA
LOS JAIVAS
JOE VASCONCELLOS
17 ENERO
LA SERENA
ANITA TIJOUX
FUNK ATTACK
ENERO 18
LA SERENA
SAIKO
LOS BUNKERS
12
RECITALES
DE
VERANO
CRISTAL
en VIVO
ASI NOS GUSTA

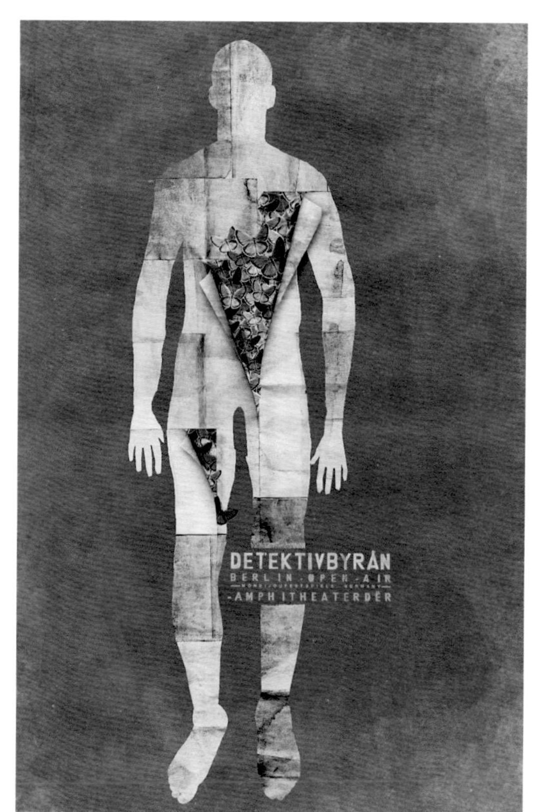
DETEKTIVBYRÅN
BERLIN · OPEN · AIR
-AMPHITHEATER DER

Ricardo Villavicencio [CHI] www.delrancho.org

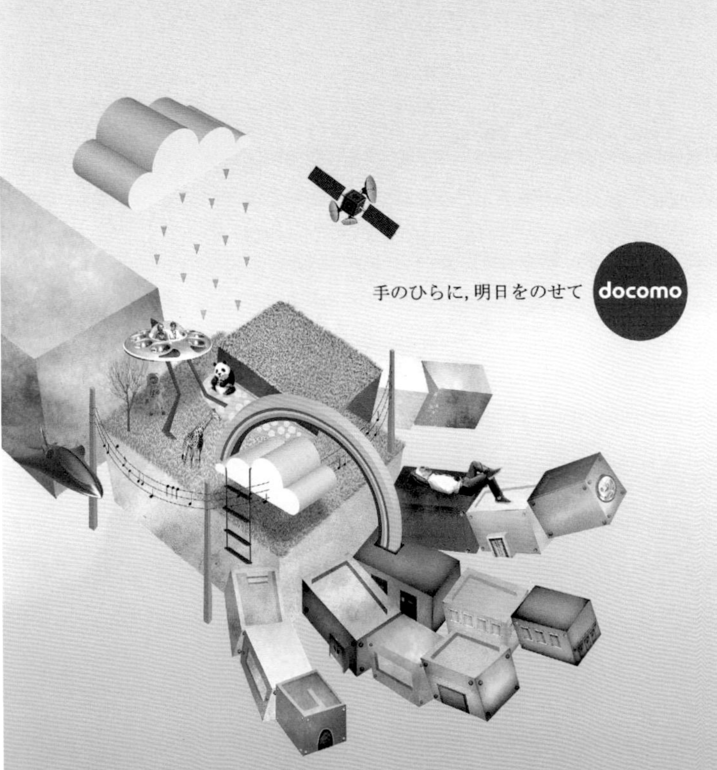
手のひらに,明日をのせて
docomo

Timo Böse (GER) www.lowerground.com

Karoly Kiralyfalvi (HUN) www.extraverage.net

MAXIM GORKI
NACHTASYL
SZENEN AUS DER TIEFE
REGIE ALEXEY ANDROWA
AUSSTATTUNG SARAH SCHNEIDER
BUEHNENBILD KATJA JANOSCH
PREMIERE AM 21 OKTOBER UM 20 UHR

WLADIMIR MAJAKOWSKI
DIE WANZE
EINE ZAUBERKOMOEDIE IN 9 BILDERN·REGIE VON IGOR KARLOWS
PREMIERE AM 10.08.06 UM 19.30 UHR IM HAUS DES
RUSSISCHEN THEATERS BERLIN

Andreas Maldei (GER) www.myspace.com/andimacht

29.02.
Poetry Slam
SCHEUNE, 21:00 U 7€/5€ (erm.
www.livelyrix.de
SCHEUNE

***

SongSlam***

Jeden 3. Freitag, ab 21 Uhr in der SCHEUNE

18. April & 16. Mai (letztes Mal vor der Sommerpause)

Infos unter www.songslam.de ✱ www.scheune.org

SCHEUNE

Tim Jockel (GER) www.timjockel.de

PLASTIK
3 FLOORS OF THE DEEPEST
DARKIEST SEXIEST ELECTRO
OCTOBER SIXTH
TWO THOUSAND
& SEVEN
EXPLOSIVE LINE - UP/
FEATURING
ERIC PRYDZ
KENNY PALMER
LEFTFIELD
9PM - 4AM
ADMISSION
£7 BEFORE 12
£8 AFTER

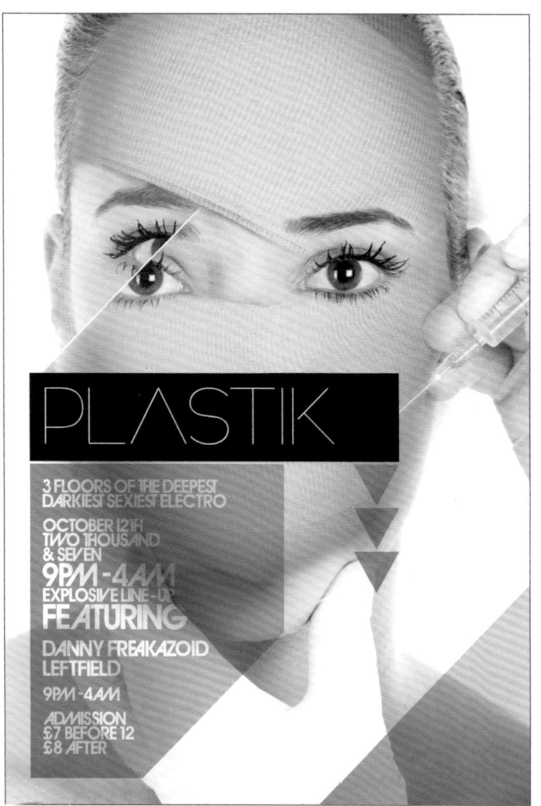
PLASTIK
3 FLOORS OF THE DEEPEST
DARKIEST SEXIEST ELECTRO
OCTOBER 12TH
TWO THOUSAND
& SEVEN
9PM - 4AM
EXPLOSIVE LINE-UP
FEATURING
DANNY FREAKAZOID
LEFTFIELD
9PM - 4AM
ADMISSION
£7 BEFORE 12
£8 AFTER

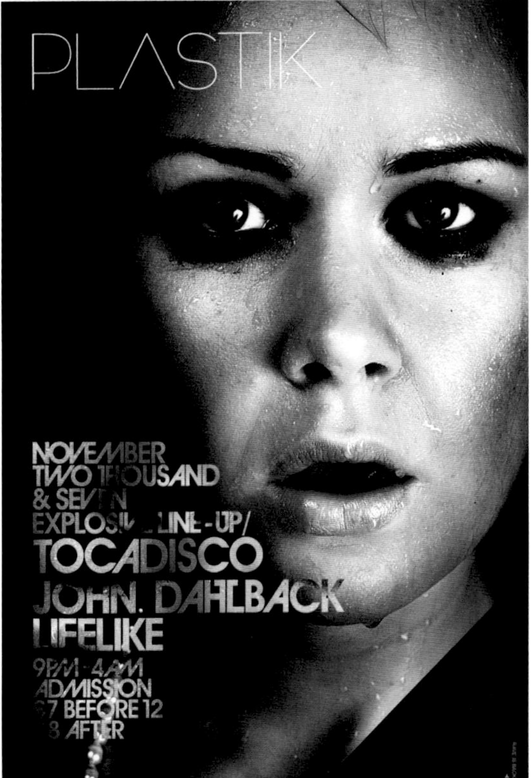

Alex Haigh (GBR) www.thinkdust.com

Alexandra Oriol (ESP) www.flickr.com/photos/alexandraoriol

IUP ARTS APPLIQUÉS
COULEUR IMAGE DESIGN
PORTES OUVERTES
CENTRE UNIVERSITAIRE DE TARN-ET-GARONNE
vendredi 8 et samedi 9 février 2008
centre universitaire
116, boulevard Montauriol
B.P. 794
82013 MONTAUBAN CEDEX
tél. 05 63 91 88 77

Judith Reiser (GER)

Frankfurter

KINOWOCHE

KINO AN UNGEWÖHNLICHEN ORTEN

11. - 18. Juli 2008

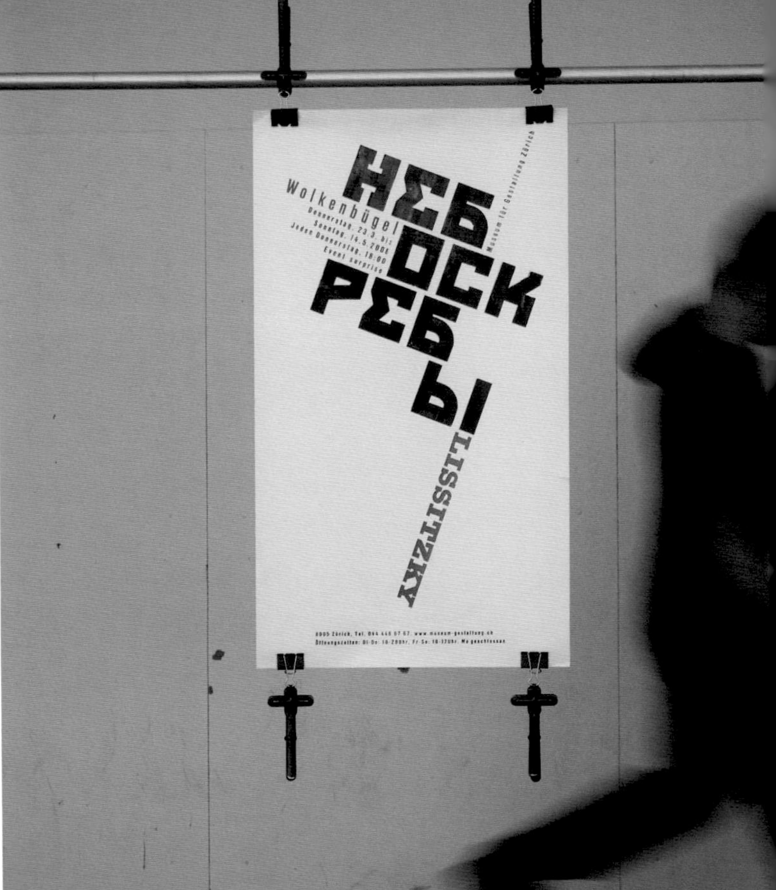
Museum für Gestaltung Zürich
НЕБ
ОСК
РЕБ
Ы
Wolkenbügel
Donnerstag, 23.3. bis
Sonntag, 14.5.2006
Jeden Donnerstag, 18:00
Event surprise
LISSITZKY

Museum für Gestaltung
WOLKEN
BÜGEL
LISSITZKY

NORTHSEA JAZZ FESTIVAL '07
13 – 15 JULY, AHOY ROTTERDAM
JVC

WAR SUCKS
1983
EISBERG
STUDIOS
BASSDAS SHAKEDOWN
drum and bass
MDC
THE STOLEN DIAMOND
UK
AUGEN
die medizin mit stil
berg
maisonduchill highsociety
MAISONDUCHILL LABEL NIGHT 18.10.03
Funky Nujazz-beatz
DRUM&BASS
IDENTITY
studios eisberg
NT Cutter
A-300
drum and bass
TEA TIME
GRAFIK FOR MUSIK
LACHEN MACHT SPASS!
es
eisberg studios
WAR SUCKS
MAISON DU CHILL
FLYING TONI'S
DELIKATESSEN SERVICE
PLAY the PIANO
KERZEN ZIEHEN
MIT BEIZLI!
omdc
vol 4
SMITH & HSU
TEA COMPANY
DJ NIGHT@NETWORK
KRÄNZLIN
eisberg studios
HAT, SHOES & MUSTACHE
WG PARTY
kost
120
BPM
JUNGLIST MOVEMENT
HIMMEL
Erdbeere Deluxe
WORK
Gusler

Henry Kage (BRA) www.flickr.com/poneis

nada surf
PAPER BOATS

Evan Melnyk (CAN) www.curseofthemultiples.com

Me

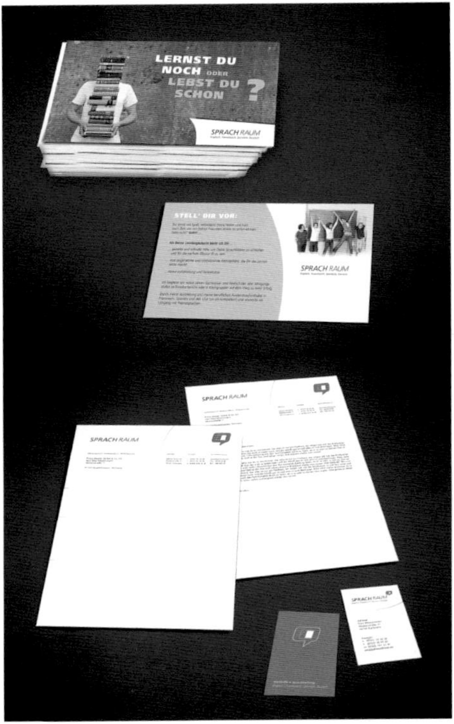

Christoph Seiler (GER) www.upshapes.de

Rico Maier (SUI) www.ricomaier.ch

DE LUX
SATURDAY
30.08.08
GLOBAL
BEAT
CLUB

DONATE FURNITURE
EXERCITO DE SALVACAO

MANGA B FRENTE
GOLA FRENTE
CORPO A FRENTE

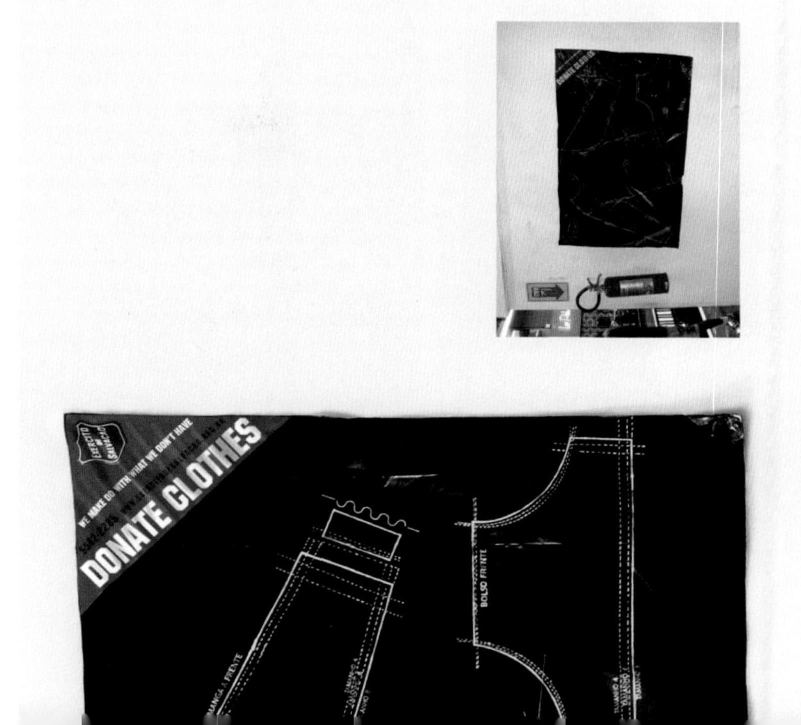
EXERCITO DE SALVACAO
WE MAKE DO WITH WHAT WE DON'T HAVE
DONATE CLOTHES
MANGA A FRENTE
TAMANHO 4
BOLSO FRENTE
TAMANHO 4

Alexandre Silveira (BRA)

Alexandre Silveira (BRA)

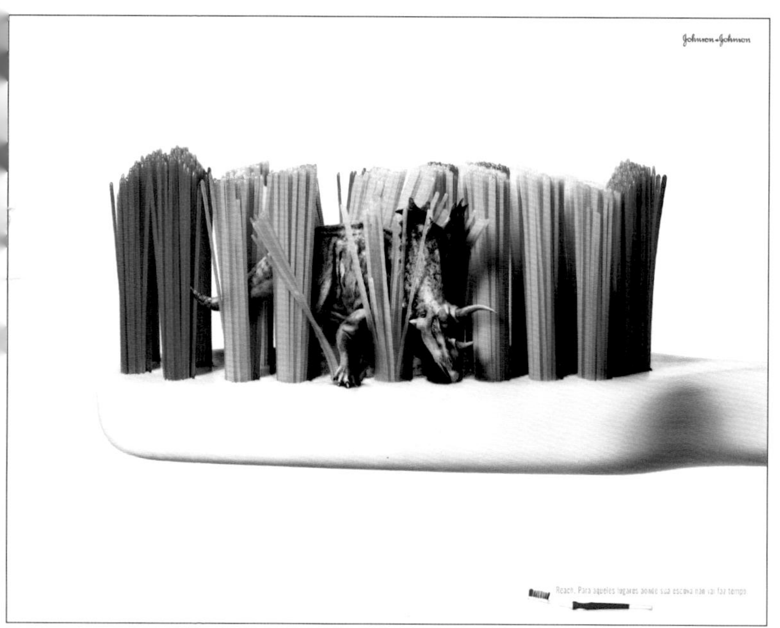
Johnson & Johnson
Reach. Para aqueles lugares onde sua escova não vai faz tempo.

Johnson & Johnson
Reach. Para aqueles lugares aonde sua escova não vai faz tempo.

Alexandre Silveira (BRA)

TRACKER
4X4
CHEVROLET

Alexandre Silveira (BRA)

The rough guide to TEXAS

NEW YORK

The rough guide to DALLAS

lonely planet Boston

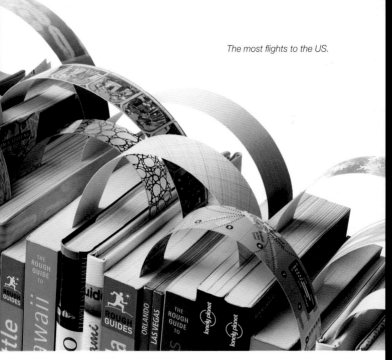

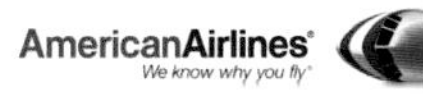
AmericanAirlines
We know why you fly

The prick is so small...

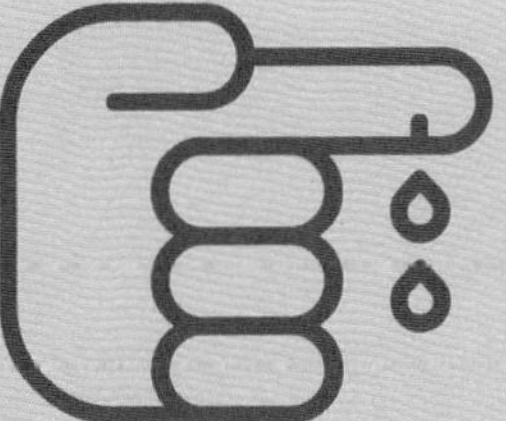

you'll forget size mattered!

Getting tested for HIV is quick, easy and only requires a drop of blood and five minutes of your time. It's a test that is worth every minute!

Love your life, get tested for HIV regularly!

Everyone is nervous their first time...

but it'll get easier the more you do it!

Getting tested for HIV is quick, easy and only requires a drop of blood and five minutes of your time. It's a test that is worth every minute!

Love your life, get tested for HIV regularly!

Kevin J. Furst (USA) www.kevinfurstdesign.com

It happened so quick...

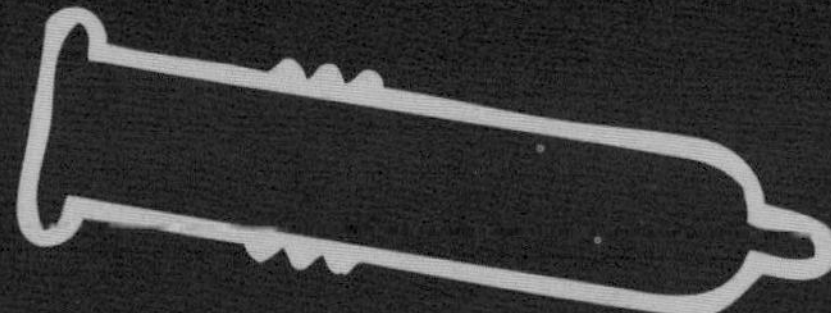

you'll forget you came!

Getting tested for HIV is quick, easy and only requires a drop of blood and five minutes of your time. It's a test that is worth every minute!

Love your life, get tested for HIV regularly!

Bernhard Moosbauer (GER) www.exsample.org

MERLIN
AND
PERFECT
WELDS.
THERE ARE
942 of them
on this bike.

Bryan Kahrs (USA) www.id29.com

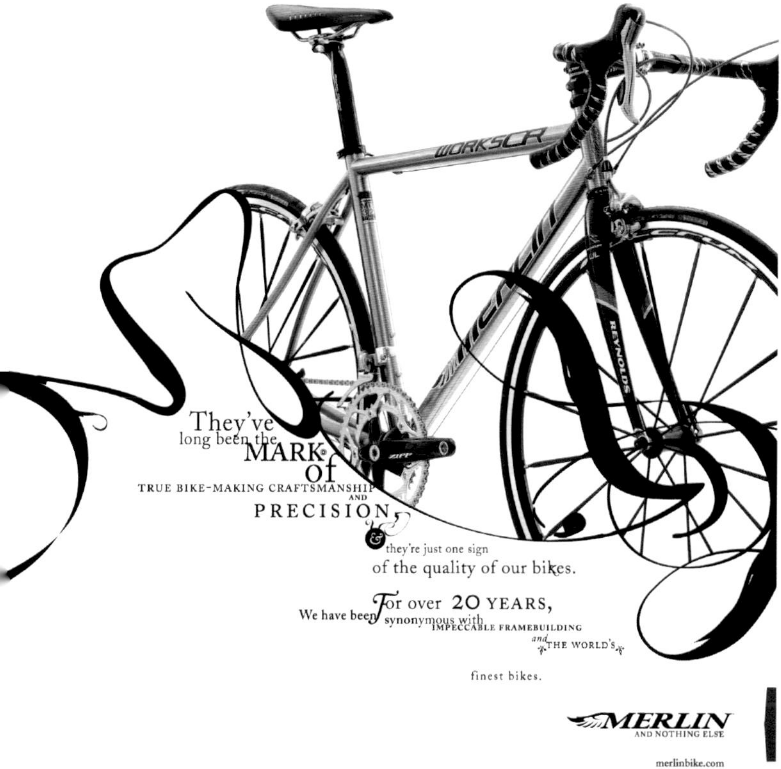

WORKSCR
REYNOLDS
ZIPP
They've
long been the
MARK
of
TRUE BIKE-MAKING CRAFTSMANSHIP
AND
PRECISION,
&
they're just one sign
of the quality of our bikes.
We have been
For over 20 YEARS,
synonymous with
IMPECCABLE FRAMEBUILDING
and THE WORLD'S
finest bikes.
MERLIN
AND NOTHING ELSE
merlinbike.com

MERLIN
AND
SMALL.
We're kind
of SMALL
AS A MATTER OF FACT, we only build 4 frames every day.

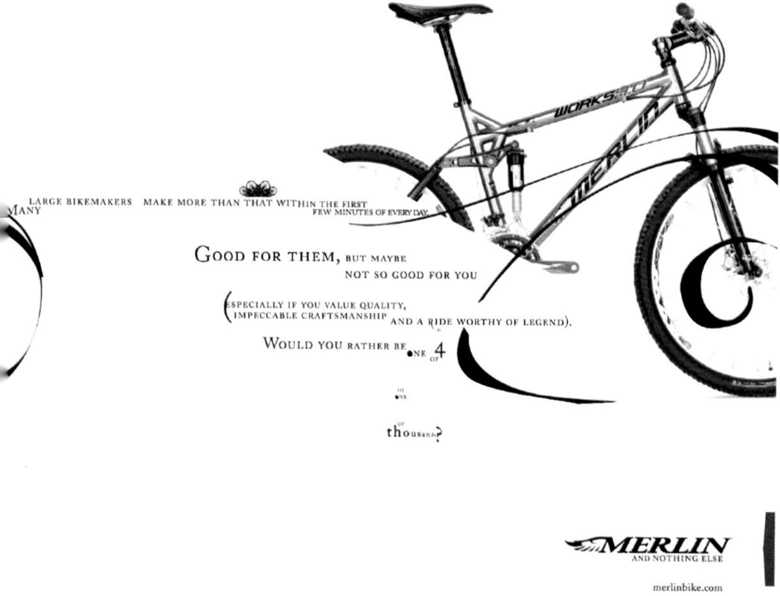

MANY LARGE BIKEMAKERS MAKE MORE THAN THAT WITHIN THE FIRST FEW MINUTES OF EVERY DAY.

GOOD FOR THEM, BUT MAYBE NOT SO GOOD FOR YOU

(ESPECIALLY IF YOU VALUE QUALITY, IMPECCABLE CRAFTSMANSHIP AND A RIDE WORTHY OF LEGEND).

WOULD YOU RATHER BE ONE OF 4

OF ONE

OF thousands?

merlinbike.com

MERLIN AND HANDS.
HANDS are good.
They're nice if you NEED to Hold on to handleba
use a steering wheel,
wear gloves or zippe

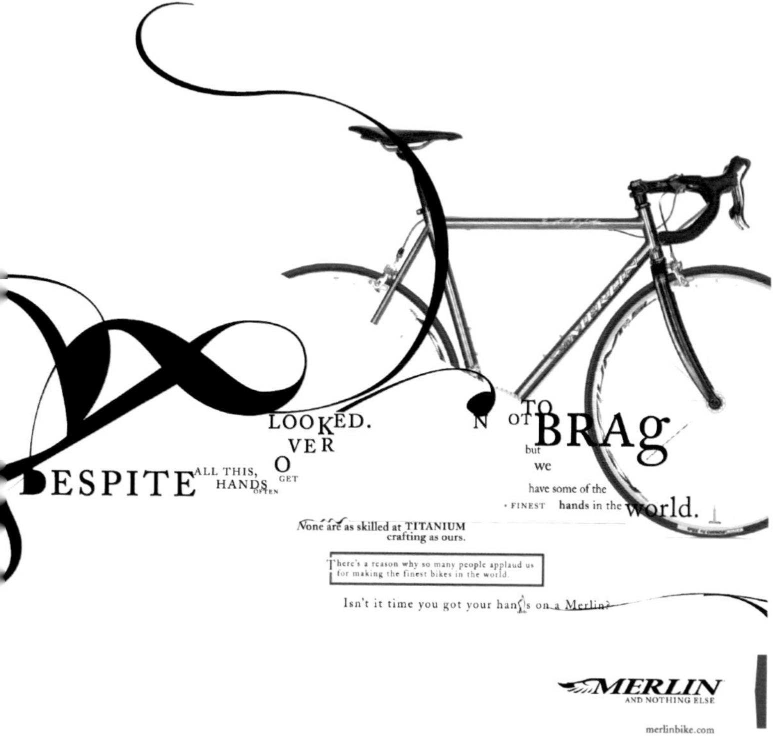

DESPITE ALL THIS, HANDS OFTEN GET OVERLOOKED.
NOT TO BRAG but we have some of the FINEST hands in the world.
None are as skilled at TITANIUM crafting as ours.
There's a reason why so many people applaud us for making the finest bikes in the world.
Isn't it time you got your hands on a Merlin?
MERLIN
AND NOTHING ELSE
merlinbike.com

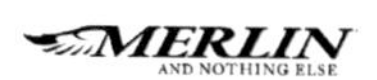

SUPER BASTONELIGHT

Light — abcdefghijklmnopqrstuvwxyz / ABCDEFGHIJKLMNOPQRSTUVWXYZ

Light Italic — abcdefghijklmnopqrstuvwxyz / ABCDEFGHIJKLMNOPQRSTUVWXYZ

Light Small Caps — abcdefghijklmnopqrstuvwxyz / ABCDEFGHIJKLMNOPQRSTUVWXYZ

Studiocharlie 2007

SUPERB
ASTONER
EGULARS
UPERBA
STONER
EGULAR

/// Superbastone Regular / Studiocharlie 2007 //

abcdefghijklmnopqrstuvwxyzABCDEFGHIJKLMNOPQRSTUVWXYZ#0123456789

{[(¡¿¼½¾?!)]}±-×÷*<=>%‰µ$ƒ€£¥¢◊¦|†‡¯–—_•˙·@«¬»™©® ‹›.:;…•§¶

äàáâãåèéêëìíîïòóôõöùúûüýÿçšžñþðøæœÄÀÁÂÃÅÈÉÊËÌÍÎÏÒÓÔÕÖÙÚÛÜÝŸÇŠŽÑÞÐØÆŒ&ß

/// Superbastone Regular Italic / Studiocharlie 2007 //

abcdefghijklmnopqrstuvwxyzABCDEFGHIJKLMNOPQRSTUVWXYZ#0123456789

{[(¡¿¼½¾?!)]}±-×÷<=>%‰µ$ƒ€£¥¢◊¦|†‡¯–—_•˙·@«¬»™©® ‹›.:;…•§¶*

äàáâãåèéêëìíîïòóôõöùúûüýÿçšžñþðøæœÄÀÁÂÃÅÈÉÊËÌÍÎÏÒÓÔÕÖÙÚÛÜÝŸÇŠŽÑÞÐØÆŒ&ß

/// SUPERBASTONE REGULAR SMALL CAPS / STUDIOCHARLIE 2007 //

ABCDEFGHIJKLMNOPQRSTUVWXYZABCDEFGHIJKLMNOPQRSTUVWXYZ#0123456789

{[(¡¿1/41/23/4?!)]}±-×÷*<=>%‰µ$ƒ€£¥¢◊¦|†‡¯–—_•˙·@«¬»™©® ‹›.:;…•§¶

ÄÀÁÂÃÅÈÉÊËÌÍÎÏÒÓÔÕÖÙÚÛÜÝŸÇŠŽÑÞÐØÆŒÄÀÁÂÃÅÈÉÊËÌÍÎÏÒÓÔÕÖÙÚÛÜÝŸÇŠŽÑÞÐØÆŒ&SS

SUPE RBAS TONE BOLD

BOLD – Studiocharlie 2007 – abcdefghijklmnopqrstuvwxyz / ABCDEFGHIJKLMNOPQRSTUVWXYZ

#0123456789

BOLD SMALL CAPS – STUDIOCHARLIE 2007 – ABCDEFGHIJKLMNOPQRSTUVWXYZ / ABCDEFGHIJKLMNOPQRSTUVWXYZ

#0123456789

Superclosed-A
Studiocharlie2007
abcdefghijklmnop
qrstuvwxyzABCDE
FGHIJKLMNOPQR
STUVWXYZ#01234
56789{[(¡¿¼½¾?!)
]}±-×÷*=%‰µ$ƒ€
£¥¢◊àáâãäåèéêëì
íîïòóôõöùúûüýÿçšž
ñþðøæœ‹›.:;,…ÀÁÂ
ÃÄÅÈÉÊËÌÍÎÏÒÓÔÕ
ÖÙÚÛÜÝŸŠŽÑÞÐØ
ÇÆŒ&ßl|¯_•˙·@«»
©®™•§¶

Superclosed-B
Studiocharlie2007
abcdefghijklmnop
qrstuvwxyzABCDE
FGHIJKLMNOPQR
STUVWXYZ#01234
56789{[(¡¿¼½¾?!)
]}±-×÷*=%‰µ$ƒ€
£¥¢◊àáâãäåèéêëì
íîïòóôõöùúûüýÿçšž
ñþðøæœ‹›.:;,…ÀÁÂ
ÃÄÅÈÉÊËÌÍÎÏÒÓÔÕ
ÖÙÚÛÜÝŸŠŽÑÞÐØ
ÇÆŒ&ßl|¯_•˙·@«»
©®™•§¶

SUPERCLOSED-A
SUPERCLOSED-B

VISUALISIERUNG DES FLAMENCOS

» LOKALANALYSE SEVILLANA

Sevillanas ist ein Folkloretanz, der vorwiegend in Andalusien getanzt wird. Es sind viele Elemente des Flamenco enthalten. Sevillanas zählen jedoch genaugenommen nicht zum Flamenco. Sevillanas sind „relativ" leicht zu erlernen, da vor allem die Anforderungen an die Fußtechnik deutlich geringer als beim Flamenco sind. Schwierig bleibt jedoch die Koordination von Tanzschritten und zugehörigen Arm-/Handbewegungen. Die Lieder haben eine festgelegte Struktur und der Tanz hat eine feste Choreografie.
Sevillanas werden paarweise getanzt. Man steht sich gegenüber und hat keinen oder wenig direkten Körperkontakt. Die Körpersprache spielt eine große Rolle.
Sevillanas bestehen aus 4 Strophen mit einer Einleitung und einem Instrumentalteil zwischen den Strophen.

Anstatt nur in Flächen zu visualisieren, werden in der rechten Informationsgrafik die einzelnen Bewegungsabläufe der Sevillana heraus kristallisiert. Anhand der blauen Linien sind die Arm-/Handbewegungen erkennbar. Die orangenen Bereiche stellen die Beinbewegung dar.
Charakteristisch in diesem Zusammenhang sind die vielen, einzelnen Arm-/Handbewegungen, welche sich weit vom Körper wegbewegen.

In den unteren Infografiken wird indes separat auf Arm-/Handbewegungen sowie Beinbewegung eingegangen. Bei der Beinbewegung sind sogar zwei Basen zu erkennen, eine links und eine rechts, welche durch große Beinbewegungen (Pasada) direkt angesteuert werden.

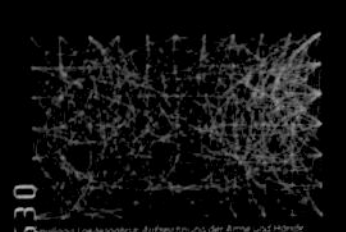

Sevillana Lokalanalyse: Aufzeichnung der Arme und Hände

Sevillana Lokalanalyse: Aufzeichnung Beine

Melanie Esteban (GER)

VISUALISIERUNG DES FLAMENCOS

» ZEITANALYSE SEVILLANA / RUMBA

Nachdem die Lokalanalyse die Bewegungsabläufe in einem Koordinatensystem veranschaulicht hat, ist es interessant die einzelnen Aktionen während dieses Tanzes visualisiert darzustellen. Das linke Diagramm zeigt diese Aktionen während einer Rumba. Da die Rumba ein sehr freier Tanz ist, könnte das Diagramm je nach Tänzer variieren, die Kernelemente sind jedoch enthalten. Wobei Grundschritte nicht vorhanden sind.

Bei der Sevillana ist der klare Ablauf gut erkennbar. Einleitend jeder neuen Strophe ist ein Klatschen gefolgt von einer kleinen Pause.
In den unten angezeigten Kreisdiagrammen werden die einzelnen Aktionen zusammengefasst und die Sekunden summiert. Dadurch ist der jeweilige Anteil am gesamten Tanz erkennbar, woraus sich neue Schlüsse zur Variierung des eigenen Tanzstils schließen lässt.

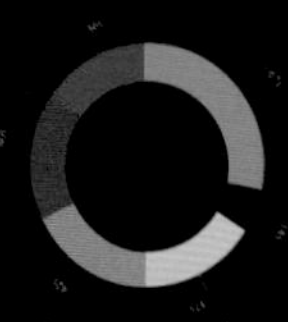

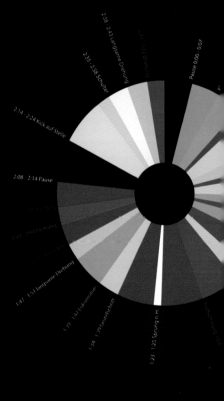

Pause 0:00 - 0:07
2:38 - 2:43 Langsame Drehung
2:35 - 2:38 Schulter
2:14 - 2:24 Kick auf Stelle
2:08 - 2:14 Pause
1:47 - 1:51 langsame Drehung
1:39 - 1:47 Lokomotive
1:34 - 1:39 Grundschritt
1:23 - 1:25 Sprung n.H.

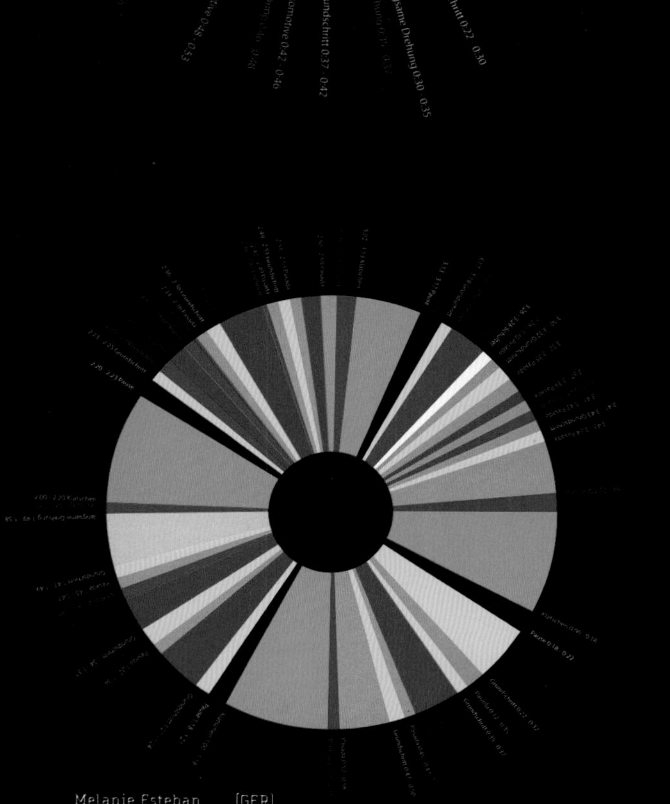

 Melanie Esteban [GER]

VISUALISIERUNG DES FLAMENCOS

» LOKALANALYSE VERGLEICH SEVILLANA / RUMBA

Der Flamenco ist ein Volkstanz, der einerseits von den Gitanos, andererseits durch die andalusische Beeinflussung stark entwickelt worden ist. Kurz gesagt, repräsentiert er eine Mischung aus andalusischer Folklore und dem Flamenco der Zigeuner.

Der Flamenco wurde von den andalusischen Zigeunern entwickelt, die von Indien kamen. Da das Leben vieler Einheimischer von Armut geprägt war, spiegelt sich dieser Zustand in den Tänzen wider. Im Mittelpunkt des Tanzes bzw. Gesanges stehen: „Trauer, Leid, Verlorene Liebe, Tod...". Der Tanz drückt die Auseinandersetzung des Menschen mit der Macht aus, die ihn bedroht. Emotionen werden in den Tanz umgesetzt, wobei der erdig / sinnliche Fusstanz, sowie die Bewegungen der Arme und Hände stark ins Spiel kommen.

Zwei Flamenco-Tänze, die Sevillana (gelb) und die Rumba (rot), wurden analysiert und in Form einer Lokalanalyse gegenübergestellt, sowie einzeln (unten, in klein) dargestellt.

Durch diese Visualisierung ist es möglich detailiert und präzise die Kernbereiche eines Tanzes in Form einer Infografik zu visualisieren. Durch die Verwendung von halbtransparenten Flächen und Linien werden die stark tangierten Bereiche farbintensiver, sowie erkennbarer.

Unten sind beide Tänze isoliert dargestellt. Anhand der Orange-Bereiche kann man die Fußbewegung erkenen und die Türkis-Bereiche symbolisieren die Hand- /Armbewegungen.

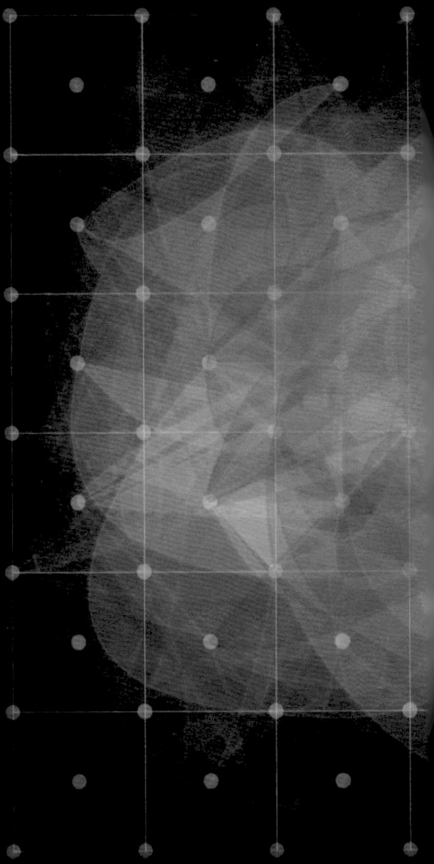

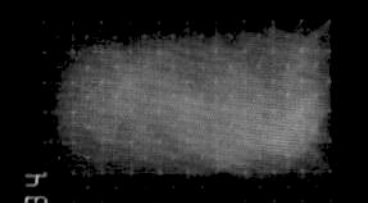

Sevillana Lokalanalyse Laura / Flächendarstellung

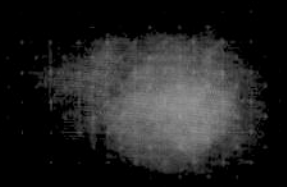

Rumba Lokalanalyse Laura / Flächendarstellung

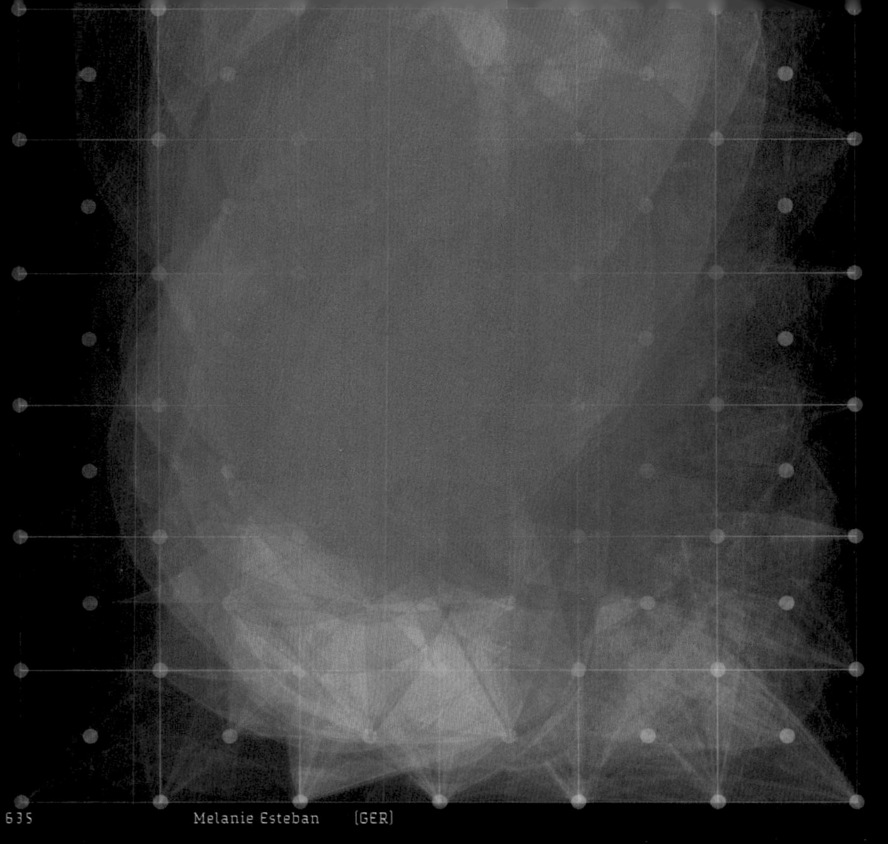

Melanie Esteban [GER]

architektur

Rico Maier (SUI) www.ricomaier.ch

KAMERA
TECHNIK

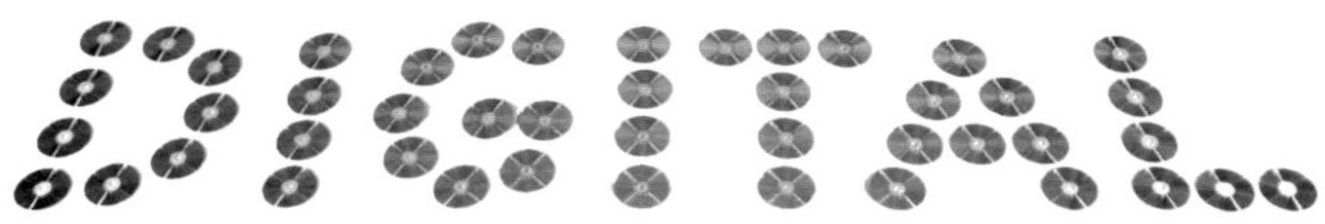

Max Ruf (GER) www.maxruf.com

allez
les autres

ZARRAPASTROSA
HIJA DE PUTA
SOY EL FAMOSO REVIENTA CAJAS

ROCK
'N'
DIOS
AG
IÓN
29
WOO!
WOO!
WOO!
Fabolous · Breathe.mp3
Fabolous
8R 347H 3!
NYC

Ace John Cabos [PHI] www.acejohn.multiply.com

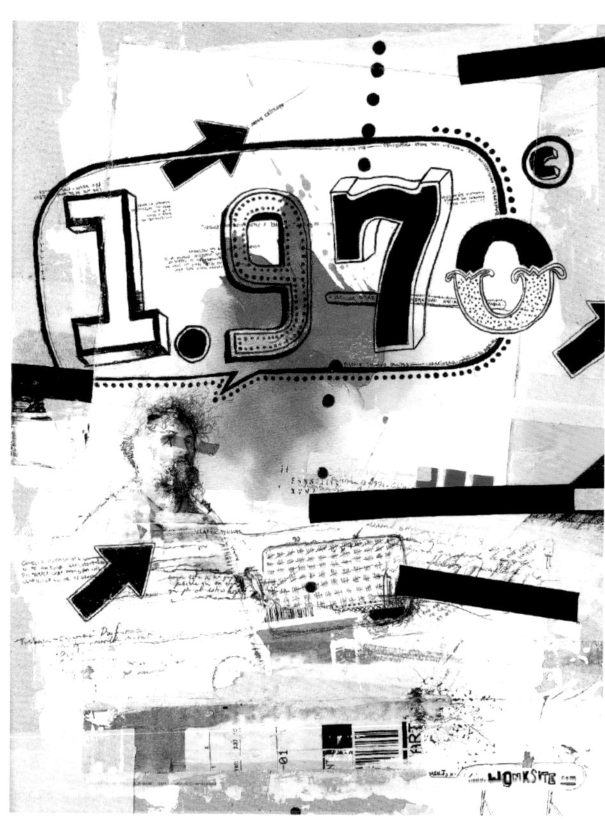

Jorge Restrepo (COL) www.wonksite.com

„breakthrough innovators set the agenda disturbing the sleep of incremental innovators"

delivering breakthrough innovation

developing striking ideas

discovering new opportunities

breakthrough

CULTURE

think big,
work hard,
play fair,
take risks and
have fun!

OUR VALUES: THE FIVE Ps

PROVOCATION: Rough-edged fresh approaches and provocative ideas are essential to all breakthrough innovations. But provocation also means courage. Courage to call a spade a spade. Courage to break rules and dogmas, to be curious, to experiment and to search for new solutions.

PASSION: Passion is what moves people. It makes ideas happen. It's the difference between "O.K." and "WOW". That is what breakthrough innovation is all about.

PURITY: No frills, no fuss! Creativity is vital, but not an end in itself. Simplicity reveals the truly great innovations.

PLEASURE: Enjoying your job is vital when working in self-directed teams in a highly liberal and open environment.

PERFORMANCE: Ultimately, only output counts. We are result-driven, action-oriented and are walking the talk. We are the first innovation company to offer a money-back guarantee.

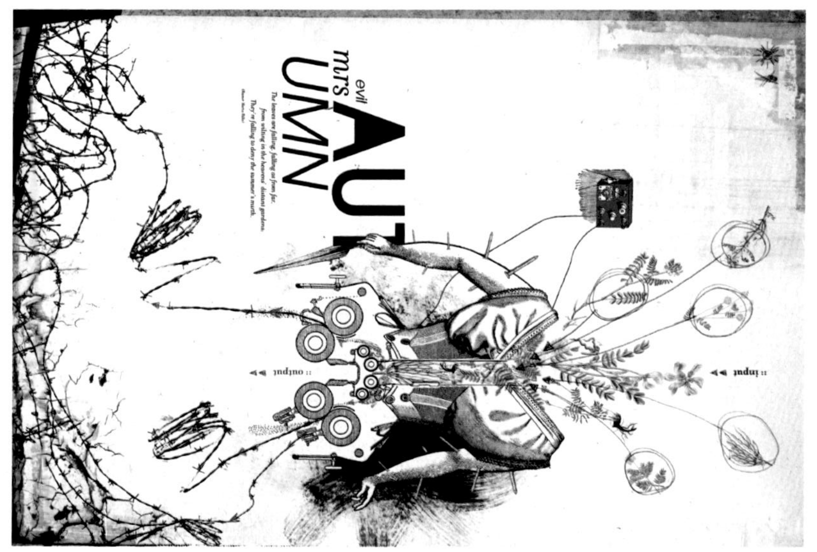
:: input
:: output
evil
mrs AUT
UMN
The leaves are falling, falling as from far,
from wilting in the heavens' distant gardens.
They're falling to deny the summer's mirth.

Chrisse Kunst [GER] www.chrissekunst.de

BrokenArrow

eps51 (GER) www.eps51.de

concept

de sign

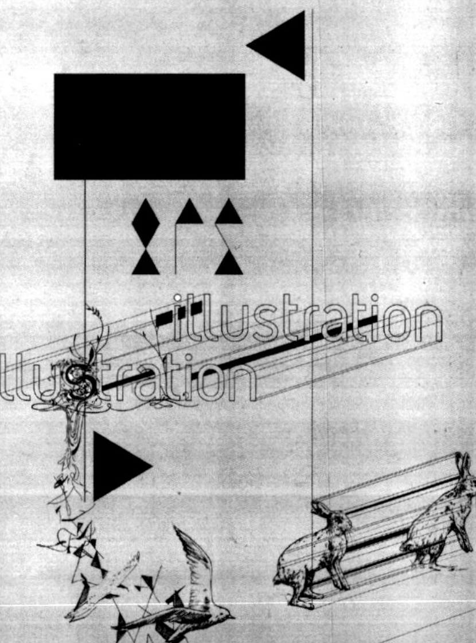
illustration
illustration

SPOKES

Erika Prib (GER) www.myspace.com/erikaprib

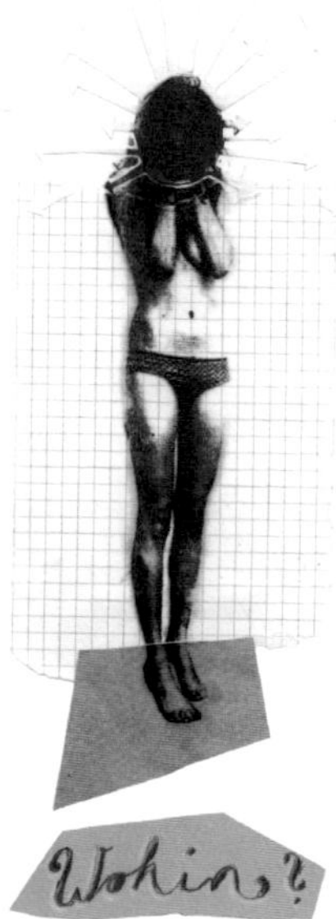

VOR
SICHT

Erika Prib (GER) www.myspace.com/erikaprib

»LOS LOS LOS«

index

all featured artists in
alphabetical order

Surname , Prename	Loc.	Contact
Alfieri, Pablo	(ARG)	pablo@pabloalfieri.com www.pabloalfieri.com
Allport, Lara & Barrett, Simon	(AUS)	www.thenationalgrid.com.au
Arber, Adam	(GBR)	adam@roadkilltoys.com www.roadkilltoys.com
Aspinall, Jamie Oliver	(SUI)	info@schnuppe.ch www.schnuppe.ch
Barco, Renan	(PHI)	renanbarco@gmail.com www.december1985.com
Bayer, Johannes	(GER)	jotopia@gmx.de www.jotopia.de
Becker, Katja M. & Podobinski, S.	(GER)	www.beau-bureau.de
Bell	(POL)	cheer_up_girl@wp.pl www.flickr.com/cheer_up_bell
Bertell, Emil	(FIN)	emil.bertell@gmail.com www.fenotype.com
Biniwersi, Ruth	(GER)	melddich@bei-ruth.com www.bei-ruth.com
Blauert, Simone	(GER)	Blauert@4teog.de www.4teog.de
Bogucki, Dorota	(POL)	dorota@boghukey.com www.boghukey.com
Böse, Timo	(GER)	boese@lowerground.com www.lowerground.com
Bowman, Jeffrey	(GBR)	info@mrbowlegs.co.uk www.mrbowlegs.co.uk
Bretzmann, Daniel	(GER)	input@eyegix.com www.eyegix.com
Brotons, Guillermo	(GBR)	contact@guillermobrotons.net www.guillermobrotons.net
Brumnjak, Boris	(GER)	boris@brumnjak.com www.brumnjak.com
Bupla	(FRA)	contact@bupla.com www.bupla.com
Cabos, Ace John	(PHI)	ace_728@yahoo.com www.acejohn.multiply.com
Campiche, Pedro	(POR)	pedro.campiche@gmail.com www.flickr.com/photos/corle1
Chessa, Roberto	(GER)	info@stilfreund.de www.stilfreund.de
Chrisse Kunst	(GER)	chrissekunst@gmx.de www.chrissekunst.de

Pages

Surname , Prename	Loc.	Contact
ciah-ciah	(POL)	info@ciahciah.com www.ciahciah.com
Claudius, Stefan	(GER)	stefan@claudius-design.de www.claudius-design.de
Cless	(ESP)	cless@picnic.la www.cless.info
Contentismissing	(GER)	nadim@contentismissing.net www.contentismissing
Cuddyre, Alexis	(GBR)	acuddyre@gmail.com www.alexiscuddyre.com
Dahlmann, Alexander	(GER)	alexanderdahlmann@web.de www.alexander-dahlmann.de
Dath, Caroline	(BEL)	yourlastchance@kidnapyourdesigner.com
de Sousa Matoso, Diana	(GBR)	info@dsway.co.uk www.dsway.co.uk
Derodit, Clementine	(FRA)	clementine.derodit@free.fr www.monordinateurmagik.free
Dunkel, Susanne	(GER)	hello@susannedunkel.com www.susannedunkel.com
Eisermann, Susanne	(GER)	s-eisermann@web.de www.susanne-eisermann.de
EMP Pfisterer	(GER)	emp@empp.de www.empp.de
eps51	(GER)	mail@eps51.de www.eps51.de
Escobar Beckwith, Eduardo	(MEX)	escobas@escobas.com.mx www.escobas.com.mx
Esteban, Melanie	(GER)	melanie.esteban@gmx.de
Feldner, Astrid	(NOR)	astrid@bleed.no www.bleed.no
Ferrari, Sarah	(GBR)	ferrari.sarah@yahoo.com www.sarahferrari.com
Fetz, Michael	(AUT)	m.fetz@fetzdesign.com www.fetzdesign.com
Fiset, Annabelle	(CAN)	info@annabellefiset.com www.annabellefiset.com
Flaccus, Christian	(GER)	flaccus@schoeneneuekinder.de www.schoeneneuekinder.d
Forbrig, Heike	(GER)	heike@coklat.de www.coklat.de
Frey, Stefan	(GER)	stevo@schwarzschild.de www.schwarzschild.de
Furst, Kevin J.	(USA)	furst2@gmail.com www.kevinfurstdesign.com
Gehrmann, Isabelle	(GER)	stefan.ruetz@ahdaad.com www.ahdaad.com

Pages

Surname , Prename	Loc.	Contact
Geiger, Lorenzo	(SUI)	hello@lorenzogeiger.ch www.lorenzogeiger.ch
Gimbel, Heiko	(GER)	info@formgrad.de www.formgrad.de
Grillon, Benjamin	(GBR)	studio@paperpop.com www.paperpop.com
Groismaier, Birgit	(AUT)	office@erwinbauer.com www.erwinbauer.com
Hahn, Evelyn	(GER)	evelynhahn@gmx.de www.evelynhahn.de
Haigh, Alex	(GBR)	info@thinkdust.com www.thinkdust.com
Halderman, Chris	(NED)	chris_halderman@hotmail.com
Halton, Steven	(GBR)	www.themiracleshop.blogspot.com
Hartmann, Daniel	(GER)	dotsch86@googlemail.com
Hartung, Benjamin	(GER)	hartung@blattgolddesign.com www.blattgolddesign.com
Hasieber, Sandro	(GER)	S.hasieber@gmx.de
Henning, Bernardo	(ARG)	bernardohenning@gmail.com www.holabosque.com.ar
Hofacker, Sandra	(SUI)	info@apfel-z.de www.apfel-z.de
Hoffmann, C. & Skala, N.	(GER)	www.charlie-hoffmann.de, www.nicoleskala.de
Hucker, Florian	(GER)	florianhucker@web.de www.thelager.de
Jakober, Florian	(SUI)	flo@floriangrafik.ch www.floriangrafik.ch
Jockel, Tim	(GER)	tamitum@hotmail.com www.timjockel.de
Jordan, Martin	(GER)	martin@martinjordan.de www.martinjordan.de
Kage, Henry	(BRA)	123poneis@gmail.com www.flickr.com/poneis
Kahrs, Bryan	(USA)	bryan@id29.com www.id29.com
Kiefer, Cedric	(GER)	ck@dec32.de www.dec32.de
Killen, Heath	(AUS)	hello@illuminationink.com www.illuminationink.com
Kingdrips	(GER)	www.kingdrips.de
Kiralyfalvi, Karoly	(HUN)	hello@extraverage.net www.extraverage.net

Pages

Surname , Prename	Loc.	Contact
Klammt, Andreas	(GER)	info@breitengrad535.de www.breitengrad535.de
Klobes, Miriam	(GER)	www.mk-kommunikationsdesign.de
Knaack, Alex	(GER)	alex@born-clothing.de www.born-clothing.de
Knüwer, Thomas	(GER)	mail@tknuewer.de www.tknuewer.de
Kohl,C. & Pauli, C.	(GER)	christian-kohl@gmx.net / chrispauli@gmx.de
Koop, Andreas	(GER)	www.designgruppe-koop.de
Kratz, Hélène	(GER)	info@helenekratz www.helenekratz.com
Krebernik, Lilo	(AUT)	hello@0717.at www.0717.at
Kühnel, Martin	(GER)	mail@martin-kuehnel.de www.martin-kuehnel.de
Kuiter, Hendrik	(GER)	info@buerosiebzehn.de www.buerosiebzehn.de
Kümpel, Carina	(GER)	carinakuempel@gmail.com www.carina-inside.de
Lambert, Sam	(GBR)	s_lambert0@yahoo.co.uk www.samlambert.com
Lampert, Philipp	(AUT)	communication@phla.at www.phla.at
Lapierre, Audree	(CAN)	audree@audreelapierre.com www.audreelapierre.com
Laurenti, Luca	(ITA)	info@mklane.com www.mklane.com
López García, Diego	(COL)	lopezgrafico@gmail.com www.lopezgrafico.com
Lowman	(NED)	mail@hellowman.nl www.hellowman.nl
Maier, Nadine Jeannette	(GER)	Nadine.J.Maier@gmx.de
Maier, Rico	(SUI)	Rico.Maier@gmx.ch www.ricomaier.ch
Maldei, Andreas	(GER)	andreas.maldei@freenet.de www.myspace.com/andimacht
Marchionna, Sandra	(GER)	sandra.marchionna@freenet.de www.klimashirts.spreadshi
Marpeau, E. & Colomina, M.	(FRA)	edouard@frenchieslitchies.fr www.frenchieslitchies.fr
Martins, Evandro	(BRA)	evandro@bluebossa.art.br www.bluebossa.art.br
Martus, Hanna	(ESP)	hanna@netzwerg.biz www.netzwerg.biz/hanna

Pages

Surname , Prename	Loc.	Contact
Masoni, Jasmine	(SUI)	lajas@lajas.ch www.lajas.ch
Melnyk, Evan	(CAN)	info@curseofthemultiples.com www.curseofthemultiples.cor
Meneses, Daniel	(MEX)	daniel@vectormedia.com.mx www.vectormedia.com.mx
Merkel, Daniela	(GER)	merkel@bemerkt.net www.bemerkt.net
Michalski, Lukas	(GER)	michalski@hundert10prozent.de www.hundert10prozent.de
Millard, Dave	(GBR)	davidmillard@hotmail.co.uk www.cpluv.com/www/galleries/
Mira	(ITA)	mira@lovepics.it www.lovepics.it
Montes de Oca, Hector	(MEX)	hector@serif.com.mx www.serif.com.mx
Moosbauer, Bernhard	(GER)	ex@exsample.org www.exsample.org
Muller, Jarrik	(NED)	icanrollallday@hotmail.com www.getbusyfoklazy.nl
Neubronner, Julia	(GER)	julia@neubronner.tv www.neubronner.tv
Nowak, Magdalena	(GER)	sweetdreams@hellucinations.de www.hellucinations.de
Öland, Axel	(GER)	axeloeland@gmail.com www.2-3-5.info
Oriol, Alexandra	(ESP)	www.flickr.com/photos/alexandraoriol
Otto, Alexander	(GER)	pride@diftnorm.com www.diftnorm.com
Penkin, Alexander	(GER)	alex@la-pesch.com www.la-pesch.com
Persson, Henrik	(SWE)	henrik.persson@become.se www.become.se
Philipp, Roberto	(GER)	info@geschmacksverteiler.de www.geschmacksverteiler.de
Poitiers, Jeff	(LUX)	jeff@spitshiny.com www.spitshiny.com
Prib, Erika	(GER)	eripri@googlemail.com www.myspace.com/erikaprib
Puclin, Marko	(GER)	mp@puclin.com www.puclin.com
Putick, Katharina	(GER)	kp@dakapu.com www.dakapu.com
Putzer, Philipp	(ITA)	philipp@gruppegut.it www.gruppegut.it
Rampazzo, Lucas	(BRA)	www.flickr.com/photos/lucasrampazzo

Pages

Surname , Prename	Loc.	Contact
Reiser, Judith	(GER)	jreiser@web.de
Rentzsch, Julian	(GER)	post@julianrentzsch.de www.julianrentzsch.de
Restrepo, Jorge	(COL)	wonksite.studio@gmail.com www.wonksite.com
Ricchi, Giovanni	(ITA)	giovanni@minimalsonic.net www.minimalsonic.net
Richardson, Mark	(GBR)	mark@superfried.com www.superfried.com
Rios, Drew	(USA)	aanoigroove@yahoo.com
Ruf, Max	(GER)	mail@maxruf.com www.maxruf.com
Rühl, Sebastian	(GER)	info@sebastianruehl.de www.varietegraphique.de
Schäfer, Nastasja	(GER)	mail@nacoscha.de www.nacoscha.de
Schlosser, Timo	(GER)	digitalink@mulonation.com www.designbydigitalink.com
Schmidt, Mario	(GER)	marioschmidt@webalive.de www.webalive.de
Schmidt, Mathias	(GER)	partikeldsgn@mac.com
Schondelmaier, Diana	(GER)	ds@markkom.de
Schröder, P. & von Manteuffel, D.	(GER)	info@sosumi.net www.sosumi.net
Seiler, Christoph	(GER)	seiler@upshapes.de www.upshapes.de
Seo, Heesun	(KOR)	def0021@naver.com
Serradura, Luca	(ITA)	lserradura@hotmail.com
Silveira, Alexandre	(BRA)	alexandre.silveira@mccann.com.br
Skala, Nicole	(GER)	mail@nicoleskala.de www.nicoleskala.de
Skala, Nicole & Tilhard, Tina	(GER)	mail@nicoleskala.de
Skarek, Sergio	(ARG)	sskarek@fibertel.com.ar www.skarek.com.ar
Soh, Ee Venn	(MAS)	e3ven@yahoo.com www.behance.net/vennsoh
Stawinski, Gregor	(GER)	herr@gregorstawinski.de www.gregorstawinski.de
Stokes, Lee	(GBR)	stokes20@hotmail.co.uk www.leestokes.co.uk

Pages

Surname , Prename	Loc.	Contact
Studiocharlie	(ITA)	mail@studiocharlie.org www.studiocharlie.org
Tanneberger, Sandro	(GER)	info@remood.net www.remood.net
Tieri, Luca	(ITA)	lucatieri@lucatieri.com www.lucatieri.com
Tolley, Stuart	(GBR)	info@thisistransmission.com www.thisistransmission.com
Tonizzo, Rick	(LUX)	rick@hookepuk.com www.hookepuk.com
Tratz, Matthias	(GER)	matthias@hkant.de www.hkant.de
Turner Duckworth	(GBR)	www.turnerduckworth.com
UREDD	(NOR)	staale@uredd.no www.uredd.no
Vega, Miguel	(USA)	hello@accent.tv www.accent.tv
Velasquez, Julian	(COL)	julianvelasquez314@hotmail.com
Villa, Viviana	(COL)	vivita2021@gmail.com www.vivianavilla.com
Villavicencio, Ricardo	(CHI)	info@delrancho.org www.delrancho.org
Waldron, Steven	(SCO)	steven@tangentgraphic.co.uk www.tangentgraphic.co.uk
Weiss, Benjamin	(GER)	info@bnweiss.com www.bnweiss.com
Weiß, Sebastian	(GER)	post@herrweiss.org www.herrweiss.org
Weßling, Sabrina	(GER)	sabrina.wessling@freenet.de
Weyer, Stefan	(GER)	mail@stefan-weyer.com www.stefan-weyer.com
Wilton, Allison	(USA)	allisonwilton@gmail.com www.allisonwilton.com
Witt, Katja	(GER)	contact@schnuppenalarm.de www.schnuppenalarm.de
Yang, Edmond	(NOR)	edmond@yangmedia.com www.yangmedia.com
Zechel, Eva	(GER)	eva@exmono.de www.exmono.de

Pages